INSTITUTIONAL CHARACTER

Cultural Frames, Framing Culture

Robert Newman, Editor
Justin Neuman, Associate Editor

INSTITUTIONAL CHARACTER

Collectivity, Individuality, and the Modernist Novel

Robert Higney

University of Virginia Press • *Charlottesville and London*

University of Virginia Press
© 2022 by the Rector and Visitors of the University of Virginia
All rights reserved
Printed in the United States of America on acid-free paper

First published 2022

9 8 7 6 5 4 3 2 1

Library of Congress Cataloging-in-Publication Data

Names: Higney, Robert, author.
Title: Institutional character : collectivity, individuality, and the modernist novel / Robert Higney.
Description: Charlottesville : University of Virginia Press, 2022. | Series: Cultural frames, framing culture | Includes bibliographical references and index.
Identifiers: LCCN 2022005244 (print) | LCCN 2022005245 (ebook) | ISBN 9780813948591 (hardcover ; acid-free paper) | ISBN 9780813948607 (paperback ; acid-free paper) | ISBN 9780813948614 (ebook)
Subjects: LCSH: English fiction—20th century—History and criticism. | Modernism (Literature)—Great Britain. | Characters and characteristics in literature. | Public institutions—Influence. | Individuality in literature. | Imperialism in literature. | Narration (Rhetoric)
Classification: LCC PR888.M63 H54 2022 (print) | LCC PR888.M63 (ebook) | DDC 823/.9109112—dc23/eng/20220204
LC record available at https://lccn.loc.gov/2022005244
LC ebook record available at https://lccn.loc.gov/2022005245

Publication of this volume has been supported by New Literary History.

Cover art: Stocksy 3482609, 3197504

CONTENTS

	Acknowledgments	vii
	Introduction	1
1	Joseph Conrad and the Institutions of Empire	25
2	Virginia Woolf and Political Possibility in the Gendered Institution	63
3	Institutional Picaresque: Mulk Raj Anand from Bloomsbury to Bombay	100
4	Elizabeth Bowen: War, Welfare, and the Institutional Impersonal	139
	Conclusion: The Institution as Promise and Limit	175
	Notes	179
	Index	215

ACKNOWLEDGMENTS

This book has been a long time in development, and I owe debts to many individuals and institutions that have shaped it. Frances Restuccia, Robin Lydenberg, and Marjorie Howes were formative influences on me when I was an undergraduate at Boston College, and their courses made me want to teach and write. My appreciation of the time I spent in the English Department at Johns Hopkins University has only increased over the years, and I am grateful to many people with whom I first crossed paths there. I am lucky to have had Douglas Mao as an advisor; this project would not have been possible without his brilliant suggestions, support, and patience. I thank him for his friendship and for the lessons I continue to learn from him, and I cannot imagine my intellectual life without his example. Frances Ferguson modeled rigorous critical engagement alongside institutional citizenship, and she helped me to feel like I belonged in graduate school. Sharon Cameron taught me to approach intellectual work seriously. Francis Mulhern's seminar was where I first began thinking about questions that led to this project, and I still appreciate his generosity and encouragement. Every day of class, I try to practice what Patricia Kain and Will Evans taught me about teaching. For the education I received in seminars, as a teaching assistant, at department talks, and in conversation, I owe Amanda Anderson, Simon During, Jared Hickman, Drew Daniel, Kevin Attell, Isobel Armstrong, Hollis Robbins, Jesse Rosenthal, and Jonathan Kramnick. I was fortunate to be part of an extended graduate school cohort who made Baltimore home. For their camaraderie and insight in Baltimore and beyond, I thank Hadley Leach, Elisha Cohn, Simon Glezos, Andrew Sisson, George Oppel, Doug Tye, Patrick Fessenbecker, Nick Bujak, Cristie Ellis, Daniel Stout, Dave Hershinow, Stephanie Insley Hershinow, and many others. The sustaining friendship of Anthony Wexler and Robert Carson has been indispensable.

My colleagues at the City College of New York have humanized what is at once the most inspiring and bewildering of institutions. For their friendship, and for questions and criticism that have made this book immeasurably better, I thank especially Daniel Gustafson, Harold Veeser,

András Kiséry, Kedon Willis, Václav Paris, Andreas Killen, and Mikhal Dekel. As department chairs, Elizabeth Mazzola and Renata Miller (and Mikhal and András, in interim capacities) upheld an unsurpassed commitment to the success of junior faculty, and their guidance was crucial as I found my footing at City College. I thank Yana Joseph for her help and guidance in more matters than I can say. The Rifkind Center for the Humanities and the Arts has provided a stimulating intellectual environment; I'm grateful to many interlocutors in seminars there, as well as for its programming and research support. Early in my time at City College, the Faculty Fellowship Publication Program at CUNY helped me begin to turn the manuscript into a book, and I thank organizer Carrie Hintz and fellow group members George Fragopoulos, Anita Baksh, Miles Parks Grier, Daly Guilamo, Lucia Cedeira Serantes, and Tanya Zhelezcheva for Saturday morning conversations and detailed comments. I am grateful to my union, the Professional Staff Congress, for its advocacy and for several PSC-CUNY grants that furnished time to write. And I thank my students across institutions for their enthusiasm, readiness to engage with difficult texts and ideas, and for prompting me to think harder.

For careful reading and feedback that immensely improved this project, I thank Victoria Rosner; Scott Selisker; Matthew Eatough, Tara Harney-Mahajan, Kelly Sullivan, Lori Cole, and the NYU Global Modernisms Group; and Megan Faragher, Caroline Krzakowski, and the contributors to the "Modernist Institutions" cluster at *Modernism/modernity*. Other colleagues, in modernist studies and across the profession, have read, listened, and contributed in a variety of ways to the development of my thinking and my capacity to navigate academic life, perhaps more than they know: I thank Allan Hepburn, John McGowan, Marshall Brown, Lisa Siraganian, Janice Ho, Ramesh Mallipeddi, Nicole Rizzuto, Rebecca Colesworthy, Jonathan Goldman, Rebecca Walkowitz, Sarah Cole, Matthew Hart, Caroline Levine, Lisa Mendelman, Patrick Deer, Emily Bloom, Tanya Agathocleous, and Nico Israel. Audiences and fellow speakers asked acute questions and offered helpful suggestions when I presented portions of this work at the conferences of the Modern Language Association, the Modernist Studies Association, and the American Comparative Literature Association, as well as at the City College of New York and at Yale University.

I couldn't be happier that this book landed at the University of Virginia Press. I owe a great deal to series editors Robert Newman and Justin

Neuman; Justin's enthusiasm and belief in my work were simply transformative. Angie Hogan, Morgan Myers, and the entire team at the Press saw this project to completion with virtuosity and more than a little patience. The anonymous readers of the manuscript were astonishingly insightful and generous and improved it greatly. I thank Joanne Allen for her acute and clarifying copyediting and Enid Zafran for her expertise in preparing the index.

Portions of chapter 1 first appeared as "'Law, Good Faith, Order, Security': Conrad's Institutions," in *Novel: A Forum on Fiction* 48.1 (Spring 2015): 85–102. Part of chapter 3 appeared online as "Institutional Picaresque" in the essay cluster "Modernist Institutions," edited by Meghan Faragher and Caroline Krzakowski, *Modernism/modernity Print+* 5, cycle 2 (November 2020). Early work on Virginia Woolf appeared at the Yale Modernism Lab. I thank the editors for permission to republish this material and for their feedback. I first thought through parts of this book's conclusion in the form of a talk delivered at the Langston Hughes Festival at the City College of New York, and I am grateful to the Festival for the invitation.

Friends and family have lived with this book for as long as I have, in some cases under the same roof. Across several cities and many years, I've been especially grateful for the companionship of Matthew Wilga, Christopher Hydal, Gregory Matthews, Joseph Klifer, Christopher Hawkins, Billy Hurley, Maureen McDonnell, Kaitlin Murphy, Tom Rossmeissl, Brian Kelly, Abby Tranel, Alison Leonard, David Fleit, and Ashley Spierer. I could not have moved forward on this project without the benefit of Hod Tamir's insight and understanding. I'm glad to know Bill Dendor. Ken and Annmarie Rubin's humor and hospitality have been a gift.

Most of all, I thank my family for a lifetime of laughter and care: Ken and Suzanne Higney; Michelle, Gill, Kelsey, and Kyle Higney; Mary, Paul, Christopher, and Jennifer Litchfield. The years I worked on this project saw the passing of Bernard Moulson, Charlotte Moulson, Raymond Higney, and Irene Higney; they encouraged me at its beginning, and I know they would be proud to see it completed. I'm grateful for the kind spirits and good nature of Mike Morace, Nick, and Mason. My niece Amelia has brought more joy into more people's lives, including mine, than anyone I know, and my sister Lauren has been my truest, funniest, and most enthusiastic friend since we were little. My longest-standing debts are for the unwavering support and love of my mother, Christina

Higney, and my late father, Wayne Higney. Both lifelong teachers of English, they raised me in a house filled with books and gave me a love of reading, language, and stories. Finally, Carly Rubin read every word of this book more than once and made it possible for me to finish it. She has supported me unconditionally and filled my life with her intelligence, determination, kindness, and laughter. I thank her for everything, especially the institution of our life together.

INSTITUTIONAL CHARACTER

INTRODUCTION

NEAR THE BEGINNING of E. M. Forster's *A Passage to India,* City Magistrate Ronny Heaslop gets into an argument with his mother. Ronny is indifferent to how British colonial officials treat their Indian subjects, but Mrs. Moore is not. When she suggests that he take a greater interest in "behaving pleasantly," he says, "I am out here to work, mind, to hold this wretched country by force. I'm not a missionary or a Labour Member or a vague sentimental sympathetic literary man. I'm just a servant of the Government; it's the profession you wanted me to choose myself, and that's that."[1] Ronny, that is, justifies his actions by appealing to the position he occupies. To feel or behave differently, in his account, one would have to be a different kind of person, "servant" to another institution: to the church, a political party, or the literary establishment. Mrs. Moore is "impressed" by his words, "but when she heard the self-satisfied lilt of them . . . she felt, quite illogically, that this was not the last word on India. One touch of regret—not the canny substitute but the true regret from the heart—would have made him a different man, and the British Empire a different institution" (51). In contrast to her son, Mrs. Moore imagines that if people would change, "from the heart," the institution they serve—hyperbolically, the whole British Empire—would be altered in turn.

To what extent are we shaped by our institutions, and to what extent do we shape them? No literary form poses this question more pointedly and sustainedly than the novel, in its historical ambition to capture both the minutiae of individual lives across time and the enduring hold of the structures of society. And in their argument, Ronny and Mrs. Moore present two clarifying if reductive responses: Ronny is an institutionalist in his assertion that the person is shaped entirely by the institution, that he is "just a servant." Mrs. Moore is an individualist in suggesting that the institution itself is servant to the right-feeling person. As a whole, though, *A Passage to India* significantly complicates this opposition. Mrs. Moore's sympathetic individualism, driven by a faith in personal relationships

1

and reflective of Forster's stated sense of his own perspective as "the fag-end of Victorian liberalism," will sour in British India; she departs the novel midstream, in a "spiritual muddledom."[2] And the novel concludes by affirming that the empire runs on something like Ronny's institutional determinism: the friendship between its central characters Fielding and Aziz, an English school administrator and a Muslim doctor, is finally impossible, not because of their feelings about each other but because those feelings appear irrelevant to the force of the hierarchies in which the men are implicated or to questions of how the empire might become "a different institution." A novel that presents a sensitive liberal exploration of relationships among individuals across lines of gender, race, religion, and national identity, *A Passage to India* nonetheless cannot finally sustain the faith in the individual by which it is animated. But in thematizing so clearly its own inability to reconcile the individual and the institutional, Forster's novel opens onto issues of institutionality—as a problem for literary form, for politics, and for writers' own careers—that are central to the history of the modernist novel that I present in this book.

Institutional Character argues that from the era of high imperialism to the rise of the postwar welfare state, the idea of the institution became central to modernist approaches to character and narrative form. Shaken loose from the ambivalence Victorian liberal individualism held for it, and not yet subject to what Scott Selisker has termed the "antiinstitutional ethos" of the Cold War era, questions about the power of institutions to shape character, and about how the lives of institutions themselves might be given narrative shape, were raised anew, and the concept of the institution was made available to a wider range of literary uses than ever before.[3] For an array of modernist writers, character becomes an attribute not so much of the unique individual as of the institutions of the state, international trade and finance, communication and media, labor, education, public health, the military, the law, and more. For all their differences, Forster shares with, for example, Joseph Conrad a powerful distrust of institutions like the corporation and of imperial governance. Conrad in the first decade of the twentieth century undertook an extended, multiwork exploration of the ways in which institutional life can (and cannot) in fact become *constitutive* of character. Decades later, colonial modernists like Mulk Raj Anand turned in often surprising ways to modern institutions for their capacity to ameliorate conflicts driven by tradition, culture, and identity, and to shape authorial careers.

In such modernist works—however such works invite us to evaluate the ramifications of institutional life that they narrativize—institutions emerge as durable collections of shared norms and practices that constitute individuals, and as collective actors in themselves. This is also to say that within the modernist novel lies a robust formal engagement with, and theorization of, institutions that anticipates literary scholarship that has approached the twentieth-century literary field sociologically and historically.

The term *institutional character* denotes the variety of ways that modernists imagined character as inhering in the workings of institutions rather than in the development of the singular individual—even as character in the novel necessarily finds expression in and through individuals. The novel has typically been thought of as the aesthetic genre of the individual par excellence, evident, for example, from nineteenth-century realism's creation of deep interiority as essential to the depiction of a self, to Ian Watt's suggestion that the novel's "primary criterion was truth to individual experience," to what Georg Lukács terms its irreducibly "biographical form," to the extensive body of scholarship on the bildungsroman.[4] Even across the familiar story of modernism's turn inward to consciousness and perception, to more recent critical attention to affect, the modernist novel too retains strong associations with the exploration of the individual consciousness. But works like Virginia Woolf's *The Years* or Elizabeth Bowen's *The Heat of the Day* largely reject psychological depth, biographical form, and the narrative satisfactions that accompany them. In novels like these, character is evoked most often through typology, shared gestures, and generic description, and narrative form is often distended, following, for instance, the rhythms of bureaucratic delay, technological acceleration, and the extended timescape of the life of an institution rather than an individual. While such forms of fragmentation have long been associated with modernist writing—such that the relevance of the term *character* has often been called into question—such fragmentation cannot be understood as indicating only the dispersal of the unitary subject. In *The Years,* patriarch Abel Pargiter is an institutional character in that he coheres as a collection of values, tics, and behaviors that are characteristic of the Indian Army and civil service of which he is a product. His daughter Sara, as a woman denied entry into institutions like journalism and the university, ultimately makes little sense as a character, speaking in abstruse riddles, snippets of song, and free association, acting unpredictably and ineffectually, and in essence disintegrating on the page. Individuals, in these works, are constitutively involved—or not—in institutional life; seemingly paradoxically, the features that individuate them are also the features of a collective form, shared by innumerable others.

Modernism may seem like odd terrain on which to pursue questions of how character is related to large social structures; this kind of inquiry is more often associated with the classical realism of the nineteenth century (think *Bleak House,* or Balzac) or perhaps with the "network novels" of postmodern and contemporary American fiction.[5] But one aim of this study is to contribute to the ongoing breakdown of the division between modernism and its precursors in telling the history of the novel and then to gesture toward some of the subsequent legacies of institutional character.[6] In depicting the operation of institutional forms as they are manifested in the details of individual behavior, the works I examine here direct our attention to how modernism might constitute an amplification of realist concerns with the social and representative aspects of character rather than their undoing. As scholars have demonstrated, the realist novel is in fact less individualist than critics have long assumed; its minor characters especially (such as Dickens's grotesques) are constituted in relation to an array of collectivities. *Institutional Character* takes up this phenomenon at the moment when those collectivities shifted from the national to the imperial scale and argues that institutional character itself moves from the edges to the center of novelistic narrative. While this book's primary approach is formalist, and my argument focuses less on specific institutions than on how the idea of the institution and its logic comes to inform character in modernism, I also suggest that institutional character offered modernist writers a means to reimagine the character of their own profession and their place in it, casting and recasting themselves in new roles, as rebels, managers, or representatives of a more stylish era when it came time to negotiate a place (and a salary) in the postwar institutions of international culture. In proposing that institutional character was key both to modernist narrative and to authorial self-fashioning, I hope to reorient our sense of the representational work modernist form could do, across the boundaries of the modernist and postcolonial eras and of art and life.

New Institutionalisms

A critical consensus that modernism and twentieth-century literatures more generally have been shaped by relatively durable institutional structures that they have shaped in turn has been some time in development. At the inception of the new modernist studies, Lawrence Rainey's *Institutions of Modernism* set a historicist and sociologically inflected agenda for the field that drew attention to how modernists both withdrew from and intervened in public cultures by creating new institutions to support their art, troubling the distinctions between high and low culture, artistic creation and commodification. Rainey's account was posed in opposition to, on the one hand, the notion that modernism was the creation of elite avant-gardes with no regard for audiences and, on the other, approaches to institutions that take the term as a metaphor for genre, a "framing category" for art, or for the world of letters as such.[7] Since then, works such as Peter Kalliney's *Commonwealth of Letters* and Jeremy Braddock's *Collecting as Modernist Practice* have shown how modernism inspired and was incorporated into a range of institutions, not only in the metropolitan centers but also in newly independent nations, that employed and funded writers and artists and put modernist aesthetics to work in the market across the twentieth century.[8] This work has by and large also been shaped, implicitly or explicitly, by a common understanding of what is meant by *institution* that Rainey's germinal work also shared: "the specific social structures that mediate between works and publics."[9] This middle-range approach, addressing itself less to abstractions like Literature or Empire than to the academic departments, extension schools, advertising agencies, publishing houses, museums, government agencies, corporations, and other identifiable collective entities, is anticipated, I would suggest, by the interest modernist writers themselves took in institutions.

This expanded perspective on the institutions *of* literature has been paralleled by a revitalized attention to institutions *in* literature, primarily in criticism focused on state power. When I began presenting work from this project, the first question I often received was a version of "What about Foucault and Althusser?" One answer has been provided by literary-critical scholarship that has moved away from viewing institutions primarily as epiphenomena of more diffuse fields of culture, power, discipline, or ideology that consolidate social control (and by extension from previously dominant ways of engaging the work of these theorists).¹⁰ Much of this work has focused on the state, attending to the ways that, as Amanda Claybaugh notes in a key 2008 essay, "Government is Good," literature and literary criticism can make state power visible, "rescuing government from the default academic critiques."¹¹ In *Geopolitics and the Anglophone Novel*, John Marx proposes a more active role for literary discourse in governmentality, positing that literary fiction of the early twentieth century, in depicting critically governmental administration and its failures, "helped forecast a world after European imperialism by identifying problems with Empire's administrative strategies and by laying the conceptual foundation necessary to generate new schemes."¹² Such work illuminates how modernism emerged during, and expressed the anxieties of, the age of (late) empire and how literature can affirm, productively critique, or formally adapt state power to its own purposes. The institutions of the welfare state, in a sense, play a role internal to literary form analogous to the role played by institutions in the production of literary texts: they are the enabling conditions of literary narrative and literature itself, their constraints and enablements the condition of the very existence of the text, even as the text offers us new—and not only critical—perspectives on the state. While my own analysis here is indebted to this body of scholarship, the ways in which it manages to address a variety of issues gesture toward the limits of the state as a category of literary analysis: from the state as such, this statal literary criticism has tended to move quickly toward concepts like sovereignty, citizenship, infrastructure, insurance, and administration—to more concrete, middle-range institutions.

Modernist scholarship has begun to highlight the usefulness of focusing on institutions, rather than the state, in part because modernist texts frequently depict state power as attenuated and inextricable from private interest, imperial competition, and a wide variety of collective forms that cannot be understood as subgenres of the state. My own approach to these issues has been aided by work from the "new institutionalism" in the social sciences. Starting in the 1980s, political science, sociology, economics, and other related fields sought to bypass the shortcomings of monolithic concepts of the state by developing a robust set of theoretical approaches to institutions. No longer so new—James March and Johan Olsen's 1989 study *Rediscovering Institutions* is often mentioned as an important early contribution—the new institutionalism encompasses an array of concepts and definitions of institutions, taking them most broadly as "the rules of the game" (property rights, free markets) and most narrowly as specific material structures (parliaments, courts). What these approaches share is an understanding of institutions as autonomous. Analysis begins at the level of the institution, rather than viewing institutions as merely expressive of the underlying preferences of powerful individuals, classes, interest groups, or other elements of society. The new institutionalism has also tended to emphasize the extended temporal scale on which institutions operate; the ways in which they exceed individual choice and the interchangeability of particular individuals with regard to institutional functioning; and their development of "path dependency," enabling but also restricting future directions for development.[13] And in their introduction to the *Modernism/modernity* online forum "Modernist Institutions," Megan Faragher and Caroline Krzakowski survey a new institutionalism in modernist studies itself, suggesting that "modernism, in particular, deserves unique consideration as an era defined by the rise of the institution."[14] Drawing on new institutionalist work from the social sciences, Faragher and Krzakowski demonstrate how the analyses brought together in the forum and other recent work in the field can move across a wide range of fields, including architecture, world literature, film, disciplinary history, visual art, design, information science, and more, all of which touch on modernist institutionality and aesthetics. Gabriel Hankins's *Interwar Modernism and the Liberal World Order* is perhaps the most ambitious work of institutionalist criticism in modernist studies so far, focusing on "the importance to modernist aesthetics of the specific language, politics, and institutional life of liberal order, not simply as background context but as the intimate ground of aesthetic creation."[15] And Caroline Levine's *Forms: Whole, Rhythm, Hierarchy, Network* has put institutionalism on the agenda for literary studies generally.[16]

While work in modernist studies' new institutionalism (and in modernist studies broadly over the past two decades) has been weighted toward historicist approaches, my approach is primarily formalist and characterological. As March and Olsen put it, the institution is "a relatively enduring collection of rules and organized practices, embedded in structures of meaning and resources that are relatively invariant in the face of turnover of individuals and relatively resilient to the idiosyncratic preferences and expectations of individuals and changing external circumstances." Institutions "prescrib[e] appropriate behavior" and make individuals "more or less capable of acting" by providing contexts within which those behaviors take on meaning and have their effects.[17] And institutions can be actors themselves (as in when we hear on the news that "the White House issued a statement"). The novel, I suggest, with its capacity for both granular interiority and sweeping description, is the form most capable of linking everyday individualized institutional practices to institutions themselves, and vice versa. I thus follow Levine and formalist critics like Anna Kornbluh in attending less to histories of specific institutions than to the institution as a form with this particular set of attributes, and thus institutional thinking from the social sciences informs my readings of literary texts not as a context or theory to be rigorously applied but as a way of looking for the shaping action of institutions in the formation of novelistic character.[18]

Institutional character, then, is social but not particularly a matter of moral inquiry or psychological depth. My theorization of character here resonates with a broad rethinking of the term, exemplified by the work of (among others) Alex Woloch, Aaron Kunin, Marta Figlerowicz, Matthew Burroughs Price, and Omri Moses, all of whom seek, in Figlerowicz's words, to "move away from an emphasis on [the novel's] value as an affirmation of the complexity and depth of first-person experience."[19] Jill Galvan suggests that this broad retheorization of character offers "cross-period resonances" through which both Victorian and modernist studies have undergone a salutary "posthuman shift: a serious consideration of how we might read characters and their shared embodiment in light of the fallacies of liberal humanism."[20] Rules, actions, habits, and values, more than deep interiority, are the bases of institutional character, and the individual emerges through the repetition and accumulation of these elements in narrative; as Levine writes, "Whether acting as administrators or parents, macho men or diligent students, poker players or welfare recipients, we play parts set out for us by institutions, and, as we do so, we reproduce the institution itself."[21] Character in the novel cannot, perhaps, ever be entirely posthuman; but there is a sense in which when we look at an imagined human being in these works, we are looking at what Joseph Conrad would call an "inhuman" institution too.[22]

While the texts I examine here are drawn from the period traditionally considered modernist, I also frame this discussion in terms of the history of the novel more broadly to de-emphasize, first, the sense of exceptionality that still clings to modernism, and second, the still prevalent understanding of modernism as constituting a break or rupture with prior conventions of nineteenth-century realism. In one sense, these may not seem like pressing concerns: much scholarship in the subfield of modernist studies has been dedicated over the past two decades to pluralizing and globalizing modernisms, to reconceiving modernism outside the logics of style or even period.[23] But beyond modernist studies of Anglophone literature particularly, in scholarship focused on other periods, forms, or the history of the novel, the impact of this work has been uneven. In *Populating the Novel* Emily Steinlight argues for understanding the nineteenth-century novel less as pursuing the reconciliation of the individual with society and more centrally as grappling with unimaginably large, impersonal collectivities—"mass life"—in narrative form.[24] I follow Steinlight in finding in the novel "a politics for which the individual is no longer the basic integer" (17). The terms on which Steinlight's argument concludes, though—that concerns with population in the novel persist in the modernist period with a "shift from society to consciousness as the novel's primary object" (212)—recapitulate a model of modernism as defined by inwardness and psychology, which I contest. Steinlight argues that "this . . . is what happens to the concept of population and to the novel form at the century's end: both, in effect, are psychologized. And this psychological turn . . . makes the unconscious the site of political collectivity" (221). Certain strands of modernism are understood as psychologizing for good reason, of course, but modern governance developed concrete means of managing social pressures around large collectivities that were neither biological nor psychological, but institutional.[25] In embedding those institutional forms in novelistic character, and vice versa, the modernist novel takes up questions of collectivity at the moment those questions shift decisively from the level of the nation to the level of the empire. The works I read here show how modernism perpetuates realist concerns—indeed, is itself a mode of realism—into the twentieth century and the postwar era.[26]

Victorian Prehistories

The economist Douglas Allen argues that the Industrial Revolution in Europe was also an "institutional revolution," in which improvements in the measurement of time and distance drove a transition from premodern institutions, characterized by patronage and venality, to what we now recognize as modern institutional forms relying on measurement and merit. The staffing of the civil service, for example, went in a relatively short period of time from appointment on the basis of status and trust accrued through "political power, social status, and wealth" to appointment "based on exam performance, professional standards, and input monitoring."[27] By about 1850, Allen argues, this shift had generated institutional forms that remain with us today. Individuals interacted with government, businesses, the legal system, and the military in ways that twenty-first-century observers would recognize.

The institutional revolution did not go unnoticed by those who experienced it, and the Victorian prehistory of institutional character is legible across canonical texts of the mid-nineteenth century. In British intellectual life, the problem of modern institutions was commonly figured in terms of an opposition between an order evolved organically out of a national tradition and one imposed in the interests of collective alteration and improvement. As early as 1829, Thomas Carlyle's "Signs of the Times" diagnosed the spirit of the age as "mechanism," in which "all is by rule and calculated contrivance . . . nothing follows its spontaneous course, nothing is left to be accomplished by the old natural methods," "politics" is replaced by "mere political arrangements," and "[men] hope and struggle . . . for external combinations and arrangements, for institutions, constitutions."[28] To this Carlyle opposes "dynamism," "the primary, unmodified forces and energies of man." "Science and Art," Carlyle writes, "rose up, as it were, by spontaneous growth . . . They were not planted or grafted, not even greatly multiplied or improved by the culturing or manuring of institutions . . . it is the noble people that makes the noble Government; rather than conversely. On the whole, Institutions are much, but they are not all."[29] In his essay "The Literary Influence of Academies" (1864) and in *Culture and Anarchy* (1869), Matthew Arnold reasons along similar lines, linking institutions to the national spirit: a nation characterized by "energy and honesty," like the English, "will not be very apt to set up, in intellectual matters, a fixed standard, an authority, like an academy. . . . Nations have their own modes of acting, and these modes are not easily changed."[30] An academy, Arnold suggests, is a fitting institution for the French, whose "open and clear mind[s]" and "quick and flexible intelligence" incline them to the requisite deference to authoritative reason, but "the very faults . . . which have hindered our having an Academy and have worked injuriously in our literature, would also hinder us from making our Academy, if we established it, one which would really correct them."³¹

In this central line of nineteenth-century British thought, the right kind of institution complements natural characteristics, whether of the group, as in the analyses of Carlyle and Arnold, or of the individual, as in the Victorian novel. Jane Eyre, on arrival at Lowood Institution, immediately engrosses herself in "pondering the signification of 'Institution,'" but she is at pains to tell us that her first interaction there "was contrary to my nature and habits": "I hardly know where I found the hardihood thus to open a conversation with a stranger."³² Jane moves from charity home to aristocratic house to village school and nearly into missionary service, and while she responds to and is clearly shaped by the challenges she faces in each of these archetypal Victorian institutions, hers is ultimately a story of innate disposition asserting itself in episode after episode. "My first quarter at Lowood," she says at the beginning of the novel, "comprised an irksome struggle with difficulties in habituating myself to new rules and unwonted tasks" (71), while near its end, as she studies to be the missionary wife of St. John Rivers, Jane finds "that I must disown half my nature, stifle half my faculties, wrest my tastes from their original bent, force myself to the adoption of pursuits for which I had no natural vocation" (460). *Jane Eyre*'s explicit focus on its title character's "natural vocation" constitutes Jane as separate from the institutions through which she passes, and the action of the plot hinges on her relationships with other individuals. As Nancy Armstrong puts it, Jane is individuated by virtue of possessing "an interiority in excess of the social position that [the] individual is supposed to occupy."³³ And as the virtuous manufacturer John Thornton says in Elizabeth Gaskell's *North and South*, putting the issue in political terms, "No mere institutions, however wise . . . can attach class to class as they should be attached, unless they bring the individuals of the different classes into actual personal contact. Such intercourse is the very breath of life."³⁴ This might be called the methodological individualism of the Victorians: an account of the social order begins with "actual personal contact" between individuals of "natural vocation," and activity at the collective level amounts to the sum of these contacts.

Institutions in this scheme may be much, but they are not all, and where they are not, the individual is. To think otherwise is to make a kind of category mistake that often plays out as comic oddity, as in Charles

Dickens's innumerable grotesque peripheral characters. Such figures' characterological deformity and minoritization are not only, as Alex Woloch has compellingly argued, a product of their constricted role in an economy of narrative labor; not infrequently, these qualities result from characters' seemingly excessive attachment to the protocols of some institution or other. As *Great Expectations*'s law clerk Wemmick says, "It's not personal; it's professional, only professional."[35] But when Wemmick's "post-office"-shaped mouth reappears a century later, on a character in Elizabeth Bowen's World War II novel *The Heat of the Day*, it follows the arc traveled by character in the twentieth century: no longer grotesque, identity generated by institutional attachment has become the norm and moved closer to the center of the novel. As Joe Cleary argues, "Nineteenth-century realism already contained latent modernisms that broke strongly to the fore only in conditions of systemic crisis," while at the same time, "modernism might now be viewed not as a liquidation but as an attempted sublation of realism into more spatially and cognitively expansive forms."[36] This humorous, minor feature of two characters, migrating from one of the canonical texts of classical realism to one of the monuments of late modernism, stands as a metonym for both the differences and the continuities in the history of the novel, and of institutional character, from the nineteenth to the twentieth century.

If this suggests that modernism's engagement with the institution grows out of realist forebears, it is also the case that the liberal individual in the nineteenth century was never as unitary as critics long seem to have believed. As Daniel Stout argues in *Corporate Romanticism: Liberalism, Justice, and the Novel*, the pursuit of justice reveals the impossibility of ever knowing for sure where persons end and collectivities begin.[37] Institutions, for the Victorians, manage this uncertainty. Novelists like Gaskell and Charlotte Brontë seek to narrate the possibility of balance or rapprochement between institutions and individuals. Likewise Carlyle, at least early in his career, envisions a mechanism that would become "our pliant, all-ministering servant," while Arnold foresees "academies with a limited, special, scientific scope" complementing the English national spirit.[38] Institutions figure predominantly as a means of reinforcing and perpetuating certain aspects of individual or collective character whose wellsprings lie elsewhere. But the desire for synthesis was overtaken by the expansion of the British Empire and state facilitations of the market in the late Victorian period, and with regard to these historical shifts the line of thinking I identify here contains important gaps. As Paul Johnson points out in his *Making the Market: Victorian Origins of Corporate Capitalism*, from the late eighteenth to the late nineteenth century "the market" was typically figured as "an absence of institutional structures . . . a natural and neutral trading-ground."³⁹ Yet in a series of acts passed in the 1840s and 1850s, Parliament established the most elaborate form of what would become arguably the most important non-state institution of modernity: the joint-stock company. "In fact," Johnson writes, "the market of Victorian England was a deliberate, and thus far from natural, construction of ideas, conventions, beliefs, customs, law and enforcement mechanisms" (24). These developments stand at odds with an intellectual milieu in which ideals of inherent character and natural institutions retained a certain hegemonic sway.⁴⁰ Whatever the continuities, by the beginning of the twentieth century, and during the definitive expansion of the discourse of the market from a national to an imperial one, the intellectual climate was quite different.

The Inevitability of Institutions

The status of imperial institutions was hotly debated at the turn of the century in London and throughout the empire—often in what can appear in retrospect to be superficial ways, considering that at the same moment in Germany Max Weber was writing *The Protestant Ethic and the Spirit of Capitalism* (1905), while in France Émile Durkheim had published *The Rules of Sociological Method* (1895), establishing sociology as "the science of institutions, their genesis and their functioning."⁴¹ By contrast, as Perry Anderson suggests, "Britain . . . never produced either a classical sociology or a national Marxism. British culture was consequently characterized by an absent center. For both historical materialism and classical sociology . . . were totalizing enterprises—attempts to capture the 'structure of structures,' the articulation of the social whole itself. Britain has for more than fifty years lacked any significant form of such undertaking."⁴² Anderson wrote this in 1968, as editor of the *New Left Review* and just after the founding of the Center for Contemporary Cultural Studies at the University of Birmingham, a project that was nothing if not aiming to fill the "absent center" to which he alludes. And yet, as Jed Esty points out, cultural studies can be understood as having taken on, however critically, a distinctly *English national* object of study after the loss of a *British imperial* one.⁴³ By contrast, empire had been interrogated more deeply in the previous "fifty years" on the terrain of culture itself. Anderson's terms for what such an interrogation would have involved—totalization, "the articulation of the social whole"—are frequently cited as the distinctive features of the form in which I argue it *was* in fact carried out: the novel. To give a sense of the range that debates about institutions did attain in Britain, though, I turn here to two turn-of-the-century examples from the political discourse of the time and then to a canonical modernist figure.

In 1901, prompted in part by the Boer War still raging in South Africa, the journalist Arnold White published *Efficiency and Empire*, an assault on the British imperial status quo. The book is an exhaustive inventory-taking of the empire's key institutions: Parliament, the Foreign Office, the Colonial Office, the Church of England, the public health services, the City of London, the courts, the army, the navy, the Treasury, and the education system from primary school to university. The verdict is not good, and the final chapter of *Efficiency and Empire* opens in mourning: "As I write the last lines of this book, the Queen's reign ends. The Victorian era of comfort and progress already belongs to the irrevocable past. Herself the most efficient of the servants of the nation, the Queen's legacy to small and great is the priceless example of Efficiency she leaves to her people. . . . If we were all like the Queen, the British Empire would be safe."⁴⁴ But all Britons are not like the queen, and "incapable administration is the rule" (311). White was an enthusiastic racist, anti-Semite, and misogynist. He did not hesitate to indict "the influence of bad foreign Jews on bad smart society" (80), "disreputable women" (84), and "pauper voluptuaries" (117) as among the causes of what he refers to as nothing less than the "decline of the British Empire" (14). "What," White asks, "is to arrest our Gadarene rush down the steeps of inefficiency to the sea of national destruction?" (312). Given the quality of the rhetoric here, one could be forgiven for expecting that the answer to this question would involve a reassertion of white racial supremacy and a reinvigorated ethos of heroic, masculine, imperialist self-sacrifice. But the culmination of Queen Victoria's "Efficiency" is less thundering than we might expect. After three hundred pages of existential doubt and scathing indictment of the empire and its administrators, *Efficiency and Empire* offers politely only a kind of golden rule for imperial administration: "Restore responsibility, and enforce it on high and low; and, secondly, open a career to talent. These are hard sayings, but worthy of all acceptation, for nothing else can save us" (312).

This attitude toward institutions proved appealing to commentators at the opposite end of the political spectrum as well. At almost the same moment, and in response to the same imperial war, George Bernard Shaw published a manifesto titled *Fabianism and Empire*. Shaw was a member of the Fabian Society and played an important role in shaping its gradualist, social democratic politics. Though not yet the towering dramatist he would become, he was a noted left-wing intellectual and activist. Where *Efficiency and Empire* is frankly jingoistic, *Fabianism and Empire* grudgingly accepts the imperial order as an emergent fact. The latter's table of contents, like that of the former, lists a series of institutions that Shaw finds wanting: the Foreign Office and the Home Office, the press, the education system—and pubs, which the Fabians proposed nationalizing. But *Fabianism* conceives of empire as something closer to a problem of the world-system than of national character and determines to optimize Britain's role within that system:

> The problem before us is how the world can be ordered by Great Powers of practically international extent.... The partition of the greater part of the globe among such Powers is, as a matter of fact that must be faced, approvingly or deploringly, now only a question of time; and whether England is to be the centre and nucleus of one of those Great Powers of the future, or to be cast off by its colonies, ousted from its provinces, and reduced to its old island status, will depend on the ability with which the Empire is governed as a whole[.][45]

That optimization is framed largely as one of humanitarian necessity, and perhaps more striking, it is framed in what we might conceive of as pluralistic, multicultural terms: "We are no longer a Commonwealth of white men and baptized Christians," writes Shaw. "The vast majority of our fellow-subjects are black, brown, or yellow; and their creed is Mahometan, Buddhist, or Hindoo. We forbid the sale of the Bible in Khartoum, and punish British subjects in India for blasphemy against Vishnu" (15). Managing that diversity thus raises questions of discrimination among institutional models: "The primary conditions of Imperial stability are not the same throughout the Empire. The democratic institutions that mean freedom in Australasia and Canada would mean slavery in India and Soudan" (15). And finally, while for Shaw the ultimate answer to the question of empire is "International Socialism" (101), the content of that socialism leads to conclusions that—like those of White—are not quite what we might have expected. "What the British Empire wants most urgently ... is not Conservatism, not Liberalism, not Imperialism, but brains and political science" (93). That is, the solution to "mismanagement and disruption from within" (15)—for Shaw as for White—is institutional reform.

Shaw and White occupied quite different places on the map of British culture and on the continuum of British political affiliation at the turn of the twentieth century. Nonetheless, both take for granted the transformative power of the relationship between large institutions and the individuals who occupy them. For White, those individuals are the rulers; for Shaw, the ruled. For all the vehemence with which they addressed their audiences, and beyond the South African war whose conduct both protested, White and Shaw wrote at the dawn of a decade in which, as one historian puts it, "British rulers ... had squared the circle of domestic reform, imperial unity and great power rivalry."[46] For solutions to more immediate problems, they turned to the institutions that maintained the empire, relatively secure in their assumption that those institutions, properly managed, would value "responsibility," "talent," and "brains" and be set right by them in turn. The discourse of institutional formation, if it never achieved the sophistication or critical attention to totality that Anderson might have wished for, nonetheless saturated British political and literary culture across the modernist era.

Four decades later, on the eve of another war and near the end of her life, Virginia Woolf drafted a memoir titled "A Sketch of the Past," which ranges widely over her youth and London intellectual society at the turn of the century. Many sections take the form of character sketches. Woolf's cousin Herbert Fisher, whose life she addresses in one passage, had been one of those men of responsibility, talent, and brains. But Woolf's account of his "career" is less interested in the ordering of imperial institutions than in the men they produced and how they produced them:

> What, I asked myself, when I read Herbert Fisher's autobiography the other day, would Herbert have been without Winchester, New College, and the Cabinet? What would have been his shape had he not been stamped and moulded by that great patriarchal machine? Every one of our male relations was shot into that machine at the age of ten and emerged at sixty a Head Master, an Admiral, a Cabinet Minister, or the Warden of a college. It is as impossible to think of them as natural human

beings as it is to think of a carthorse galloping wild maned and unshod over the pampas.⁴⁷

In this memoir, Woolf imagines the schools, universities, military, and Parliament of the British Empire functioning as a "great patriarchal machine," generating administrative types: the headmaster, the warden, the admiral, the cabinet minister. Herbert Fisher's life, according to Woolf, would not only have been different without the machine; his very existence would be inconceivable. The liberty denied the men "stamped" by the machine is rendered as unimaginable as a carthorse—slow, drowsy, bred for work—galloping across the imperial hinterland those men were created to govern. This single sentence at once evokes and undercuts the heroic imagery of imperialism that Woolf had long viewed with a mixture of contempt, amusement, and anger, while at the same time tying the men's formation to the British Empire as a whole. In the course of "A Sketch," which also discusses at length her half-brother George Duckworth, Woolf repeatedly deploys the machine as a figure for the operation of institutions not only political, military, and "intellectual" but also social: the "social machine," from which George "emerged at the age of sixty with a Lady Margaret for a wife, with a knighthood, with a sinecure of some sort, three sons, and a country house" (132). Woolf emphasizes the "patriarchal" nature of the machine, suggesting that men are its main product, but she refers too to the "machine into which our rebellious [female] bodies were inserted in 1900" (152). If women are not always the bearers of the machine's imprint, neither do they exist outside a relationship to it.

Much of "A Sketch" is bleak, and not only because of the allusions made elsewhere to the sexual abuse that George Duckworth inflicted on Woolf when she was a child and young woman. It evokes a world in which large institutions have metastasized to dominate the social landscape. Woolf suggests that the dominance of institutionalized life has two primary and related effects, one social and one aesthetic. First, despite the social capital provided by the roles for which it forms them, the machine's products are totally ineffectual when confronted with experiences outside the world for which they have been prepared: George, she writes, is "almost brainless," incapable of meeting "any opposition" and "offer[ing] none." He possesses "no instinct, no ability to make him stray beyond the circle of the upper middle class world" (152); he is panicked by the young Virginia's appearance one evening in the wrong green dress. George's total embodiment of convention—"he never went an inch out of his orbit"—leads him to accept the world immediately and without reflection, and this, along with the dominance of his "physical passions" over his intellect, make him seem less than human. Unaware of themselves as selves, the men of the machine seem incapable of ever inhabiting the perspective that the writer herself relies upon as she turns the past into prose.

Second, the machine leads to an aesthetic dead end. Woolf writes that "[t]he spectacle of George, laying down laws in his leather armchair so instinctively, so unhesitatingly, fascinated me," recalling with disappointment that when "I wrote a sketch of his probable career . . . his actual career followed almost to the letter" (154). George "flow[s] into the mold without a doubt to mar the pattern," a "fossil" of more interest to the "archaeologist" (151) than to the novelist. The institutional configuration of a social landscape, in which any George or Herbert may as well be any other headmaster, admiral, minister, or warden, is an unrewarding object for the writer who, constructing a persona in the memoir by exploring the seemingly contingent associations among her own memories, finds nothing so deep or unpredictable in these imperial men. As the particular Herbert is revealed to be interchangeable with the generic cabinet minister, what at first appeared to be a substantial character dissipates as Woolf draws closer to him. And yet, despite this apparent impasse, as character is flattened into type by the machine's gears, the machine itself moves into the narrative foreground. George, though uninteresting in terms of his interiority or the analysis of motives and decisions privileged by classical realism, becomes a vehicle for the exploration of a world of "school reports," "scholarships," "triposes and fellowships," "social hoops," "required acts," and "tests" (152–54). Conjured into being by these prods and constraints, George reproduces them in "laying down laws" himself. "A Sketch of the Past" suggests that the evocation of character might produce not a progressively deeper excavation of self-sufficient individual subjectivity but rather an aesthetic map of the processes by which individuals become legible through, and in turn reproduce, the habits, practices, and procedures of the modern, fully institutional world.

What is unnerving about this section of "A Sketch" is that it suggests the hermetic nature of the relationship of the individual human being to the institution. George and the social machine form a closed feedback loop, where the stability of the individual relies on his adherence to accepted practice and institutional practice is validated and sustained by the conformity of the individuals it produces. Although this world is an undesirable one, it is not immediately obvious, in the scenario Woolf envisions, how novelty or change could enter into this process of static reproduction. In "A Sketch," though, writing that the power of convention "impresses even the outsider by the sweep of its current" (153), Woolf emphasizes that at the very least outsider status is never absolute; that is, it always produces and maintains itself in relation to an institutional inside. A social and an aesthetic problem intertwine: if the situation of Woolf's characters captures the reality of institutionalized life, it becomes difficult to imagine a position from which the writer herself could achieve the detachment necessary to "[c]onsider what immense forces society brings to play upon each of us, how that society changes from decade to decade, and also from class to class." She writes that she can "see myself as a fish in a stream; deflected; held in place; but cannot describe the stream" (80).

This question, of how the writer might take sufficient distance from her own formation to "describe the stream," was one Woolf engaged throughout her career. Long before she made it a punch line in her reminiscence of Herbert Fisher, Woolf viewed as naïve the notion of the "natural human being," independent and self-sufficient, whether in psychological or political terms. She strove to capture, through character, what she called "the invisible presences" that give shape to human lives. This practice suggests an ongoing negotiation with the ways that such "presences" might shape the perspective of the writer, but "A Sketch of the Past"—a product of 1939, a late and difficult moment in Woolf's career—is not especially optimistic about this negotiation.[48] The Virginia Woolf who speaks in "A Sketch of the Past" stands at an angle to the machine, "seeing the circus going on" (153). The cultivation of this perspective has a great deal to do with gender, and with the proximity of women to professional institutions. Woolf's perspective finally comes not from a rupture in institutional production or from a preexisting position outside it but from the routine and effective functioning of the institution itself: "Sometimes when I hear God Save the King I too feel a current belief but almost directly I consider my own splits asunder and one side of me criticises the other" (153). This split gives rise to "perceptions, however slight and transient . . . [that] gave my attitude toward George a queer twist. . . . There was a spectator in me who, even while I squirmed and obeyed, remained observant" (154). When the machine in the very moment it creates the individual produces a self-consciousness of her determination on the part *of* the individual, it echoes the constitution of Woolf's famous Outsiders Society in her 1938 essay *Three Guineas,* whose members become "outsiders" (indeed, have "positive existence" at all) only in the historical moment of their incorporation into the institutions of professional life. In short, the institutions that appeared to political writers like White and Shaw as the solution to a political problem appeared to a novelist like Woolf as the beginning of an aesthetic one.

I dwell on "A Sketch of the Past" for two reasons: First, its juxtaposition to the works of White and Shaw sets out the generic and chronological scope of the central argument of this book, from the turn of the century to around World War II. Second, while not engaging directly in the textual and extratextual strategies that I bring together under the term *institutional character,* "A Sketch" functions as a metacommentary on some of the key questions that writers would employ those strategies to address: How does one narrate "the machine"? How can a writer evoke a distinct character when so much of what constitutes character is a product of collective forms? What becomes of the individual, faced with the institution's tendency to flatten individuals into types? Where does the writer stand relative to their object, or relative to the institutions *of* literature?

To begin to address these questions, this book's first two chapters center on novel history and key modernist writers working at the center of the British Empire. Chapters 3 and 4 examine less canonical figures and move to the colonial periphery and briefly to the United States. Chapter 1, "Joseph Conrad and the Institutions of Empire," looks at Conrad's sustained novelistic examination of what he called simply "political institutions." His little-read collaboration with Ford Madox Ford, *The Inheritors* (1902), like the better-known *Nostromo* (1904) and *Under Western Eyes* (1912), encodes a profound pessimism about collective action in an attempt to hold together incommensurable modes of characterization. *The Inheritors* and *Nostromo* seek to retain the mythical Victorian liberal individual as the basis of character, even as individuals' attenuated capacity for action makes them unable to resist the "inhuman" institutions of government, finance, the military, and the press—what Conrad famously termed "material interests." Dispensing with the bildung conventions that Conrad's earlier works, such as *Lord Jim,* rely on, *Nostromo* moves a group of human ciphers through a fragmented, cyclical narrative that presents only repetition and futility. In *Under Western Eyes,* Conrad reintroduces moral individualism to investigate what possibilities remain for Victorian values of disinterest and critical rationality. Yet institutional demands foreclose, for his characters, the "effort of detachment" that he describes himself as undertaking in writing the novel.[49] The language teacher who narrates *Under Western Eyes* finds that his ability to observe events is predicated on his inability to intervene in them—a failure to yoke the moral individual to political agency that is key to Conrad's political novels. These works embody at the level of character and narrative form the institutions of high imperialism that they indict in their themes; their tonal and generic instability are products of this contradiction at their heart.

"Virginia Woolf and Political Possibility in the Gendered Institution," the book's second chapter, focuses on Woolf's optimistic evaluation of women's entry into male-dominated professions. Reading Woolf's 1937 novel *The Years* and its drafts, I argue that contrary to dominant critical understandings, Woolf conceived of her feminism in institutional terms, viewing the incorporation of individuals into collectivities as essential to novelistic character (aesthetically) and to nonviolent social change (politically). Like *Nostromo*, *The Years* uses a temporally dispersed plot and a large cast of characters to build a narrative centered on institutional rather than individual life. Woolf fully develops in *The Years* a theory of character only hinted at in her early essays on fiction: character is a function of incorporation into the university, the legal system, colonial bureaucracy, and medicine—in short, "professions." In the procedures and habits of institutional life, experience is shared and individuals cohere as part of a social structure, though that structure remains marked by differences of gender and class. The generic nature of institutionalized traits suggests, for Woolf, a limit on radical individuality that is necessary both for character in fiction and for women's agency. Peggy Pargiter, a dissatisfied young doctor, manifests a critical sensibility that looks toward women's growing presence within the institution of medicine; her cousin Sara, however, embodies the deforming effects of institutional exclusion, as a rich but unstructured aesthetic sensibility leads her to speak in illegible riddles, disintegrating on the page. In *The Years*, Woolf ultimately seeks to elaborate institutions as a means to what she calls "the old fabric insensibly changing without death or violence into the future."[50]

Chapter 3, "Institutional Picaresque: Mulk Raj Anand from Bloomsbury to Bombay," addresses Anand's long career. His work as an author took him from a childhood in Punjab, to London in the 1920s, to the BBC during World War II, and extended far into the postcolonial world, to the cultural institutions of nonaligned India in the Cold War and beyond (he died in 2004). I seek to grasp the broad scope of Anand's career by tracking his reliance on picaresque tropes in both his fiction and his self-presentation as an author and cultural functionary. Those tropes—the roguish, comic (male) protagonist; his persecution at the hands of authority; his irrepressible desire to succeed and fit in anyway—serve in Anand's literary writing, especially his novel *Coolie* (1936), to indict both "native" identitarianism and imperial universalism, while also evoking stability in institutions such as banks, public health agencies, and labor unions. In its indifference to the development of its picaresque hero, Munoo, and the contingency of his fate, *Coolie* draws the reader's attention less to individual exploitation than to the structures that produce that exploitation, while offering fleeting glimpses of how those structures might be put to work to ameliorate it. Through readings of correspondence around "The Barber's Trade Union," a short story published in 1937 by the Hogarth Press; of Anand's 1981 memoir *Conversations in Bloomsbury;* and of his "Self-Obituary," written in 1995 and published after his death, I argue that Anand cast himself as a picaresque figure—an outsider—as a means of securing his positions *inside* Bloomsbury publishing, the world of postwar Indian letters, and the liberalizing Indian state. Writers and cultural workers like Anand bridged the epochal divide of World War II and decolonization, often returning from sojourns in the metropolitan centers of modernism to their countries of origin to participate in the project of developing a postcolonial national literary culture. Such careers can be difficult to place in standard periodization, as they evolved across very different literary and cultural economies in the pre- and postwar worlds. To "think institutionally," in the words of the political scientist Hugh Heclo, helps to illuminate how such authors' work both addressed life in modern institutions across midcentury and helped pave those same authors' way through those institutions.[51] I conclude by examining moments when, his position secured, Anand turned to writing *as* an institution, dropping the picaresque mode for the security of collective authorship in his 1954 *Story of the Indian Post Office* and in his longtime editorship of the remarkable art and architecture journal *Marg*.

Finally, chapter 4, "Elizabeth Bowen: War, Welfare, and the Institutional Impersonal," opens on Bowen's family chronicle *Bowen's Court*

(1941). In this work, which covers some three hundred years in the history of Bowen's family, their Anglo-Irish landowning class, and the titular house in which they lived, Bowen depicts how a highly formal, aestheticized social sphere, with distinctive practices, rhythms, and "impersonal" manners, emerged in Anglo-Ireland in part because of the demands of the state power that both protected and threatened it. Tracing the Anglo-Irish class to its dissolution in Bowen's own lifetime, *Bowen's Court* ultimately disarticulates Anglo-Irish values from the so-called Big Houses in which those values were embodied, suggesting that they have continued relevance in the twentieth century. In *The Heat of the Day* (1948), Bowen resurrects Anglo-Irish style and impersonality in the shadowy complex of espionage and intelligence institutions of World War II London. The world of *The Heat of the Day*, a novel set during the Blitz, is one in which human relationships are mediated entirely through institutional roles; Bowen evokes in her heroine Stella a heroic ethos—beautiful, stylish, honorable, exciting—to which politics are largely incidental, even as this ethos is dependent on the wartime state. This purely aesthetic concept of what institutions can do for individuals (allow them to live beautifully) goes some way toward explaining the scathing satire Bowen directed at the welfare state (which provided merely for people's basic needs) in her short fiction and postwar journalism. I draw on archival materials that illustrate how Bowen figured the university in the fifties and sixties as a similarly aestheticized institution for herself, as she turned to teaching and lecturing in writing programs in the United States. The commonalities Bowen found across late Victorian Ireland, the British state, and the American university illustrate how thinking institutionally allowed modernist writers to organize narrative form, political engagement, and their own literary careers. The book's conclusion briefly follows the fate of institutional character into the present, in the work of one contemporary novelist particularly indebted to modernism, Zadie Smith.

1
Joseph Conrad and the Institutions of Empire

IN 1904, in the midst of writing *Nostromo,* Joseph Conrad took "two nights and the morning" to compose a brief essay on Anatole France.[1] The essay attributes to France's genius the notion that "political institutions, whether contrived by the wisdom of the few or the ignorance of the many, are incapable of securing the happiness of mankind," a sentiment Conrad's own work would echo for the rest of his life, but to which he was already attuned.[2] As Ford Madox Ford would put it, Conrad had, "as a Papist, a profound disbelief in the perfectibility of human institutions."[3] This passage from a minor essay functions as a sort of epigraph for the series of novels and essays upon whose threshold Conrad then stood. The imminent publication of *Nostromo* would be followed by *The Secret Agent* in 1907 and *Under Western Eyes* in 1911, not to mention the major essay "Autocracy and War," on the Russo-Japanese War (1905), and the story collection *A Set of Six* (1908), which deals extensively with themes of revolution and social upheaval. Across the decade, the ambit of Conrad's work expands from a concern with the ethos of the seafaring men who worked for the empire to the institutions that administered it. Yet critics have generally found in these works little in the way of a positive concept of politics as such. Conrad's emphasis on individual action, his skepticism of rationalist improvement schemes and collective agency, and his divided attitude toward imperial practices remains more ethical than political, affirming little aside from solitary endurance.

This chapter, however, argues that despite his antipathy toward the development of modern institutionality, the logic of institutions and institutionalization contributes in a significant way to important formal effects in Conrad's writing, particularly to his construction of character. When read against a historical moment in which the idea of the institution was of heightened concern, Conrad's political novels—particularly *The Inheritors, Nostromo,* and *Under Western Eyes*—suggest that institutionality erodes the aspiration to social cohesion, while curtailing the potential for individual action to counter this erosion. And even as Conrad insists on the necessity for literary writing of a liberal ideal of detachment from institutional life, these novels repeatedly stage scenarios in which that detachment is revealed to be an impossibility or a doomed aspiration. The confluence of the political Conrad and the national Conrad has generated a criticism highly sensitive to the unsaid and the contradictory in Conrad's work, first, because Conrad's own national context is so apparently illegible, and second, because he seems not to have produced in his work a positive vision of politics.[4] Yet as the essay on Anatole France hints, Conrad tends to address not politics as such but "political institutions." Indeed, the term *political institution* (or *institution* alone) appears with considerably greater frequency than does *politics* in the period in which Conrad seems to have been most engaged with political questions. That he seems to have reflexively chosen to discuss the political in terms of the institutional suggests, on Conrad's own terms, a means of understanding his engagement with collectivity that does not lead down the path to the nation. Critical attention to Conrad's politics has taken his writing to be organized around the *absence* of a collective form he admired but despaired of seeing instantiated in the conditions of early-twentieth-century modernity: the organic nation. But the figure of the institution, critically neglected but a persistent presence in Conrad's political writing and which he viewed with deep suspicion, can be seen as an organizing and active *presence* in the formal innovations of his work—as what Jed Esty, discussing modernism's inheritance from the realist tradition promoted by George Lukács, calls an "aspect of the world-system understood as a global fact susceptible to positive representation."[5] Conrad's relative illegibility in terms of national context is a product of his investment in the institutionalizing imperial order of the late nineteenth century. This age of institutions underwrites the imaginative universe of his work.

Avrom Fleishman, in his classic *Conrad's Politics*, was the first to situate Conrad's engagement with collective forms in a primarily English tradition of organic nationalist thought reaching back to Burke and Rousseau, through Coleridge, Thomas Carlyle, Thomas and Matthew Arnold, George Eliot, and the Oxford neo-Hegelians T. H. Green and F. H. Bradley, among others.[6] Fleishman argues that Conrad was not, as many of his Cold War–era American interpreters insisted, a prophet of radical individualism. Instead, like his predecessors, Conrad aimed to resolve the tensions between dynamism and mechanism, spirit and authority, individual and institution. Properly understood, organicism offers a "critique of individualism": the individual's existence takes on meaning only in the context of the organic community.[7] The right kind of institution complements natural characteristics, whether of the group, as in the analyses of Carlyle and Arnold, or of the individual, as in the Victorian novel, most especially the English-language bildungsroman. If Conrad seems particularly obsessed with individual seekers, this is because authentic community has become largely impossible to achieve under the conditions of Western modernity. Thus *Lord Jim,* for example, becomes a parable of "identification with the higher claims of the community"; for Jim, rejected by the industrial West, "the only refuge outside civilized atomism lies in creating an organic native community."[8] And for Conrad the concrete form of community is the nation: "'National temperament' is Conrad's term for the popular sentiments, manners, and sense of identity which the organicist tradition made the basis of political organization."[9] As Conrad writes in *The Mirror of the Sea* (1906), "We must turn to the national spirit which, superior in its force and continuity to good and evil fortune, can alone give us the feeling of an enduring existence and an invincible power against the fates."[10] For these thinkers and ultimately for Conrad, according to Fleishman, the life of the individual is lent meaning by their spiritual identification with a national whole that expresses itself in the formation of a state that relates through commerce and diplomacy to other naturally ordered states for the benefit of all. Nations are the units within which individual lives gain meaning, and any extranational order is premised on the prior existence of a group of nations properly constituted. Thus Conrad is assimilated to an intellectual genealogy in which the horizon of politics is ultimately national.

A subsequent critical tradition followed Fleishman in foregrounding the category "national," while showing it to be a problematic (if also productive) means of understanding Conrad. The Polish aristocracy into which Conrad was born was a former ruling class, denied sovereignty since 1795 by the imperial ambitions of Russia, Prussia, and Austria and inclined to conceive of the Polish nation as, in Geoffrey Galt Harpham's words, "a theoretical entity, the absent cause of a defiant but literally groundless patriotism."[11] Both sides of Conrad's family included nationalists and revolutionaries who rallied to this cause. Conrad himself, of course, decided at a young age to go to sea, adopted French and then

English as his primary languages, and settled in England to write novels populated by an exceedingly cosmopolitan cast of characters and deeply indebted to French realist models—choosing both personal and artistic self-exile from a nation itself thought to exist in spiritual and political exile in its own homeland.[12] Because of this, even Zdislaw Najder, whose authoritative biography and volumes of historical documents have done as much as any work to bring to light Conrad's Polish inheritance, argues that "his unusual, polycentric background" makes national contextualization futile.[13] F. R. Leavis includes Conrad in his great tradition only by establishing a tradition that, its stated Anglocentricity aside, has as little as possible to do with national origin, turning instead to the English *language* as a medium conveying "essential human values."[14] And when Harpham focuses on Conrad's Polishness, Poland itself functions in his reading as a vanishing point on which converge all the seemingly opposed lines of thought to be found in Conrad's work. For Harpham, the difficulty of pinning Conrad down on almost any issue is symptomatic of Poland's contradictory, nonexistent nationhood: "The real significance of Poland in Conrad's work is that the real significance is elsewhere; or, to put the matter otherwise, where the real significance is elsewhere in Conrad, there Poland is."[15] Poland is less a context or object of analysis than a principle of indeterminacy, the figure of an ambivalence about which Conrad is perfectly unambivalent, a quality that marks him as unique. Or again, as Christopher GoGwilt puts it, even as Conrad ceaselessly interrogates concepts of nationhood there is a "significant *lack* of national affiliation informing Conrad's imaginative and creative work."[16]

Readings that seek to position Conrad beyond the nation have read his work against the history of global capital. Stephen Ross, in his *Conrad and Empire*, argues that accounting for Conrad in terms of nation-state-led imperialism is ultimately futile because of the author's "grander, more oblique, and less articulate concern with what we might now call incipient globalization . . . the emerging post-imperialist modernity that Michael Hardt and Antonio Negri have christened Empire."[17] Regina Martin situates *Lord Jim, Nostromo,* and *Victory* amid the development of "absentee capitalism": the transition from "an imperialist system of capitalism based on the modern corporation" to one "organized around the family-owned firm," the latter of which (for Conrad) grounds an ethical imperialism in the affective ties of kinship.[18] Both critics look to Conrad's engagement with institutions: Ross at a relatively high level of abstraction, finding in

Nostromo, for example, an Althusserian conception of "the Law" (120), and Martin in the development of the corporation as described by V. I. Lenin and Eric Hobsbawm. In many ways, I follow these critics' institutional focus, but in examining Conrad's treatment of institutions as such, my own approach is both more specific and more general; in what follows, I read Conrad's political works as structured around a range of institutions—more specific than "the Law," more varied than the corporation. *The Inheritors* features the popular press and weighs different conceptions of what an institution is for. In *Nostromo*, character is a product of the collective forms of the military, modern communications, the financial institution, and the state—the "material interests" that are the real actors in the drama of late empire. Conrad renders the ascent of these institutions as "inevitable" even as he consistently portrays this inevitability as lamentable. *Under Western Eyes*, while set in imperial Russia rather than the British sphere of influence, allegorizes the same set of issues around institutional life; the novel generates alternatives to, and suggests postures of detachment from, institutionality only to reveal those alternatives' and postures' inadequacy and ultimate failure. These novels pattern major elements of character on the very forms of institution that their plots mercilessly deride.[19] In his essential reading of *Heart of Darkness*, Michael Levenson argues that that novel "begins . . . by defining character in firmly institutional terms, asking in effect what happens to the self when it has been thoroughly assimilated into a social form."[20] In what follows, I suggest in effect that Conrad spent the long decade that followed working out answers.

Historians, political scientists, and economists have traced how the life of the European empires from the 1880s onward was characterized by the increasing prominence of formal institutions, whether state-, market-, or civil society–based. Ronald Hyam describes the expansion of state and financial power throughout the empire in the late nineteenth and early twentieth centuries as the birth of a "new Leviathan": the "masterful modern State" untethered from the popular spirit or geographic contiguity of the organic nation. "At its most basic level," he writes, "[the new Leviathan] represented a shift from society to state, from local linkages of regulatory social integration to networks of rationalizing bureaucracy and intrusive policing, ever-widening and ever-tightening in their grip. This Leviathan was more interventionist in economic life than Western states were in their own home bases."[21] Historians have amply documented the upheavals in local societies initiated by this process of violent modernization, while a vast critical literature has theorized the effects of the process whereby the non-West was incorporated into Western systems of knowledge and control, demonstrating how fundamental this process was to notions of identity for both colonizers and colonized. The new Leviathan, Hyam argues, ultimately "provided the framework within which Afro-Asian nationalist protest was effectively articulated, and within which alternative 'post-colonial' states could be constructed" (61). While the imperial state's specific methods and emphases varied widely—the directly administered empire-within-an-empire of India, the chartered company and "indirect rule" in Africa, financial hegemony in South America—each form of imperial activity in this period consistently formalized administrative, economic, and educational systems in particular ways in attempts to alter collective behavior. As Hyam points out, this shift was often first enacted and most intensely felt on the periphery of the empire rather than in the metropolitan center.

Adding an economic perspective to this historical story, Daron Acemoglu, Simon Johnson, and James Robinson argue that European colonialism and Atlantic trade from the sixteenth to the early nineteenth century fueled the development of political and economic institutions, especially in Britain, that enabled economic growth and laid the groundwork for the era of high imperialism.[22] And in his *Rational Empires,* Leo J. Blanken pursues this institutional analysis through the nineteenth century, arguing that European imperial activity in its various forms was provoked and guided by institutional incentives within states, in competing imperial powers, and in areas targeted for imperial exploitation.[23] The changing institutional environment these analyses reveal presupposes relationships among global institutions, whether state or non-state, that no longer sustain any obvious connection to the natural inclinations of individuals who occupy those institutions. At this distance from the individual, institutions appear as ends in themselves, relating only to other globalizing institutions. As Conrad himself writes, "We have all heard that well-known view that trade follows the flag. And that is not always true. There is also this truth that the flag, in normal conditions, represents commerce to the eye and understanding of the average man."[24] In his distinctly imperial understanding of international relations, Conrad points not to the conflict between states and private interest but to the specter of their becoming indistinguishable: rather than trade following the flag, or vice versa, the two seem to collapse into a single phenomenon in which, at least to the "average man," one bewilderingly represents the other.[25]

Imperial institutions appear throughout Conrad's work; for example, in a well-known passage in *Heart of Darkness*, Marlow finds "a large shining map" that shows the division of Africa among the European governments in the office of the quasi-private Company that administers the Congo River trade, and whose employ he is about to enter. *Heart of Darkness* incorporates the late imperial institutional world in a referential manner—for example, the map clearly situates the narrative in the years following the actual Berlin Conference; Kurtz's International Society for the Suppression of Savage Customs is an ersatz version of King Leopold's Association Internationale Africaine; and the novel famously draws on Conrad's own Congo experience in its portrayal of these institutions. But Conrad's more thoroughgoing engagements with the late imperial institution are primarily conceptual, concerned less with reference to specific people and places than with ideas of the institution and institutionalization that became available in that historical moment.[26] This conceptual engagement with the age of institutions separates the major novels *Nostromo*, *The Secret Agent*, and *Under Western Eyes* from the rest of Conrad's oeuvre. *Nostromo* in particular may be seen as a pivot point not only in Conrad's career but also in the engagement of the novel form with institutional life, precisely at the moment when the representational concerns of Victorian realism ostensibly began to dissolve into the stream of modernism. In this novel, the temporal compression and distension of plot, the evacuation of individual motivation, and the dominance of material interests as actors in themselves can be seen as propelled by an attempt to capture processes of institutionalization in the era of high imperialism. *Nostromo*'s chronology figures Conrad's skepticism about the institutional codification and regularization of the imperial world-system, even as the story itself is driven by a series of episodes in this process. As Georg Lukács argues, the structure of the novel relies on its being tethered to the life of the individual—it "overcomes its 'bad' infinity by recourse to the biographical form."[27] But as the political scientists James March and Johan Olsen point out, the biography of an institution exceeds that of any given individual, both in its longer duration and in being comprised of many persons; institutions are "relatively invariant in the face of turnover of individuals."[28] The institutional timescape may be many times longer than that of a human life. The difficulties this poses for representing institutions in narrative can be felt throughout Conrad's political novels.

The Institution as Tradition and Technology: *The Inheritors*

Conrad's first engagement with imperialism not as an ethical question but as a set of institutions was *The Inheritors,* a 1901 proto-science-fiction thriller coauthored with Ford Madox Ford, in which a young journalist's assimilation into the demands of the emergent popular press figures larger questions about individual agency and institutional life. The novel involves a plot by a group calling themselves the Fourth Dimensionists (who are in fact aliens from another planet) to tie a respectable old-guard government, and in particular its Foreign Minister, Churchill, to an immoral and inept imperial development scheme undertaken in Greenland (of all places) by the Duc de Mersch. The Dimensionists wager that the venture will be exposed as the fraud it is by a newly aggressive and sensationalistic press, bringing down Churchill's government and handing power to Gurnard, the Chancellor of the Exchequer and a Dimensionist collaborator. A beguiling and unnamed Dimensionist woman insinuates herself into the aristocratic family of the narrator, Arthur Granger, by posing as a long-absent "sister" and manipulates him into writing for a prominent newspaper, while she uses the family name to gain entry to the corridors of power. With full knowledge of the Dimensionist plot, but in love with the mysterious young woman and unable to withstand the various pressures and enticements of his new career, Arthur, given editorial authority for one night, allows the publication of the exposé that ruins his friend Churchill and ushers in the new regime.

The growing power of the popular press is registered first in failed novelist Arthur's reluctance to lower himself to write a series of political and celebrity "atmospheres," or profiles, and then in the dignified Churchill's bafflement at being asked to interview for one.[29] As a year passes and he writes "fifty-two atmospheres in all" (75), though, Arthur's newspaper, *The Hour,* gains prominence such that when a damning profile of de Mersch's Hyperborean Protectorate and Trans-Greenland Railway appears it circulates widely enough to create a scandal that opens the door to Gurnard. In the course of the novel, the figure of the journalist goes from that of "some respectable tradesman that one calls in only when one is *in extremis*" (58) to "*the* man who could be believed" (184). This ascent, though, is less a product of personal virtue or ambition on the part of any particular journalist than of the consolidation and elevation of the institution itself. Arthur says that he "saw the apotheosis of the Press—a Press that makes a State Founder suppliant to a man like myself.... I was nothing, nobody; yet here I stood in communion with one of those who change the face of continents. He had need of me, of the power that was behind me.... It was nothing to me. I was just a person elected by some suffrage of accidents. Even in my own eyes I was merely a symbol—the sign visible of incomprehensible power" (99–100). Arthur himself is "nothing," "nobody," "merely a symbol"; he stands in for an "incomprehensible power." "Uniformly unsuccessful" (16) in his attempts to achieve fame as an author on his own, Arthur quickly discovers that the way to a reputation is through adherence to the dictates of his new employers: "I had been very docile; had accepted emendations; had lavished praise, had been unctuous and yet had contrived to retain the dignified savour of the editorial 'we'" (34). The novel captures not only the emergence of the press as a social force but also the processes by which it shapes the individuals it comprises. Arthur's realization of himself in the "apotheosis of the Press" evinces an ironic consciousness of his own institutional character: his more or less unquestioning, and often unconscious, adherence to the rules and practices of an institution. "Oh," Arthur says, "I never play off my own bat" (197).[30]

The Dimensionists themselves are "a race clear-sighted, eminently practical, incredible; with no ideals, prejudices, or remorse; with no feeling for art and no reverence for life; free from any ethical tradition" (9). In what appears a cynical adherence to pure process, they are also "indistinguishable" (12). Gurnard's face has "nothing distinctive in its half-hidden pallid oval; nothing that one could seize upon" (81). Arthur thinks his young Dimensionist "sister" is "American" (3), "Australian," (5) "Semitic," "Sclav," or "Circassian" (7), finally giving up as she continues to insist that she hails from "a mathematical monstrosity," the Fourth Dimension. Having as their origin not another country but another dimension altogether, the Dimensionists are an almost parodic instance of what several critics have pointed to as Conrad's "heterotopic" sensibility, a product of his globalized and non-national writing that creates spaces that "have the curious property of being in relation with all other sites, but in such a way as to suspect, neutralize, or invert the set of relationships they happen to designate, mirror, or reflect."[31] "In relation with" the Dimensionists, and ultimately ruined by them, is the decent government of Churchill, a figure strongly associated with national values and with Englishness specifically, and who, according to Arthur, "really was a sympathetic character and did stand for political probity" (29). An aristocratic amateur, he is writing a life of Oliver Cromwell, loves art in a gentlemanly way, is "sane . . . persistent," a politician by "circumstance," with "contempt for the political mind," and "little personal quaintnesses . . . a deference, a modesty, an open-mindedness" (68). These values are aligned with the English landscape itself when Churchill speaks at a village fair, surrounded by "the sunlight on the stretches of turf . . . the mellow, golden stonework of the long range of buildings . . . the sound of a chime of bells that came wonderfully sweetly over the soft swelling of the close turf" (156). Forced, though he dislikes it, to ally the government with de Mersch's Greenland scheme in the interests of political stability, Churchill takes a political gamble that is, as the young woman puts it, "a desperate effort to get in touch with the spirit of the times that he doesn't like and doesn't understand" (64).

At the novel's conclusion, Arthur sits in the newspaper office late at night, deciding whether or not to publish the report that he knows will bring down Churchill's government:

> [N]ow that the condemnation had come, it meant ruin, as it seemed to me, for everybody I had known, worked for, seen, or heard of, during the last year of my life. It was ruin for Fox, for Churchill, for the ministers, and for the men who talk in railway carriages, for shopkeepers and for the government; it was a menace to the institutions which hold us to the past, that are our guarantees for the future. The safety of everything one respected and believed in was involved in the disclosure of an atrocious fraud, and the disclosure was in my hands. (184)

This central passage in the novel's institutional plot is also one of a very few that Ford singled out as having been written by Conrad alone.[32] Arthur becomes a character in embodying a set of distinctive traits drawn from the collectively shared rules, expectations, and incentives of the new journalism. But here he also makes explicit a second logic of institutionality, one that has been implied throughout, gesturing to another force behind this apparently simple narrative: the opposition between competing concepts of the institution itself. Arthur's description of these institutions as things "which hold us to the past, that are our guarantees for the future" emphasizes the preservation of existing social arrangements, and their inclusion within the sphere of "everything one respected and believed in" imputes an element of moral value to their operation.

An institution in this sense is what Mark McGurl calls "an embodiment of *tradition*, a place where the authority of past practices is contained and conserved," and here it is closely affiliated with the nation, indeed with the organic nation.[33] Arthur's list of those elements that stand to suffer from the disclosure of de Mersch's scheme builds, as does the organicist order, from the individual (Churchill), to the delimited group ("shopkeepers," echoing the line famously attributed to Napoleon that the English were "a nation of shopkeepers"), to the "government," culminating with an "us" that refers clearly to the English people. Conrad writes approvingly of institutions in this sense in his 1919 essay "The Crime of Partition," in which he discusses the "liberties" and "institutions" of the "Polish temperament." "The Polish State," Conrad writes, "in its Parliamentary life as well as its international politics, presented a complete unity of feeling and purpose."[34] A noble people make a noble government. These might be called *institutions* that have not been *instituted*; they arise naturally and are essentially reflective of the temper of the people and nation, changing only as that temper changes and acting to ensure the continuity of past and future.

The Dimensionists imagine institutions not as tradition but as technology, and the terms of the conflict in *The Inheritors* lies in the distance between these two ideas of institutions. Forced from their own overpopulated world, the Dimensionists arrive on Earth without "ideals, prejudices, or remorse," but this does not mean that they plan a violent overthrow of the existing human order. Instead, they will be "irresistible because indistinguishable" (12), like humans but without the "scruples that acted like handicapping weights," which prevent us from following the logic of our social forms to its amoral extreme: "There would be no fighting, no killing; we—our whole social system—would break as a beam snaps, because we were worm-eaten with altruism and ethics" (13). The Duc de Mersch, whose machinations are essential to their scheme, presents himself as "first and foremost a State Founder" (31), and his "System for the Regeneration of the Arctic Regions" as a liberal imperialist utopia: "They had laid down so many miles of railways, used so many engines of British construction.

They had taught the natives to use and to value sewing-machines and European costumes. So many hundred of English younger sons had gone to make their fortunes and, incidentally, to enlighten the Esquimaux—so many hundreds of French, of Germans, Greeks, Russians. All these lived and moved in harmony, employed, happy, free labourers, protected by the most rigid laws. Man-eating, fetich-worship, slavery had been abolished, stamped out" (99). This is obviously at odds with the Englishness of the cabinet's "Churchill strain"; indeed, de Mersch's "*Systeme Groenlandais*," an inversion of the organicist ideal, is a state without a nation, its legitimacy further dissipated by its taking sanction not from a people but from a supranational institution: "The great international society for the preservation of Polar freedom watched over all, suggested new laws, modified the old" (99). Its diverse community of "Esquimaux . . . French . . . Germans, Greeks, Russians" is not self-regulating but rather sustained only "by the most rigid laws." And it's a fraud: the advertised humanitarian aspects of the Greenland "system" are nonexistent and serve only to justify to the world "a corporate exploitation of unhappy Esquimaux" (32). In this respect *The Inheritors* offers a popular-novelistic version of a work like J. A. Hobson's *Imperialism*, which appeared in the same year and offered a similar indictment of deceptive imperial practices and economic motives. But, as in Conrad's better-known engagements with empire and colonialism (that is to say, most of his other major writings), critique is really not the point. The hypocrisy of the Greenland scheme matters only insofar as it exploits public morality to kick Churchill out; in this sense, the nation would in fact benefit from being less sympathetic about the fate of "Esquimaux."

Greenland is but one of the "corporate" arrangements—which also include the new print media, the activist imperial administration, City financial firms, and even the tatters of hereditary aristocracy—that the Dimensionists seek to occupy and manipulate. Indeed, they often play them against one another, in a version of what might be termed, in a phrase often attributed to Antonio Gramsci, "the long march through institutions."[35] For them, the institution acts as what McGurl terms "a social *technology*, a way of mobilizing human and other resources."[36] This demands both the remobilization of older forms (e.g., Arthur's, and the Dimensionists', reliance on his pedigree for access) and the creation of new ones (the founding of *The Hour* as an institution of the new journalism). Either way, institutions are seen as creating opportunities for collective change, not as providing a guarantee that things will stay the same. "They had no joy, these people who were to supersede us," Arthur says; "their clear-sightedness did nothing more for them than just that [sic] enabling them to spread desolation among us and take our places" (205). The nature of those "places," and the means of delimiting them, is changing as the social value of the concept of the institution shifts from traditionalism to technology. The novel's critique of imperialism, such as it is, is subsumed into the representation of this larger, what the novel terms "inevitable," process.

Institutional Agency in *Nostromo*

The narrator of *Nostromo* tells of "a certain prominent man. . . . then a person in power" in the Costaguanan capital of Sta Marta, who "had exclaimed with a hollow laugh, once . . . at a time of political crisis": "You call these men Government officials? They? Never! They are officials of the mine—officials of the Concession—I tell you. . . . The political *jefe*, the chief of the police, the chief of the customs, the general, all, all are the officials of that Gould."[37] What his listeners overlook, the prominent man suggests, is that Charles Gould's silver mine has overtaken the Costaguanan state as guarantor of official authority. And indeed, the mine will go on to become, at the novel's climax, "big enough to take in hand the making of a new State" (323). But the prominent man takes for granted that the officials must derive their authority from some extrapersonal source. His apparent confusion lies in how to figure that source: is it "the mine," the land and infrastructure? "The Concession," the legal fiction that forced ownership of the mine on Gould's father? Or is it "that Gould" himself?

Conrad's narrator has already offered a seemingly less ambiguous account of this "power in the land": "The San Tome mine was to become an institution, a rallying-point for everything in the province that needed order and stability to live" (119–20). But as literary critics—including Caroline Levine, Jeffrey Williams, Lisi Schoenbach, and Mark McGurl—have turned to institutions, they have also pointed out that *institution* itself is a notoriously mutable term. As McGurl writes, its "meaning . . . ranges so easily in our usage from social organizations housed in buildings and supplied with proper names . . . to individuals like Henry James or James Joyce, who become 'institutions' of a kind, to a more diffuse sense of institutions as 'established practices,' as in the institution of the family, or literature, or slavery" (132). Institutional character is not so diffuse; the prominent man's seeming confusion about the source of official authority comes to look more like precision. It is exactly as products of an institution that the officials can be "of" the mine (a social organization with a material structure), the Concession (a quirk of the established practices of law), and "that Gould" (a distinct individual). *Nostromo* has long been read as what Eloise Knapp Hay calls "a modern political novel": it "laments the loss of individual self-control and the defeat of will power by anonymous social forces."[38] But as the prominent man indicates, one would be hard pressed to find "individual self-control" or autonomous "will power" in the novel's universe to begin with, and the "social forces" are hardly so "anonymous": they are "material interests," institutions as technologies, and the mine is only one among many.

Rather than merely bemoaning the relative commonplace that the ascendance of modern institutional life is at odds with the development of the individual, *Nostromo* turns this tension into a central feature of its construction of character. In contrast to Fleishman's argument that *Nostromo* "represents the history of a society as a living organism," what he terms "the fulfillment of Conrad's political imagination" (167) is better understood as inhering in his representation of institutions. *Nostromo* contravenes Franco Moretti's assertion that the idea of collective forms as "constitutive of individual identity—and not just destructive of it" has "remained an unexplored possibility in Western narrative," even as it stands as a remarkably pessimistic evaluation of the historical trends its formal explorations strain to represent.[39] The novel may thus be seen as a pivot point not only in Conrad's career but also in the engagement of the novel form with institutional life. In *Nostromo*, the temporal compression and distension of plot, the evacuation of individual agency, and the dominance of material interests as actors in themselves can be seen as propelled by an attempt to capture processes of institutionalization in the era of high imperialism. The novel's disfigured chronology thus figures Conrad's skepticism about the institutional codification and regularization of the imperial world-system, even as the story itself is driven by a series of episodes in this process. Conrad ultimately needs to import an older set of conventions, those of the romance, to bring a stop to the otherwise potentially endless narrative of institutions—potentially endless because of the institutional narrative's relative indifference to the life of any particular individual.

Across this period, Conrad's works dispense with the synthesizing impulse of the nineteenth century while equally refusing to adapt the conventions of the coming-of-age novel. The connection between empire, institutionalization, and the modernist novel has been drawn most tightly in scholarship on the bildungsroman. The coming-of-age novel, in Moretti's influential account, was the nineteenth century's privileged genre, symbolically mediating between individual "self-determination" and "socialization" into the collective: in the bildungsroman, "One's formation as an individual in and for oneself coincides without rifts with one's social integration as a simple *part of a whole*" (16). Esty's *Unseasonable Youth* argues that as the age of empire disrupted the self-sufficiency of nationhood, it did the same to narratives of development: "As the national referent was increasingly embedded in the matrix of colonial modernity, the destinies of persons, and the peoples they represent, had to include not only the story of progress, but also stories of stasis, regression, and hyperdevelopment. Modernism's untimely youths—Woolf's Rachel Vinrace, Conrad's Lord Jim, Joyce's Stephen Daedalus—register the unsettling effects of the colonial encounter on humanist ideals of national culture."[40]

Yet one aspect of Moretti's concluding argument in *The Way of the World* has received less explicit attention than others. The death of the bildungsroman is linked to the slaughter of the Great War, yet "the war was the final act in a longer process" (229). What precipitated this process, Moretti suggests, was that in place of what I have termed the methodological individualism of the Victorians, "social institutions began to appear as such" (230). The nineteenth-century bildungsroman preserved "neutral spaces," areas of life in which the individual could grow into reconciliation with society on what appeared to be one's own terms: "what he must do is also symbolically right" (230). But the institutions of the twentieth century produce "functional integration," in which even the illusion of individual assent to institutional norms is erased. The totalizing reach of "institutions as such" presented an insoluble problem for the novel of development, and thus a change in the social world produced a change in novelistic form—in this case, the end of a form. Moretti's account thus closes with the declining importance in the novel of both youth and the institutions that housed (and stifled) it. While other readers of the twentieth-century bildungsroman have countered by demonstrating the continued relevance of the youthful protagonist developing in time, the works these accounts examine tend to persist in imagining large institutions as inimical to the development of individual persons.

This story, about the fit between the coming-of-age novel and late empire, is compelling and gets at important truths. But as a now dominant account of the Anglophone modernist novel's relation to history, that story also obscures genres and formal features that are also important to understanding the history of the novel, and it gestures toward an issue in the historiography of the modernist novel generally. The historiography is based in a Marxist account of imperial economy that has been largely displaced within the discipline of history itself but spans majors works of the twentieth century, from J. A. Hobson's *Imperialism*, to Lenin's *Imperialism: The Highest Stage of Capitalism*, to Hannah Arendt's *Origins of Totalitarianism*, to Eric Hobsbawm's *The Age of Empire, 1875–1914*.[41] What unites these works is a strongly teleological account of the nineteenth and early twentieth centuries that divides them into periods of "informal" and "formal" imperialism. Nation-based capitalism driven by the middle classes of European states turns around 1880 to what Esty, ventriloquizing Arendt, terms "a new phase of unrestrained capitalist relations outside the national boundaries and moral limits of middle-class progress"—in other words, "the age of empire."[42] In the novel, meanwhile, straightforward realist bildung plots (in Austen, Dickens, Thackeray, the Brontës) that align the maturing individual with the maturity of the nation give way to broken, distorted, negative or anti-bildungsroman in modernism, in which frozen or prematurely accelerated plots of maturation stand in for the uneven development and conflicts of colonial settings in the age of empire. The two stories, first of empire and of youth, then of history and aesthetics, allegorize each other.

Part of why this narrative of imperialism syncs up with generic changes within the bildungsroman so effectively is that both present a powerful monoplot: a single global force figured in the biography of a single individual. From the perspective of historiography, though, this narrative does a poor job of accounting for the development of *British* imperialism in particular, inaccurately making territorial expansion central to its story and flattening and abstracting the longer continuities of the British Empire into phases separated by an epochal break. From the literary side, the empire/bildungsroman thesis rests a great deal of weight on a single genre, one that is itself unstable, for reasons that are suggested by, but go beyond, the need to import a German term from a distinct national-cultural context alien to many of the authors hailed by its use here. Critical overinvestment in the bildungsroman also pushes aside many important, multiply plotted, temporally complex works that one would think are undeniably central to the history of the novel—and others that have yet to be acknowledged as such, including the works I address in the following chapters. And finally, the thesis reasserts the kind of epochal break that has become less and less compelling in modernist scholarship: it turns out that human character did change, but in 1880, not in or about 1910.

Revised approaches to British imperialism offer a more nuanced account. As early as 1953 the historians John Gallagher and Ronald Robinson's brief essay "The Imperialism of Free Trade" offered a different political-economic model of British imperialism, demonstrating convincingly the incoherence of any account that divides the history of the British Empire into "informal" and "formal" phases underwritten by broad changes in global capitalism. Instead, they claim "a fundamental continuity in British expansion" from the early nineteenth century to the empire's contraction in the mid-twentieth, foregrounding the plurality of ways that the empire actually expanded (economic and commercial hegemony, lopsided political treaties, settlement, and military power—the former two far more regularly than the latter two) and the differing rates at which such forms of expansion moved.[43] This essay founded what came to be known as the Cambridge school of historiography, and its influence can be felt in such works as P. J. Cain and A. G. Hopkins's *British Imperialism 1688–2015* and John Darwin's *The Empire Project: The Rise and Fall of the British World-System 1830–1970*.[44] This imperial historiography defies correspondence with the plot of the bildungsroman. But in bringing together the many things that "imperialism" actually was (settlement, treaty, finance, etc.) and the divergent temporalities at which it functioned across a broadly continuous history, this account of imperialism maps and can be mapped by the formal features and narrative structures of novels like *Nostromo*, which feature plots that are themselves multiple and uneven, and they might invoke, but are hardly exhausted by, the category "bildung." The characterological consequences of this revisionist historiography are such that, as Stephanie Insley Hershinow puts it, we can avoid "conceiving of novelistic character tout court as operating according to the protocols and expectations of bildung" and "refuse to consider the depiction of character over narrative time as conterminous with psychological maturity."[45] Narratives that are not bounded by the lifetime and development of the individual, but by the longer and less teleological arcs of collectivities and institutions—and resonate with a different historiography of imperialism—should be central to a more coherent and considered history of the novel in relation to the empire.[46]

Unlike *Lord Jim* and Conrad's other bildung narratives (e.g., *The Shadow Line*), *Nostromo* lacks a deep concern with individual experience. For Fredric Jameson, this apparent shift from the individual to the social is in fact a "dialectical intensification" of a shared problem: that of the meaning of acts that are "at once irrevocable and impossible."[47] In Jameson's reading, Jim's leap off the *Patna* prompts an existential examination of individual responsibility that stands in for broader questions about modernity, value, and ideology; in *Nostromo*, Decoud and Nostromo's escape with the boat full of silver, through which "capitalism arrives in Sulaco," gets "appropriated by collective history . . . as the founding of institutions" (278). These institutions, which herald a new historical epoch, make unrecognizable the acts of heroic individualism that founded them, and thus the novel becomes a meditation on the impossibility of developing a narrative form that would adequately capture the "always-already-begun" (279) nature of its own story. In what Jameson calls an "unplanned harmony," though, this "always-already-begun"-ness is the dynamic not only of *Nostromo*'s story but also of its "historical content"—that is, capitalism itself, which thus turns out to be written into the novel's form at the very moment that that form seems to abandon it. But *Nostromo*'s address to institutions means that it deals with substantially different problems from those of *Lord Jim*. While in the "negative Marxist hermeneutic" of Jameson's *Political Unconscious* capitalism itself may only ever be manifested in literary texts negatively, symptomatically, or through a "wondrous transfer" (280), *Nostromo*, in certain features of its plot and methods of characterization, actually does develop its institutions as, in Esty's phrase, "susceptible to positive representation," though this representation brings with it the evacuation of character as a property of the individual.

Some clear differences from *Lord Jim* enable *Nostromo*'s representational feat. Michael Valdez Moses cites a key passage from the earlier novel in which Marlowe asks: "But do you notice how, three hundred miles beyond the end of telegraph cables and mail-boat lines, the haggard utilitarian lies of our civilisation wither and die, to be replaced by pure exercises of imagination, that have the futility, often the charm, and sometimes the deep hidden truthfulness, of works of art? Romance had singled Jim out for its own."[48] Moses argues—compellingly, and in accord with the consensus that has made *Lord Jim* an important text for histories of the Anglophone bildungsroman—that in placing himself outside civilization, Jim "hopes . . . to find once again an arena in which personal courage and political action become historically meaningful."[49] This reading of *Lord Jim*, though, immediately throws into relief the extent to which Conrad emphasizes the placement of *Nostromo*'s plot very much *within* the reach of "telegraph cables and mail-boat lines." The novel's second chapter opens by invoking "the wooden jetty which the Oceanic Steam Navigation Company (the O.S.N. of familiar speech) had thrown over the shallow part of the bay," its inclusion in "familiar speech" reinforcing the extent to which the company is an established presence, its ships appearing "year after year . . . disregarding everything but the tyranny of time" (i.e., the regulations of their schedule) (43). By the time of the novel's central events, Charles Gould's development of the silver mine in the mountains above Sulaco has brought with it a telegraph line that extends down the coast and as far north as San Francisco—though it does not yet connect the province to the distant Costaguanan capital of Sta Marta. The telegraph thus links Sulaco directly to Holroyd, the mine's American financier, while failing to integrate the province into the national whole of Costaguana—foreshadowing in infrastructure Sulaco's pending secession from Costaguana and its total incorporation into the circuits of global finance. The steamships and telegraph lines, along with the railroad, are the "material" manifestation of the "material interests" that drive *Nostromo*'s narrative. All, despite their avowed neutrality ("We are not a political faction," says the chief railway engineer [268]), play pivotal roles in the climactic events of the novel: the telegraph office alerts the Sulaco separatists that the rebel Sotillo and his troops are headed for them by sea; the O.S.N. helps to store and hide Sulaco's main bargaining chip, a shipment of silver from the mine; and the National Central Railway "consent[s] to let an engine make a dash down the line" bearing Nostromo. Nostromo recalls troops that have been sent to the neighboring port of Cayta; their return helps to liberate Sulaco from the occupying forces of the Monterist rebellion in Costaguana, after which the province secedes.

Given their "interestedness," it is not merely as infrastructure that these "material interests" operate; like Gould's silver mine, each is also "an institution, a rallying point for everything in the province that needed order and stability to live" (119–20).[50] Here, on the developing edge of global capital, Conrad's narrative folds together ideas of the institution as a technology of development (the mine, railway, telegraph, and steamship all rest on the importation of previously unavailable forms of infrastructure; previously operated by "lashes on the backs of slaves ... it had ceased to make a profitable return, no matter how many corpses were thrown into its maw" [75]) and the institution as preserver of tradition (the stated aim is continuity, "order and stability"). In pursuit of "order and stability," the mine, the railway, the telegraph, and the steamship company promise to authorize individual action in the interest of institutional continuity, in a place where "governing" has long been like "ploughing the sea" (178). Ultimately, however—and this is where Conrad's real pessimism about this process inheres—action that is both enabled and demanded by the logic of institutional perpetuation ceases to be the property of the individual and thus renders individual agency relatively insignificant. Acts are performed by individuals, but it would be more accurate to say that agency in the world of *Nostromo* has moved to the "inhuman" (432) institutions outside of which those actions would be meaningless.

Thus, while *Lord Jim* and *Nostromo* both foreground the centrality of their protagonists in their very titles, and while Jameson's canonical reading of the two works holds that they share a set of ideological concerns, the geopolitical move *Nostromo* makes into the purview of a modernizing institutional order ultimately demands of Conrad a fundamentally different approach to the construction of novelistic character. Tobias Boes suggests that Jim's search for community in the imperial hinterland marks the moment in Conrad's career in which his deployment of the conventions of the bildungsroman arrives at an impasse; that Jim must die to ensure the integrity of the Patusan community that he had helped to create and that had provided a social context for his bildung obviously creates problems for any notion of "character development" (130). Accordingly, Nostromo's own physically mobile but essentially static subjectivity becomes the ideal instantiation of character in a world where development is a property of institutions rather than individuals. Depictions of the internal states of *Nostromo*'s significant figures invariably demonstrate their fixations on particular objects rather than their development over time. Charles Gould's "imagination had been permanently affected by the one great fact of a silver mine." For Martin Decoud, it is his love of Antonia Avellanos; for Emily Gould, her love of Charles;

for Dr. Monygham, his love of Emily Gould; for Giorgio Viola, "liberty and Garibaldi . . . his divinities" (48); for Nostromo, his reputation and the silver that he has stolen and on which he tries to "grow rich very slowly" (417). There is little qualitative distinction in this sense between the primary figures in the novel and more peripheral characters such as the rebel second-in-command, Pedrito Montero, whose *bovarysme* births in him a desire "to be a sort of Duc de Morny to a sort of Napoleon" (214, 328, 239, 340), or Don Juste Lopez, with his pathetic wish "to save the form at least of parliamentary institutions" (304), "the precious vestiges of parliamentary institutions" (314). Nostromo and the novel's other central figures occupy more space on the page, and the things they are induced to do make up the substance of the narrative, but it cannot exactly be said that they possess greater *depth*. In terms of the consistency and legibility of their motivations, there are few distinctions to be made among any of these characters.

Even as *Nostromo* empties out the space of the interesting individual psychology, however, it refills that space with the habits and shared traits generated by institutional life, most clearly in the career of Charles Gould.[51] We learn nothing of Gould's early education in England and on the Continent except that left to his own devices, and instructed in his father's despairing letters to stay away from the corruption and failure of Costaguana and the Gould Concession, he undertakes to become a mining engineer. Yet the science of the work is not what interests him; that remains "vague and imperfect in his mind." Rather, "[m]ines had acquired for him a dramatic interest" (81). Conrad's choice of adjective here is significant: Gould's interest is "dramatic" not only in being especially strong or striking but also in that he conceives of the development of the mine metaphorically *as a drama*, as a kind of stage on which individual action becomes meaningful. "Only in the conduct of our action can we find a sense of mastery over the Fates," the narrator says, with reference to Gould's mind-set. "For his action, the mine was obviously the only field" (86). The impression that he is an actor, in the theatrical sense, follows Gould throughout the text: petitioning the financier Holroyd for capital, he consciously produces "a vague smile, which his big interlocutor took for a smile of discreet and admiring assent" (95); he wears "a soft, grey sombrero, an article of national *costume* . . . with his English get-up" (100); his "taciturnity" is "assumed with a purpose" (311). That purpose is to make the mine "a serious and moral success" (86): "What is wanted here is law, good faith, order, security. Anyone can declaim about these things, but I pin my faith to material interests. Only let the material interests once get a firm footing, and they are bound to impose the conditions on which alone they can continue to exist. That's how your money-making is justified here in the face of lawlessness and disorder. It is justified because the security which it demands must be shared with an oppressed people. A better justice will come afterwards. That's your ray of hope" (100). This use of the mine "as a means, not as an end" (93) rests on a conception of Gould as an independent moral agent: "his character safeguarded the enterprise of their lives as much or more than his policy" (145); "it is your character that is the inexhaustible treasure which may save us all yet; your character, Carlos, not your wealth" (309). No figure in the novel is as closely associated with the idea of the specifically *moral* depth of character as Gould.

And yet the undercurrent of theatricality—of his actions' constructed or contingent significance—consistently ironizes Gould's ostensibly worthy goal. This is hinted at repeatedly: when he first decides to pursue the development of the mine, he "for a moment felt as if the silver mine . . . had decoyed him further than he had meant to go; and with the roundabout logic of emotions, he felt that the worthiness of his life was bound up with success" (101). Forced to pledge his support to the militia of the bandit Hernandez, he is "like a man who had ventured on a precipitous path with no room to turn, where the only chance of safety is to press forward. At that moment he understood it thoroughly" (309); he thinks "the mine had corrupted his judgment" (311). But where Gould is exhausted by what he sees as the constraints placed by imperfect means on an essentially moral end he has chosen to pursue, Dr. Monygham's understanding of the situation goes deeper: "The Administrador had acted as if the immense and powerful prosperity of the mine had been founded on methods of probity, on the sense of usefulness. And it was nothing of the kind. *The method followed had been the only one possible*" (315, italics mine). Monygham sees that the mine and the other institutions that have become forces in Sulaco are not in the control of the individuals who operate them and constitute not an imperfect means to a humanly chosen end but an end in themselves (i.e., in the accumulation of financial and political capital that allows their self-perpetuation): "There is no peace and no rest in the development of material interests. They have their law, and their justice. But it is founded on expediency, and is inhuman;

it is without rectitude, without the continuity and the force that can be found only in a moral principle" (423). Monygham's desire for a "moral principle" in this context is essentially a wish for the restoration of character to the self-authorizing individual; in this he echoes Conrad's own call in "Autocracy and War" for "a statesman of exceptional ability and overwhelming prestige," "a sage," and "a solemn prophet."[52]

But the world of *Nostromo* has no place for this heroic individual. Even the men behind the curtain—Sir John and Holroyd, the British magnate and the American financier—first appear in the novel weirdly subordinated to the institutions they embody: they are bodies with titles but without proper names. Sir John is "the head of the chairman of the railway board . . . [which] hovered near [Emilia's] shoulder" (62); Holroyd is "the considerable personage . . . the big-limbed, deliberate man" (94), whose name the reader only learns indirectly by the mention of the "House of Holroyd" (93) and "the great Holroyd building" (97). The moral content of character having been both asserted thematically (by Gould and those around him) and questioned formally (in the presentation of character as the staging of an institutional script) throughout the novel, character turns out to be a vessel filled by the actions and duties that were demanded of us by institutions and performed as though we had chosen them. What has been developed by "heroic" action is the institutions that were thought to be merely tools but turn out to have interests and a logic of their own, independent of any single individual. In *Nostromo*, awareness of this fact seems available, at the cost of immense "cynicism," both to Martin Decoud, who, having found a role as a propagandist and journalist, "call[ing] Montero a *gran'bestia* every second day in the *Porvenir*" (170), commits suicide from "solitude and want of faith in himself and others" (412), and to Monygham, who, ironically, finds an institutional home of his own as "the Inspector-General of State Hospitals (whose maintenance is a charge upon the Gould Concession)" (418). In neither case does the character's knowledge of the order of things enable him to escape that order.

The static, evacuated nature of individual character in *Nostromo* is both reinforced and complicated by the way characters in *Nostromo* become occasions for the proliferation of type-phrases rather than the conveyance of developing subjectivity or psychological depth.[53] This aspect of Conrad's narration might be dismissed as a stylistic tic if not for the frequency and insistence with which it is deployed and for the fact that it does not feature to anything like the same extent in Conrad's other writings. Sometimes these phrases indicate the named individual's relationship to another character or to an institutional context, but equally often they are produced and taken up by the narrator in a relatively haphazard way. With slight variations, and appearing in both narration and dialogue, the type-phrases are often contradictory and tend toward mock grandiosity or adventure-tale camp. Charles Gould, for example, is variously referred to as "Don Carlos, the administrator of the San Tome silver mine" (62), "a citizen of Costaguana" (93), "an American himself" (99), "a true Englishman" (105), "El Señor Administrador" (121, 160, 170, 244), "the Ingles of Sulaco" (144), "the Costaguana Englishman" (144), "the king of Sulaco" (145, 305), "El Rey de Sulaco" (174), "*Monsieur l'Administrateur*" (182), and "that stony fiend of a man" (341). Martin Decoud is rendered "the son Decoud" (151, 413), "an idle boulevardier" (151), "the young and gifted Costaguanero" (153), "the Costaguana boulevardier" (154), "the adopted child of Western Europe," "the brilliant defender of the country's regeneration, the worthy expounder of the party's political faith before the world," "Young Decoud" (155), "the Journalist of Sulaco" (156, 157, 187), "the voice of the party" (188), "the dilettante in life" (188), "the exotic dandy of the Parisian boulevard" (209), "the spoiled darling of the family" (413), and "the lover of Antonia" (413). Likewise, a less central figure like Giorgio Viola is "the Garibaldino" (48), "the old companion of Garibaldi" (209), "the old hater of kings and ministers" (437), "the immaculate Republican, the hero without a stain" (461). The total effect of these type-phrases is to reinforce the novel's antidevelopmental logic of character; rather than adding a layer of complexity, each repetition carries with it the suggestion that it has captured and fixed the essentials of the individual in a given moment. Characters' ostensibly defining qualities are both recapitulated and blurred as type-phrases proliferate.

As collections of these repeated but varied titles, the major characters in *Nostromo* cannot be called either round or flat, to adopt for a moment E. M. Forster's well-worn but useful vocabulary. No figure in the novel is "round," surprising us with their actions; the reader knows the outcome of the War of Separation very early on, and the kinds of internal conflict or "depth" that would produce surprising action are absent from the novel. If there is an exception to this rule, it is when Emily Gould, convinced by Decoud that a forthcoming shipment of silver will be necessary for Sulacan secession, neglects to give Charles information that would prevent its delivery—a turning point in the intricately plotted novel. But even the surprise this might produce—she is otherwise absolutely faithful to her husband and "never forgive[s] herself" (458)—is surprise not at Mrs. Gould's action but at her lack of it, her allowing things to continue as they were. Moreover, this is entirely in keeping with the logic of the mine, which exerts its power by the consistency of its operation. Silver comes down every three months, subject like the steamships of the O.S.N. only to "the tyranny of time." Because of his obsession with the mine, Charles Gould, meanwhile, is said to feel "the remorse of that subtle conjugal infidelity through which his wife was no longer the sole mistress of his thoughts" (312), but despite this "remorse," he is never shown to be in any doubt as to where his responsibilities lie. However, individuals are not exactly one-dimensional, flat types: in the words of the railroad's enigmatic chief engineer, "a nickname may be the best record of a success" (274). Each of the many type-phrases suggests a part played, a position occupied ("the King," "the Journalist," "the Republican") in the larger economy of roles produced by the antagonistic interests composing the social field of Costaguana, but "the King" is also, in a different moment, "the administrator," or again "a citizen." At the risk of belaboring the spatial metaphor, the character in *Nostromo* is a jagged assembly of overlapping type-phrases, just too varied and uneven to be "flat" but without the contiguity and change over time that would produce "roundness" or "depth."

No individual is more perplexing in this regard than the novel's namesake. Critics have seen Nostromo and Gould as connected since Conrad's own description of them, in the author's note to the novel, as "the two racially and socially contrasted men, both captured by the silver of the San Tome mine" (32). As with Gould, a multiplicity of type-phrases circulate around Nostromo; the very name Nostromo is a mistranslation, "a name that is properly no word" (53), but he is also "Gian'Battista" (53), "a phantom-like horseman" (108), "the lordly Capataz de Cargadores, the indispensable man, the tried and trusty Nostromo, the Mediterranean sailor come ashore casually to try his luck in Costaguana" (135), "this Genoese" (181, 378), "The incomparable Nostromo, the Capataz, the respected and feared Captain Fidanza, the unquestioned patron of secret societies, a republican like old Giorgio, and a revolutionist at heart" (434), "the hopeless slave of the San Tome silver" (440, 445), "the man of careless loves" (444), "master and slave of the San Tome treasure"

(456), "Comrade Fidanza" (462), and "a Man of the People" (261). The full version of his proper name—Gian' Battista Fidanza—occurs only once. While Gould is linked either to both a set of problematic and ultimately superseded national identities (Costaguanan, American, English) or to the mine whose protocols he embodies, the range of nicknames applied to Nostromo—indeed, the narrative's regular swapping out of one type-phrase for another, such that they all come to seem like proper names—suggests both a broader set of allegiances and a degree of individual freedom, in that this "universal factotum" who has "personal contact . . . with every European in Sulaco" (69) escapes being incorporated into any particular set of institutional demands. But it also suggests a more radically dispersed sense of identity. If, as I've argued above, character in the case of individuals like Gould, Decoud, Holroyd, Monygham, or Sir John is a matter of embodying one's institution whether one likes it or not, Nostromo, apparently residing outside or on the margins of any institutionally organized collectivity, seems like mere negation, groundless, without content at all.

Peter Mallios, in *Our Conrad*, traces a version of this reading of Nostromo through numerous early critics who found the character unrealistic, inappropriate to the novel's broader concerns, or otherwise unconvincing. Mallios argues that Nostromo's blankness is in fact key to the novel's investigation of the strategies by which national projects are imagined into being—what Mallios terms its "meta-national form" (233). According to Mallios, Nostromo is both "socially" central—he interacts with every part of society—and "magically" central—he exudes an almost superhuman romantic charm while doing so. These qualities combine to make Nostromo himself a consummately fictional figure; not only do other characters write about him but he often appears via the tropes of romance (an impression reinforced by the excessively heroic type-phrases that proliferate around him). His fictional, unreal quality makes him a site onto which other characters project their impossible fantasies of national belonging. This is unquestionably correct, insofar as the narrative is engaged with the discourse of the nation. But part of *Nostromo*'s irony is that these doomed fantasies of national belonging, while they fail on their own terms, have another function that they fulfill entirely effectively and with which the novel is equally concerned: they justify the material interests that are indifferent to national projects. Gould's moral concern with the mine is not national in itself, but he relies on his reputation for "a truly patriotic heart" (73) to advance it; Decoud disavows any "patriotic illusions" (179) but authors the push for Sulacan secession that births a banana republic. Near the novel's conclusion, when Monygham speaks of the various factions in the new Occidental Republic that are plotting to re-annex Costaguana and are looking "for the necessary force" to "the secret societies among immigrants and natives, where Nostromo—I should say Captain Fidanza—is a great man" (423), he makes clear that yet again national imagining is being used to further "the development of material interests," only through different institutions: the church and the emergent labor unions. This is the irony that colors the words of Scarfe, a callow railway employee who describes the Monterist rebellion, and the resultant War of Separation in Sulaco, as "one of their so-called national things" (164). "So-called" but insubstantial, nationhood is a failed concept in *Nostromo* to the very extent that material interests, and the institutional forms through which they establish legitimacy, are successful.

Nostromo's centrality to the novel, then, is performed on two levels, neither of which involves his own development but both of which establish him as crucial to the development of material interests. On one level, he enables other characters' ideologies of nationhood; on the other, he works to advance the interests for which that ideology is a cover: he is "an active usher-in of the material implements for our progress" (181). The first level props up the myth of self-sufficient moral individualism that underlies various national imaginings; for this imagining to work he must be the superficial yet multifaceted figure of the many type-phrases that circulate through the narration and dialogue. And in this sense he has a psychic, "magical" function in relation to others. But the second level is at cross-purposes to the first, and in his work for material interests Nostromo only seems like an empty character if character is seen as inhering in the psychologically interesting individual rather than in the shared protocols and demands of institutions. In his "social" role, he is at the behest not of individuals but of the material interests that are the actual agents of narrative and that are represented through character. In this sense he is not so much an empty figure as he is stuffed to overflowing. While the journeys he undertakes on his schooner—the sailing ship being the site where Conrad typically *is* concerned with the intricacies of individual psychology and subjecthood—go unnarrated, Nostromo caroms through the novel leading the workers of the O.S.N.; guiding the railway's investors through mountain passes; "disclosing to the then Chief of Police the presence in town of some professional thieves" (277); carrying messages from church leaders to Hernandez's bandits; "[making] free of the offices of the *Porvenir*"; hiding the mine's silver, which is the focal point of all the forces in contest for power in Sulaco; traveling on military transports. Although critics have tended to view Nostromo as undergoing a significant change in the course of the novel, his realization that "I am nothing!" (380)—that he is being exploited—does not change but rather reveals his role in the narrative of institutions.[54] He is subsequently persuaded by Monygham to undertake the ride to Cayta, bringing back Barrios (who promises to make him "a captain of cavalry" [408]) and his troops, and he becomes the patron of the revolutionary groups that arise in the Occidental Republic. Becoming a man of *ressentiment,* patron of a secret society run by "a somewhat hunchbacked little photographer, with a white face and a magnanimous soul dyed crimson by a bloodthirsty hate of all capitalists" (436), shows an investment in an alternate order from the one that he helped to install during the War of Separation but not a move beyond the institutional logic of the novel's social world. His deathbed refusal to give away the location of the silver to either Mrs. Gould or the radical photographer is the closest Nostromo comes to acting outside that logic, but like Mrs. Gould's own earlier decision not to interfere with the scheduled shipment from the mine, this is not a positive act but a refusal to act. It is acquiescence to an order that has made individual action unthinkable without the agency that resides in institutional authority. It is through these varied roles, and not only in his presence as a site of national projection, that he cements the novel's varied institutions to one another and to the impossible ideal of national unity. Both a meta-national and a meta-institutional figure, Nostromo holds together the imaginary projects of nationhood and of material interests.

In a sense, then, it is fitting that the death of the novel's titular figure does not come as a product of its institutional plot, where there is "no rest and no peace" and which promises to continue without him into the unnarrated future of the Occidental Republic. Instead, Nostromo's theft of the silver initiates the romance plot of the final third of the novel, in which his visits to Great Isabel Island to retrieve ingots of silver from his hoard dovetail with his visits to the lighthouse manned by Old Giorgio and his daughters Linda (whom Nostromo is to marry) and Giselle (with whom he is in love). Nostromo, returning for silver late one night, is mistaken for another jilted lover of Giselle, is shot by Giorgio, and dies. *Nostromo* overcomes the potential endlessness of institutional narrative with the reemergence of biography in the romance plot. Critics have puzzled over what some have taken to be a failure of Conrad's craft in the latter portions of the novel, as the romance plot moves to the fore and disrupts the terseness and complex structure promised by the earlier sections.[55] But it would be more adequate to the aesthetic problems *Nostromo* confronts to read the romance plot—failure or no—as a byproduct of Conrad's attempt to incorporate "inhuman" institutions into human-centered realist narrative. In providing a traditional form of closure for the narrative, the romance plot and Nostromo's death look back to a prior realist tradition, but in the process they ironically erase the possibility of an heir for Giorgio, "the old companion of Garibaldi," the avatar of a nineteenth-century revolutionary nationalism. Putting both an aesthetic and a political tradition to bed with this gesture, *Nostromo* also anticipates the more open-ended narratives of a modernist realism of institutional life. The subsequent novels of Conrad's political period, *The Secret Agent* and *Under Western Eyes*, seek but fail to find spaces of detachment and individual agency for characters bound up in complexes of state and non-state European institutions. The distended plots and absent or hollow protagonists of later texts of global modernism, such as Virginia Woolf's *The Years* or Mulk Raj Anand's *Coolie*, similarly register and represent the late imperial world in transforming development from a property of the individual into a property of the institution. *Nostromo* is thus an important instance in a modern genealogy of novelistic attempts to narrate collectivity: to show institutions as substantially "constitutive of individual identity."

In the end, Gould, Nostromo, and the rest of the "Occidentals" have won the battle, but they have lost a war they did not know they were fighting: the attempt to wrest a "moral principle" of action out of institutional life. In contrast to their struggle, Conrad presents an alternate way of living in institutions in the figure of the engineer-in-chief of the railway. Unnamed, his physical appearance never described, he is "a brave man" (268) with "an army of workers under his orders" (271), tells his stories "of ignorant prejudice and as ignorant cunning very well" (183), and sees perfectly clearly the course of all the machinations undertaken to defend material interests. He seems amoral in his readiness to defend the railway by cutting any deal necessary, yet he is moderately consoled by the thought of higher aims: "Upon my word, doctor, things seem to be worth nothing by what they are in themselves. I begin to believe that the only solid thing about them is the spiritual value which everyone discovers in his own form of activity—" (275). Most definitively, though, he never appears except when he takes action to advance the railway's interests; man and institutional role are perfectly congruent, each filling the outline of the other. Efficient and anonymous, he is individualized only by his rank in the institutional hierarchy and the physical marks of his age: we see "engineers of the railway, sunburnt and in tweeds, with the frosted head of their chief smiling with slow, humorous indulgence amongst the young eager faces" (180). Not even remarkable in his unremarkableness—he is no Kafkaesque bureaucrat—he simply appears one day to build the railway and then vanishes, at the novel's conclusion, from the independent Occidental Republic in which it is completed, moving with the impersonality and disregard for national boundaries of the institution itself. His aims and his achievements, in contrast to those of every other character, are in perfect accord. He is Conrad's zero degree of institutional character. It is easy to miss the significance and bitter irony of his success in a novel deeply committed to showing the corrosive effects of modern institutions on the potential for individual agency, but it is because of his absolute unity with the demands and authority of the railway company that, as Martin Decoud says, the engineer is "the principal European really in Sulaco" (216).

Under Western Eyes and Detachment's Diminishing Returns

Taking institutions as agents and representing them through innovative forms of character, *Nostromo* ranks as Conrad's most ambitious attempt to render a social world essentially devoid of individual agency. Alongside their exploration of institutional character, the political novels typically register Conrad's disenchantment with the institutional world they address by continually producing figures capable of perceiving, whether steadily or fleetingly, the futility of their labors. Inevitably, though, this perception fails to produce better templates for individual action. *The Inheritors* features Arthur Granger; in *The Secret Agent* this role is played by the Assistant Commissioner, who has been recalled from worthy "police work . . . in a distant part of the globe" to the cynical intrigue of London politics: "A square peg forced into a round hole, he had felt like a daily outrage that long-established smooth roundness into which a man of less sharply angular shape would have fitted himself."[56] *Nostromo* offers Decoud and Monygham; the cynicism of the first leads him to suicide, while the conscience of the second leads to acquiescence. Conrad's last political novel, *Under Western Eyes*, is structured around a character who can see but cannot affect what he sees, attempting to reintroduce the moral individual in the figure of the novel's unnamed Teacher of Languages and to investigate what possibilities remain for what Conrad terms, in an author's note appended to the novel, "analysis" and "efforts of detachment." Its story has less to say about imperialism as such but takes up conceptually the same questions of institutionality and character that preoccupied Conrad for the preceding decade. That Conrad did not again address these questions in his fiction marks *Under Western Eyes* as the point at which his attempts to deal with "political institutions" exhaust themselves.

For Conrad, the cost of making character adequate to institutionalized modernity—of using it to "make you see," as he famously writes—is the loss of the social force of character's moral aspect. Conradian detachment in *Under Western Eyes* thus follows on the historical trajectory of detachment in nineteenth-century culture traced by Amanda Anderson.[57] For the early and mid-Victorians, Anderson argues, critical detachment is in the service of moral education or of progressive systemic critique, as depicted most notably in the novels of George Eliot. A late Victorian shift, exemplified by Oscar Wilde's aphoristic style, elevates forms of detachment once judged "bad"—"irony, dandyism, and aestheticism"—to privileged status. From founding political action, detachment undergoes a subjective turn, becoming primarily an ethical practice of the self. *Under Western Eyes* gives this trend an additional twist by making the impossibility of effective engagement a condition of detachment. In *Under Western Eyes*, the futility of political action and politically motivated critique elevates the status of detachment as ethos, rendering it the only means by which a privileged individual may achieve a position from which to perceive and convey truths about the world. Detachment is thus valuable insofar as seeing clearly is the most one can do in a world where one cannot hope to affect what one sees, and what it turns out to be capable of producing is not historical change but a novel like *Under Western Eyes*: its narrator turns out to have written the story we read, using "(his) pen to create for the reader" the personality of its central figure, Razumov.[58]

At almost the exact midpoint of *Under Western Eyes,* Conrad's unnamed narrator, an English-language teacher who has "lived for a long time in Geneva," recounts his first conversation with the novel's protagonist, the Russian expatriate Razumov. Their friend Nathalie Haldin, leaving them to attend to her invalid, grief-stricken mother, has departed with the phrase, "Mr. Razumov does not quite understand my difficulty, but you know what it is." As the two men walk along, the language teacher imagines that it is his "mission" to make Razumov "understand" the effect he will have on the Haldins as the "comrade" and "intimate" of their son and brother, who has been executed for his role in a political assassination (151). But in the face of Razumov's irritation and brusqueness—"Must understand this! Not expected to understand that! I may have other things to do" (154)—the conversation takes a different turn, and the language teacher introduces a fact that he suspects Razumov does not know: that "the trouble of which I speak was caused by an English newspaper" (156). That is, the news of Victor Haldin's midnight arrest, with its implication that an insider betrayed him, has been brought out of Russia by an English journalist. When the language teacher asserts the probable truth of the report, Razumov asks, "How can you tell truth from lies?" Lest the query be thought rhetorical, or in reference only to the gossip-strewn revolutionary circles of Geneva, he broadens his inquiry: "In Russia, and in general everywhere—in a newspaper, for instance." The language teacher earnestly responds, "Well. . . . The character of the publication, the general verisimilitude of the news, the consideration of the motive, and so on. I don't trust blindly the accuracy of special correspondents, but why should this one have gone to the trouble of concocting a circumstantial falsehood on a matter of no importance to the world?" Razumov then changes tack to place the truth or falsity of the report to the side: "That's what it is," he grumbles. "What's going on with us is of no importance—a mere sensational story to amuse the readers of the papers—the superior contemptuous Europe" (156).

With regard to the novel's plot, Razumov's question is a sham; he knows perfectly well that the report is right, since he is the one who turned Haldin in. Yet this merely reinforces the sense that the conversation is really about something else. Primed by the resonating issue of "understanding," the question of how to read a newspaper instances a much larger question: "How can you tell truth from lies . . . in general?" In return, the language teacher offers a textbook example of the application of critical reason: not to "trust blindly," to use prior knowledge of the source, evaluate the evidence, consider the speaker's motivation, and so forth. Razumov's response, though, suggests that such strategies are ultimately irrelevant in a world where the effect of a statement will be determined not by its veracity according to independent standards of evaluation but by the preexisting situation of its audience, in this case "the superior contemptuous Europe." The passage is shot through with irony, but as it elevates the language teacher's exchange with Razumov above the immediate contingencies of the plot and into a pedagogical register, this passage also thematizes, as two distinct approaches to knowledge, the tension between Conrad's institutional characterization and a form of character that imagines individual discrimination as possible and desirable. The relationship between these two fundamentally different modes of characterization—one that valorizes critical reason and detachment, another that declares them irrelevant—encodes Conrad's pessimism about issues of individual and collective agency.

In an early review of the novel, Edward Garnett noted wryly that "the professor's story does not, as might be expected, suggest an interpretation of which he himself is unconscious: its last page leaves us almost as much in the dark as the first."[59] Subsequent critics have come to remarkably mixed evaluations of the language teacher; readers in the sixties and seventies tended to foreground his own professed inability to comprehend the Russians who surround him and what was taken to be his unreliability as a narrator, often in conjunction with theories about Conrad's own relationship to language and writing.[60] More recently, critics have taken a more measured view, drawing attention to the language teacher's characteristically post-Enlightenment navigation between rationality and sympathy and his embodiment of certain values of reason and detachment.[61] The latter view is exemplified in his conversation with Razumov, where the language teacher's lesson on how one tells truth from lies condenses the features that distinguish him throughout the novel and issue from Conrad's own sense of the novel's project. The language teacher neither "trusts blindly" nor argues irresponsibly; rather, he is engaged constantly in demarcating the limits of his knowledge and making explicit the norms underlying his judgments, offering, implicitly, the possibility that his opinions could be corrected or revised. Even in his lack of comprehension of the Russians by whom he is surrounded, he allows that a different position might allow him to understand more readily: "Had I been myself a conspirator, a Russian political refugee," he says at one point, "I could have perhaps been able to draw some practical conclusion" (262). Daniel Darvay argues that the language teacher, though not to be identified directly with Conrad, is "an exemplary character for whom Russian affairs appear obscure, timeworn, and illusory so that broad-minded Western values, purified of English insular nationalism, are able to be reinvented as distinctly rational, forward-looking, and modern."[62] Darvay points to the language teacher's often categorical statements about the Russian character as evidence of an irrational prejudice and thus a serious limitation to his sensibility, but these statements are in fact the product of the teacher's careful observation of the Russians with whom he comes into contact and are often carefully hedged. In this way they actually serve to reinforce his embodiment of a critical ethos.

Moreover, the language teacher's sustained performance of detachment accords with Conrad's own statements about his project in the novel in an author's note written in 1919:

> My greatest anxiety was in being able to strike and sustain the note of scrupulous impartiality. The obligation of absolute fairness was imposed on me historically and hereditarily, by the peculiar experience of race and family, in addition to my primary conviction that truth alone is the justification of any fiction which makes the least claim to the quality of art or may hope to take its place in the culture of men and women of its time. I had never been called to a greater effort of detachment: detachment from all passions, prejudices and even from personal memories.[63]

Although Edward Said dismisses the author's notes as "concerned mainly with justifying what he did as being reasonable," this was not the first time Conrad discussed novel writing in terms of "efforts of detachment."[64] In his letters, Conrad distinguishes between writings about "action" and writings of "analysis," stating that "stories of incident . . . are not studies—they touch no problem. They are just stories in which I've tried my best to be *simply entertaining*"[65] The "business of the artist," however, is "analysis" (29), and this term occurs repeatedly in his discussions of later novels, particularly *Under Western Eyes*, of which Conrad writes that "analysis—that's the *tone* of the novel" (59). *Chance*, also in process at the time Conrad was writing *Under Western Eyes*, is referred to as "analysis applied to the life at sea" (106). And elsewhere, Conrad writes to an anonymous aspiring writer, "Let me warn you against bringing emotion instead of reason to your inquiry" (66). The language teacher becomes, in the course of *Under Western Eyes,* an "exemplary" instantiation of these values. Conrad repeatedly emphasizes this ethos of detachment: the language teacher takes on depth and is marked as distinctive by virtue of traits that issue from this ethos, and his position as narrator emphasizes his authority. In effect making an imagined individual out of an ethos, Conrad makes co-present in a particularly intense way both "character" in the literary sense (a character, novelistic character) and character as a moral concern (to have a good character, to cultivate one's character).

Against the language teacher are arrayed what he terms "the ruthless workings of political institutions" (293). Institutional characterization in *Under Western Eyes,* as in *The Inheritors* and *Nostromo,* constructs individuals from the shared practices, rule-bound behaviors, and repeated actions of institutional life, but with a fixity and determinism that is absent from the earlier novels. General T—— and Councillor Mikulin, the novel's representatives of Russian autocracy and bureaucratic terror, draw their distinguishing features entirely from their institutional roles. The General does not speak any word or express any emotion that is not in keeping with an institutionally dictated role. In an echo of the momentarily surprising choices of Mrs. Gould and Nostromo, and of the chief engineer of *Nostromo*'s National Central Railway, when the General "develops . . . an unexpected thought" it is reincorporated into an institutional affirmation: "Fidelity to menaced institutions on which depend the safety of a throne and of a people is no child's play," he says. "My *existence* has been built on fidelity" (43, 45). He is "the embodied power of autocracy" (72). General T——, lacking a proper name, is reduced to a title; Councillor Mikulin has the entire history of his life related in a paragraph: he is "*one of those* powerful officials," "simply inconspicuous," whose "downfall" comes in "*one of those* state trials" (253, italics mine). This is the life of the generic councillor, not the particular Mikulin. Conrad makes the institution entirely constitutive of the individual character, though at the cost of the character's reduction to type, as the traits that character embodies are, we are given to understand, shared across an institutional context.

Opposite the representatives of autocracy are the revolutionists, who are excluded from the exercise of power through state institutions and for whom a desire to "see all the Ministries destroyed" exists alongside "the spark to start an explosion which is meant to change fundamentally the lives of so many millions so that Peter Ivanovich should be the head of a State" (290). Their relationship to Russian institutions is one of mutual reinforcement rather than negation. In a meeting on a train between Councillor Mikulin and Peter Ivanovich, the head of the expatriate revolutionaries, Mikulin, wishing to be rid of a troublesome double agent, reveals his own identity to Ivanovich, thus safeguarding both their enterprises (323). Their understanding echoes Chief Inspector Heat's insight into the relationship between police and thieves in *The Secret Agent*: "[T]he mind and the instincts of a burglar are of the same kind as the mind and the instincts of a police officer. Both recognise the same conventions, and have a working knowledge of each other's methods and of the routine of their respective trades. They understand each other, which is advantageous to both, and establishes a sort of amenity in their relations. Products of the same machine, one classed as useful and the other as noxious, they take the machine for granted in different ways, but with a seriousness essentially the same."[66] In *Under Western Eyes,* this structure produces multiple inauthentic forms of detachment. The revolutionists, though critical of Russian autocracy, spend their time making a fetish of "the people," as when Peter Ivanovich asserts, "In Russia we have no classes to combat each other, one holding the power of wealth, and the other mighty with the strength of numbers. We have only an unclean bureaucracy in the face of a people as great and incorruptible as the ocean" (119). Tekla, the *dame de compagnie* of a prominent female revolutionist, is the only figure in the revolutionist circle who has no illusions about their cynicism and futile plotting, but rather than enabling critique, her disaffection simply leads to a bad conscience and lack of agency that is figured in her intense identification with animals, in particular an omnipresent cat. "Detachment" in relation to the institutions of autocracy is deformed into either delusion or abjection.

Razumov himself finally testifies to the ultimate incommensurability, for Conrad, of reasoned detachment and institutional incorporation; his trajectory in the novel is determined by trying and failing to hold these two sets of values together. He describes himself as possessed of "patriotic instincts developed by a faculty of independent thinking—of detached thinking" (83); his political manifesto, "History not Theory. Patriotism not Internationalism. Evolution not Revolution. Direction not Destruction. Unity not Disruption," verges on a parody of conservative liberalism;

he is frequently described as "English," a term charged by its association with the language teacher. And yet he is simultaneously as pure a product of institutional life as any character in the novel. Parentless, without a relation in the world (the aristocratic Prince K——, who may be his father, notwithstanding), he seems to spring fully formed from the University, but with an education less liberating than bureaucratizing. He hopes to win the Ministry of Education essay prize, the winner of which "would have a claim to an administrative appointment of the better sort" (12). Often marked with the type-phrase "the student Razumov," he is defined by an institutional routine: "He walked to and from the University, ascended stairs, paced the passages, listened to lectures, took notes, crossed courtyards" (247). And he leaves the University only to be assimilated into Mikulin's ministry and then abandoned to deafness after a beating by the revolutionists and emotional collapse, to be visited periodically by those among whom he had spied. When Razumov defends his "attitude of detachment," Mikulin states: "For a man like you . . . such a position is impossible" (244). As Nicole Rizzuto puts it, Razumov's "'freedom' emerges at the cost of a loss of the possibility of community."[67] This loss echoes that of the language teacher, whose detachment is predicated on his removal from the social world he observes.

In the end, the novel's pessimism about political action and individual agency is given a sharper point by the pretense that the text itself is the language teacher's written composition. The language teacher's position is not that of Conrad; the teacher is an "exemplary" character drawn from the ethos of detachment. Conrad's own position, as what Hay calls the novel's "missing center," is in a sense more grim.[68] In *Under Western Eyes* Conrad looks back to nineteenth-century concepts of critical reason and detachment, embodying them in the elderly, untimely teacher of languages, who, insofar as he is able to act, does so only in reaction to the plans of those who have only "scorn for all the practical forms of political liberty known to the western world" (104). Those individuals, in turn, are possessed of political agency but lack the capacity or desire for detachment that enables the discernment of "truth from lies." Michael Levenson suggests that as the institutionalization of character erodes individuality, *Heart of Darkness* "responds by offering the Impressionist temperament as itself a basis for moral autonomy."[69] The long decade that followed would, in Conrad's political thought, strip away this aesthetic consolation. *Under Western Eyes* imagines a world in which those who can see cannot act, and those invested with power cannot see the consequences of their actions, which, effected by large institutions, are "meant to change fundamentally the lives of so many millions." *Under Western Eyes* thus brings to a close a period in which Conrad, looking at new institutional regimes, relied for his vision on the very principles of detachment whose erasure his works' characterological innovations seem to foretell.

2

Virginia Woolf and Political Possibility in the Gendered Institution

VIRGINIA WOOLF'S 1930s ended in pessimism about the institutions of the country in which she lived and the prospects for their improvement. "A Sketch of the Past," as I have already noted, considers the intertwining of the aesthetic and the political at length by tracing Woolf's own life and position as a writer. The posthumously published *Between the Acts* continues in a melancholy vein, with Woolf seeking forms of continuity in national culture and the natural world, as critics have pointed out, largely as a response to the failures of institutional politics in the thirties and the rise of Fascism.[1] But Woolf had inaugurated the decade in a mood of great optimism. On the evening of January 20, 1931, she wrote in her diary, "I have this moment, while having my bath, conceived an entire new book—a sequel to a Room of Ones Own—about the sexual life of women: to be called Professions for Women perhaps—Lord how exciting!"[2] It was mid-1932 by the time she began work on this project, which she hoped would be a new literary form based in social fact, an "essay-novel" that alternated fictional scenes with interchapters of historical explanation and critical commentary.[3] In early 1933, having evidently decided that this method of conjoining fact and vision was insufficient to both her aesthetic and her critical goals, she abandoned the experiment, compressed the fictional chapters into what would become one section of *The Years*, and reserved her social critique for *Three Guineas*. Forty years later, amid a surge of interest in Woolf's feminism and politics, the drafts of her essay-novel were edited by Mitchell Leaska and published in 1977 under Woolf's working title, *The Pargiters*.

Each of Woolf's novels brought with it new stylistic innovations. *The Pargiters* breaks sharply from the lyrical prose of *The Waves* in favor of more straightforward realist description, while at the same time incorporating *Orlando*'s interest in extended timeframes. Its innovation lies in its inchoate attempt to find a narrative form sufficient to account for all the social, historical, and institutional forces that shape women's lives. Woolf attempts to grasp, through the combination of narrative and critical commentary, every aspect of the world she portrays; at the same time, whether because of *The Pargiters*'s grounding in Woolf's increasingly militant feminism or simply because of its relatively unpolished prose, the writing feels highly personal—the voice of the narrator seems closer at times to the voice in Woolf's diaries than to that of her other novels. Then there is the essay-novel's central conceit: that its chapters about the Pargiter family are passages from a work in progress, and its interchapters a commentary on that work presented to an audience of women by a (fictional) writer. Woolf writes that the work "tries to give a faithful and detailed account of a family called Pargiter, from the year 1800 to the year 2032. Thus, if I select the Chapter which deals with the Pargiters in the year 1880, I ought to be able to show you what you were like fifty years ago: to provide that perspective which is so important for the understanding of the present."[4] There appears to be no evidence that this historical and speculative work was ever to be written in full. But its ambition signals Woolf's optimism at this moment in her career about the capacity of experiments with narrative form to provide new ways of representing the experiences of women.

After five of the most difficult years of Woolf's writing career, these experiments would produce Peggy Pargiter: "Pain must outbalance pleasure two to one, she thought, in all social relations. Or am I the exception, the peculiar person? she continued, for the others seemed happy enough. Yes, she thought, looking straight ahead of her, and feeling again the stretched skin round her lips and eyes tight from the tiredness of sitting up late with a woman in childbirth, I'm the exception; hard; cold; in a groove already; merely a doctor."[5] In this passage from late in *The Years*, Peggy contemplates her discomfort at the party that concludes the novel and that brings together nearly all the characters who feature in Woolf's most ambitious work. Aware of herself as in one sense a type, "merely a doctor," a product of medical institutions whose vocabulary and habits of perception define her presence in the narrative, Peggy is at the same time a distinctive individual: she is "the exception, the peculiar person." Indeed, the marks of her peculiarity as a character—the "pain" she finds in "social relations," her hyperawareness of her body and of the bodies of others—come not from her freestanding subjectivity and deep interiority but from her letter-perfect incarnation of what Woolf presents as the protocols and worldview of the medical professional. She embodies the push and pull, the tension and complementarity, between the individual person and the institutional practice. In one sense, Woolf addressed this point elsewhere: in *Three Guineas* (1938) she imagines a "Society of Outsiders" composed of women who would work "by their own methods for liberty, equality, and peace," adopting toward militarism and patriarchy an attitude of revolutionary "indifference." *Three Guineas* was frequently taken as an excessively strident statement of female autonomy even by sympathetic contemporaries, so it can be surprising to note how much of its text is devoted to the analysis of specific British institutions—the university, the civil service, the church, government—and to note Woolf's point that "the Outsiders have only had a positive existence for twenty years—that is, since the professions were opened to the daughters of educated men."[6] As *Three Guineas* only fleetingly suggests, but *The Years* bears out, Woolf at this moment in her career conceived of her feminism in institutional terms, viewing the incorporation of individuals into collectivities as essential to novelistic character (aesthetically) and to nonviolent social change (politically).

Woolf's use of institutional character as a way to think about women's agency via incorporation into institutions is the subject of what follows. I first address what I suggest is the overlooked importance of the concept of character and its relationship to institutions in Woolf's classic essays on fiction. I then turn to the drafts of *The Pargiters*, examining Woolf's experiments therein with a politically charged practice of fictional representation supplemented by expository prose, and to her decision to end this practice and separate what she thought of as art and politics in *The Years*. Turning to *The Years* itself, I argue that the novel is organized around the varied ways that Woolf generates character out of individuals' relationships to institutional contexts: Abel and Morris Pargiter's embodiment of the army and the legal profession, respectively; the exclusion of women such as Eleanor, Delia, Milly, and Rose Pargiter from a range of modern institutions; Sara Pargiter's professional outsiderdom (and her centrality to a set of critical debates about the novel); and Peggy's difficult, disenchanted, but ultimately productive assimilation into the medical profession. This chapter maps through these individuals how *The Years* makes character out of institutions and how the novel's plotless narrative works to reimagine the institution as a feminist mechanism of inclusion and collective change, directed toward the future rather than the past.

Consciousness or Character?

A long-standing critical tradition has understood Woolf as a key figure in modernist writing's move away from character. As Baruch Hochman writes, somewhat dismissively, "Many things did not interest Woolf, and character in its classical sense was one of them."[7] Edward Bishop, argues that "Woolf is not representing *character;* what she is exploring is the construction, and representation of, the subject."[8] Jesse Matz situates Woolf within a shift in the history of the novel from a concern with social totality to a concern with "perceptual totality."[9] Similarly, Emily Steinlight suggests that "the call to 'look within,' per Woolf's 1925 antirealist polemic 'Modern Fiction,' relocates literary truth from outward social expression to psychological subjectivity"; the Victorian "literary strategies" Steinlight examines, "which aimed at giving narrative order to collective life, would seem to lose their exigency as interiority comes to the fore."[10] Matz and Steinlight, like other twenty-first-century readers of Woolf, acknowledge that her work is animated by complex engagements with the social world; what is retained in such contemporary readings is the insistence that those engagements are conducted on the grounds of consciousness, not character.

These understandings are grounded in the texts commonly taken to make up Woolf's aesthetic manifesto. Across "Modern Fiction" (originally composed in 1919, published in 1921), "Mr. Bennett and Mrs. Brown" (1924), and "Character in Fiction" (which expanded the argument of the previous in the same year), Woolf mounted an argument against what she termed the "materialist" approach of the "Edwardian" novelists, including Arnold Bennett, H. G. Wells, and John Galsworthy, and for the "spiritual" method of the "Georgians," whom we now know as modernists: Joyce, Lawrence, and, by implication, herself. "Modern Fiction," the earliest and most quotably aphoristic of these pieces, contains lines commonly taken as Woolf's analysis of her own method:

> Examine for a moment an ordinary mind on an ordinary day. The mind receives a myriad impressions—trivial, fantastic, evanescent, or engraved with a sharpness of steel. From all sides they come, an incessant shower of atoms; and as they fall, as they shape themselves into the life of Monday or Tuesday, the accent falls differently from old.... Let us record the atoms as they fall upon the mind in the order in which they fall, let us

trace the pattern, however disconnected and incoherent in appearance, which each sight or incident scores upon the consciousness.[11]

Passages like this one have, understandably, made the exaltation of the ordinary through the rendering of consciousness a key concept for thinking about Woolf's fiction. With the emphasis on consciousness comes its entailment of a presumed turn inward in Woolf's ambitions for novelistic art that continues to pervade critical understandings of her self-conception as a writer: opposing "impressions" and their "pattern . . . upon the consciousness" to the Edwardians' "villas" and "railway carriages," Woolf seems to oppose the inner life to the outer, the private and particular to the public and general, tilting the scales toward the former in each case.

Less often noted is that across the development of these essays Woolf noticeably shifts the grounds of her discussion, from some passing mentions of consciousness in "Modern Fiction" to an intense focus on questions of character in the later pieces. "Mr. Bennett and Mrs. Brown" opens with the statement that "the novel is a very remarkable machine for the creation of human character . . . directly it ceases to create character, its defects alone are visible." "This character-making power," Woolf writes, is the "essence" of the novel—a claim that calls into question the unproblematic assimilation of Woolf to that critical tradition that associates modernist fiction with the dispersal of character.[12] The issue is not exactly (or only) one of replacing outmoded forms of realist character with the diaphanous transcription of consciousness; rather, what appear as debates at first over novelistic content (inner or outer world?) and then over literary devices (consciousness or character?) are revealed as divergent approaches to form and method: how is character, the essence of the novel, best rendered to take advantage of the unique possibilities it presents for capturing the social world, and more specifically, the collective forms that make up that world? But the idea that Woolf's essays mark a radical break in the history of the novel persists in suggestions that for Woolf the representation of *perceptual* totality replaces that of *social* totality and in the related critical tendency to see Woolf's construction of a phenomenology of perception as first among her preoccupations throughout her novelistic writing.[13]

Woolf's essays themselves ultimately belie these suggestions. In them, we can see Woolf moving toward a particular concept of character and toward a suspicion that fidelity to consciousness in itself is not a meaningful goal. Joyce she describes as "concerned at all costs to reveal the flickerings of that innermost flame which flashes its messages through the brain"; does he not, Woolf asks, "centre" us "in a self which, in spite of its tremor of susceptibility, never embraces or creates what is outside itself and beyond?"[14] Whether or not one agrees with this critique of Joyce—which, though typically described as issuing from Woolf's squeamishness about *Ulysses*'s "indecency," is more substantially about the distinction between character as social and consciousness as solipsistic—Woolf's often overlooked turn to character seems calculated to emphasize that effective novel-writing depends on precisely the relationship between the imagined individual and the social world.[15] If consciousness seems to mark for Woolf an attention to the "recording of the atoms" that threatens to become self-limiting, character suggests something like what the critic C. H. Rickword called, pejoratively, the "social crystallization" of that consciousness, its relationship to the "moral, social, political, and religious"; but for Woolf, in the 1930s, this social quality has ceased to be something to deride. It becomes instead the essential quality of a properly novelistic art.

In "Mr. Bennett and Mrs. Brown" and "Character in Fiction" Woolf returns repeatedly to the idea that character alone allows the novel to incorporate the full complexity of the social world. As Jessica Berman argues, "For Woolf, [social, historical, and political] concerns become appropriate in a novel when they are made intrinsic to the characters themselves rather than simply included as representations of its intellectual context, its material conditions, or its impact on the outside world."[16] "Mr. Bennett and Mrs. Brown" takes up William Makepeace Thackeray's *Pendennis*, suggesting that "[t]he whole country, the whole society, is revealed to us, and revealed always in the same way, through the astonishing vividness and reality of the characters" (385). Likewise, Woolf writes in "Character in Fiction" that

> If . . . you think of the novels which seem to you great novels—*War and Peace, Vanity Fair, Tristram Shandy, Madame Bovary, Pride and Prejudice, The Mayor of Casterbridge, Villette*—if you think of these books, you do at once think of some character who has seemed to you so real (I do not mean by that so lifelike) that it has the power to make you think not merely of itself, but of all sorts of things through its eyes—of religion, of love, of war, of peace, of family life, of balls in country towns, of sunsets,

moonrises, the immortality of the soul. . . . [A]ll these great novelists have brought us to see whatever they wish us to see through some character. Otherwise, they would not be novelists; but poets, historians, or pamphleteers.[17]

If the demands Woolf places on character here are, as I am arguing, of particular relevance to her own historical moment, her examples are nonetheless drawn exclusively from classical nineteenth-century realism. In this sense Woolf's point is backward-looking and literary-historical rather than methodological; hence the gently ironized, distinctively Victorian flavor of the "sorts of things" made available to the reader in the great works of nineteenth-century literature (that is, the novels and the social phenomena she lists correspond to each other; there is no suggestion here that "balls in country towns," for example, are among the proper concerns of the modern novelist). In this way the passage follows her reluctance to specify a method for modern characterization. But more broadly, what the passage highlights is Woolf's understanding of a necessary and persistent relationship between the "real[ity]" of character and the mass of habits and behaviors that are entailed by living in modern institutions. In *The Years*, what is made intrinsic to character is the institutional practices it comprises: by institutionalizing character, Woolf seeks to maintain it as the essence of novelistic art and thus by extension to maintain the self-sufficiency of the novel form itself, apart from the strictures placed on it by the Edwardians, for example.[18] But this is a peculiar and partial kind of self-sufficiency, one dependent on making institutions intrinsic to the work, and psychology is frequently obscured from the reader in favor of external details that ground character in the history the novel depicts. Character, for Woolf, can be thought of as what Andrew Goldstone terms a "fiction of autonomy": an assertion of "relative autonomy as a *mode of relation* between literature and the social world" in which "seemingly nonliterary concerns and materials become essential to modernism's claims for literary autonomy; the literary work seeks self-governance even as it extends its relations in a great variety of directions."[19] This is where *The Years* arrives, but as the long incubation of her project suggests, Woolf did not arrive at this position overnight.

Narrating Institutional Effects in *The Pargiters*

Shortly after *The Years* was published, Woolf wrote to Stephen Spender that in composing the novel she had sought

> to give a picture of society as a whole; give characters from every side; turn them towards society, not private life; exhibit the effect of ceremonies; Keep one toe on the ground by means of dates, facts: envelop the whole in a changing temporal atmosphere; Compose into one vast many-sided group at the end; and then shift the stress from present to future; and show the old fabric insensibly changing without death or violence into the future—suggesting that there is no break, but a continuous development, possibly a recurrence of some pattern; of which of course we actors are ignorant.[20]

Nowhere else in Woolf's commentary on the novel—and there is a great deal of it in her letters and diaries—does she offer so concentrated an account of the project she had undertaken six years earlier. Her aesthetic ambition to capture "society as a whole" and her political optimism in trying to imagine historical change "without death or violence" are unmistakable. Yet the letter also contains what has often been taken as Woolf's final verdict on the project: "Of course," she writes, "it was an utter failure." Yet given the extended timeframe involved (1931–37) and the mutability of Woolf's own thoughts on that matter (at around the same time, she wrote in her diary, "There is no need whatever in my opinion to be unhappy about The Years. It seems to me to come off at the end"), it seems more accurate to say that if the novel is in some sense a failure, it is primarily because over the arduous period of its composition Woolf shifted the terms according to which she could have considered it a success.[21]

What this shift entailed was a revision of how Woolf conceived of the novel embodying the relationship between her aesthetics and her politics. *The Years*, and the years of its composition, had a chastening effect on both—or, more precisely, on the extent to which Woolf envisioned either one directly fueling the other. Having embarked in *The Pargiters* on a project of "intellectual argument in the form of art," she would never again attempt so direct a synthesis of what, in her 1929 essay "Women and Fiction," she called the political "gadfly" and the artistic "butterfly."[22] By the time she published a 1936 article in the *Socialist Worker*, "Why Art Today Follows Politics," Woolf was arguing that the artist involves herself in political activity precisely to preserve her art's independence from politics; while in "The Leaning Tower," she sharply criticized the left-wing poets of the thirties for "the pedagogic, the didactic, the loud-speaker strain that dominates" their "politician's poetry."[23] Yet at the same time, *Three Guineas* is Woolf's most explicitly political work; and "Why Art" and "The Leaning Tower" both assert a relationship, however oblique, between literature and the social world in which it is composed and circulates. In "Why Art," she argues that "the writer is in such close touch with human life that any agitation in his subject matter must change his angle of vision."[24] In "The Leaning Tower" she suggests that the political creativity relies on an aesthetic sensibility: "We can help England very greatly . . . if we borrow the books she lends us and if we read them critically" (180). Even earlier, in *A Room of One's Own,* Woolf wrote that "fiction is like a spider's web, attached ever so lightly perhaps, but still attached to life at all four corners."[25] Artistic creation and political action are, in the end, distinct realms of human endeavor; yet in their distinctness they are mutually imbricated. (Woolf's friend John Maynard Keynes arrived at a similar position in the realm of public policy at exactly the moment when Woolf completed *The Years,* in his 1936 article "Art and the State": "[The artist] needs economic security and enough income, and then to be left to himself, at the same time the servant of the public and his own master.")[26] The elaboration of this position spans much of Woolf's career. In 1925, Woolf declared that in *Mrs. Dalloway* she hoped "to criticise the social system, & show it at work, at its most intense." The desire both to show and to criticize was also behind Woolf's idea, in January 1931, of an "essay-novel."

In this spirit Woolf began work the following year on *The Pargiters.* At their most ambitious, the critical interchapters of *The Pargiters* not only make explicit the fiction's implicit social critique but also seek to overcome what Woolf sees as the representational limits of the novel in her own cultural moment. In the second fictional chapter, for example, young Rose is repeatedly accosted by a suspicious man on her trip to and from the store: "When she reached the pillar box there was the man again. He was leaning against it, as if he were ill, Rose thought, filled with the same terror again; [but] he was lit up by the lamp. There was nobody else anywhere in sight. As she ran past him, he gibbered some nonsense at her, sucking his lips in & out; & began to undo his clothes . . ."[27] Later, when her sister Eleanor asks Rose why she can't sleep, Rose cowers mutely: "'But I can't tell Eleanor' she was saying to herself" (48). The interchapter commentary glosses Rose's experience in a passage worth quoting at length, as it draws together Woolf's awareness of the limits and possibilities of aesthetic creation with the structures of social and sexual repression that she was attempting to represent in this part of the essay-novel:

> This instinct to turn away and hide the true nature of the experience, either because it is too complex to explain or because of the sense of guilt that seems to adhere to it and to make concealment necessary, has, of course, prevented both the novelist from dealing with it in fiction—it would be impossible to find any mention of such feelings in the novels that were being written by Trollope, Mrs Gaskell, Mrs Oliphant, George Meredith, during the eighties. . . . In addition, there is, as the three dots used after the sentence "He unbuttoned his clothes . . ." testify, a convention, supported by law, which forbids, whether rightly or wrongly, any plain description of the sight that Rose, in common with many other little girls, saw under the lamp post by the pillar box in the dusk of that March evening. All the novelist can do, therefore, in order to illustrate this aspect of sexual life, is to state some of the facts; but not all; and then to imagine the impression on the nerves, on the brain; on the whole being, of a shock which the child instinctively conceals, as Rose did . . . and is also too ignorant, too childish, too frightened, to describe or explain even to herself, as Rose again was. (51)

Woolf thus attempts to account both for what is in the fiction and for what cannot appear there, not by naming the experience itself but by explaining why it can't be named. It's not difficult, then, to see why she became frustrated with *The Pargiters:* the explanations constantly threaten to obscure more than they reveal, as each layer of metacommentary moves further away from its object. The division of narrative labor that this technique produces ultimately embodies the work's failure to live up to Woolf's ambitions for novelistic character. Individuals in *The Pargiters*'s fiction are isolated monads whose thoughts are faithfully recorded by the narrator, while the interchapters attempt, at length and with considerable clanking of the machinery, to account for the external world of institutions that produced those individuals' thoughts.

The fourth interchapter essay analyzes Edward Pargiter and his inherited ideas about women. It combines an insistence on the institutional transmissibility of character with an almost overwrought awareness of the futility of the descriptive method Woolf had chosen: "[N]obody who was not first at Rexby or St. James's and then at Benedict's in the summer of 1880 could possibly understand the force of the traditions and influences" (76); "to give the full effect of all this ... would be entirely impossible" (77); "A highly educated foreigner failed completely to understand ... a working man would be equally at a loss" (78). And indeed, the comprehension of character is inhibited rather than enabled in passages like the following, which occur with greater and greater frequency as the draft progresses: "That scene, though it may possibly throw some light upon the problems that worried Edward's younger brother Bobby when he first went to a public school and therefore indirectly explain his sister Rose's anger in the bathroom, and her consequent refusal to go 'beetling' with Bobby in the Round Pond, is inevitably imperfect" (76). This passage—only one example among many—loops back on itself, each insight offering another connection and demanding further explication, a movement only arrested by the admission of failure in the final clause. The very syntax of *The Pargiters* moves backwards, contradicting at the level of style Woolf's stated interest in "the future" and "continuous development." Her imperative to "give a faithful and detailed account" produces an exercise in the accumulation of contextual detail, no amount of which will ever equal the whole of an individual's motivation, and a return to the tired binaries of inside/outside, private/public for which Woolf had pilloried the Edwardians some years before: the fiction shows us individuals acting, and the authorial commentary tells us why. As Leaska notes in his introduction to the drafts, the *OED* defines *pargeter* as "a plasterer; a whitewasher," and if Woolf's aim in her essay-novel was to bring to light through the Pargiters institutional aspects of the modern world that they themselves "whitewash," she was frequently tripped up by her own ambition.[28]

Woolf's abandonment of the essay-novel then, in February 1933, marks the moment when she concluded that the political and the aesthetic would remain, for her, relatively autonomous spheres, even as a deepened understanding of one might produce effects in the other—the point she would argue in "Why Art" and "The Leaning Tower." But her change of emphasis involved an expansion rather than a diminution of her plans for the project:

> I want to give the whole of the present society—nothing less: facts, as well as vision. And to combine them both. . . . It should aim at immense breadth and immense intensity. It should include satire, comedy, poetry, narrative, & what form is to hold them all together? Should I bring in a play, letters, poems? I think I begin to grasp the whole. And its to end with the press of daily normal life continuing. And there are to be millions of ideas but no preaching—history, politics, feminism, art, literature—in short a summing up of all I know, feel, laugh at, despise, like admire hate & so on.[29]

"No preaching": that is, not an argument but the created totality of a protean aesthetic form, informed by her politics but also by much else. Likewise, in advice to her nephew Julian Bell: "I don't see why you should worry yourself to write a novel. . . . What I wish is that you'd invent some medium that's half poetry half play half novel. (Three halves, I see; well, you must correct my arithmetic.)"[30] None of those halves, significantly, involves an essay. And if the finished version was finally not the all-encompassing tour de force that Woolf had hoped for in her more optimistic moments, this was in large part because she returned fully to the novel form as such, saving political commentary for *Three Guineas* and the incorporation of other forms (particularly drama, but also poetry) for *Between the Acts*. If, for Woolf, the essence of the novel lies in the creation of character, *The Years* is her most properly novelistic work.

The Years works to fulfill Woolf's goal of a mode of character in which the individual emerges out of formal tension and thematic feedback with an array of institutions. The novel's institutions overlap with the operations of sovereign power, but in their diversity and in Woolf's attention to the unintended consequences of their operation they exceed incorporation into a model of analysis based on the relationship between the individual and any unified concept of the state. Likewise, they share at points the thematic terrain covered by the Foucauldian critique of modern subjectivity as produced by the hospital, the prison, and the asylum, but Woolf in *The Years* maintains an optimism about the ordering effects of institutional life, an attention to the imperial rather than merely local or national ramifications of institutions, and a prestructuralist liberal humanism. As James March and Johan Olsen put it, institutions are "organized practices" and "constitutive rules" that are "carriers of identities and roles." They receive social and economic validation, are durable across time, and are relatively, although not absolutely, unaffected by the preferences of individuals. Institutions enable forms of action and lend meaning to individual lives, but they also impose constraints, setting limits on what actions are plausible and thus on what types of lives are imaginable. And yet, "institutions are not merely static," and so the question of institutional change is central to the project of representing a fully institutionalized social world.[31] *The Years* captures in narrative form that "changing temporal atmosphere," the "old fabric insensibly changing without death or violence into the future"; how institutions change across time and how new kinds of lives become livable.

"The Glare of the East": Abel Pargiter and Military Bureaucracy

Woolf describes the Pargiters as "one of those typical English families whose members are to be found in the Army, the Navy, and the Church; the Bar, the Stock Exchange; the Civil Services; the House of Commons; who never rise very high or sink very low."[32] And indeed, in its opening sections *The Years* seems to foreclose on the idea that an individual could occupy a social position outside of institutional life—or that such a thing as a legible character could precede the rules and practices that enable and constrain the emergence of character as such. We meet Abel Pargiter in his unnamed club, and within this space Abel first appears as merely one among many, a name only, otherwise indistinguishable from the individuals around him: "Colonel Abel Pargiter was sitting after luncheon in his club talking. Since his companions in the leather armchairs were men of his own type, men who had been soldiers, civil servants, men who had now retired, they were reviving with old jokes and stories now their past in India, Africa, Egypt" (4). The language of the passage lends causal force to the linkage of institutional history with type, and type with action or habit: "since" these individuals were formed as soldiers or civil servants, they now converse in this way. The narrator describes their conversation as pertaining to "some appointment, to some possible appointment" (4), and the indirect conveyance of this bit of dialogue, which is marked *as* dialogue only by the narrator's subtle aping of the men's slightly self-important, repetitive way of talking, implies that this is the speech not of a particular character but of a group: it is immaterial which of "the three baldish and greyish heads" has actually said it, or indeed whether exactly these words have been said at all. It is the indirect discourse not of Abel or his companions specifically but of what the narrator herself refers to as a particular imperial "type."

This narrative process, in which indirectly reported speech seems to emanate not from an individual but from a collective, is prefigured a few pages earlier, in the first of the short, broad-focus interludes that Woolf places between the chapters of *The Years*: "It was an uncertain spring . . . but in April such weather was to be expected. Thousands of shop assistants made that remark, as they handed neat parcels to ladies in flounced dresses standing on the other side of the counter at Whiteley's and the Army and Navy stores" (1). Again, via the narrator's indirect reportage, the speech of any particular shop assistant becomes the speech of the Shop Assistant, a type instantiated by any of "thousands" of particular individuals, all of whom might as well as not be saying the same words at the same moment anywhere in London.[33] Rachel Blau DuPlessis has argued that one of Woolf's feminist innovations in *The Years* is the creation of a "choral," "group," or "communal protagonist," "a way of organizing the work so that neither the development of an individual against a backdrop of supporting characters nor the formation of a heterosexual couple is central to the novel," a point relevant to the issues of individuality and anonymous collectivity that these passages raise.[34] Margaret Comstock makes a similar argument, writing that the novel is composed "on aesthetic principles that are the opposite of fascist. It has no center or central figure around which subordinate elements can be arranged."[35] But while this reading does help illuminate the structure of the relationships among the characters who actually populate the novel as discrete individuals, it does not account for those characters' processes of emergence from an anonymous though not innumerable multitude of individuals who occupy the same institutional positions. In light of the establishment of this structure on the novel's first page, Abel's emergence as a full-fledged character a few pages later cannot but seem somewhat arbitrary—there are thousands of his type sitting in the rooms of other clubs; indeed, we know there are others in the very same room.

So, a paragraph into the scene it is not immediately clear who the man speaking, "the youngest and sprucest of the three" (4), actually is; it may be Abel, though it turns out to be "Major Elkin." The description at first attaches to no individual; it is significant only relatively, in that it lessens slightly the interchangeability of the men (one is younger and sprucer than the others). Abel himself separates from the group only when he tires of the conversation, "[throwing] himself back in his chair," and his physical appearance gains specificity: "He sat staring ahead of him with bright blue eyes that seemed a little screwed up, as if the glare of the East were still in them; and puckered at the corners as if the dust were still in them" (5). Perhaps surprisingly, Abel begins to emerge as an *individual* here only by reference to his place in the military bureaucracy of "the East," a professional world in which personal distinction was subordinated, as B. B. Misra writes, to "efficiency . . . achieved within the framework of institutional and legal constraint imposed on the exercise of discretionary authority" and "rationalization . . . based on the principle of bureaucratic impersonality which was not supposed to recognize political or social differentiations."[36] Abel gains distinctiveness on the page only because he has been selected out of the many indistinguishable Englishmen in the background of the novel who similarly beheld that "glare"—that is, who participated in the project of the British Empire in India and have returned to the metropolitan center to reminisce in their clubs.[37] But this superficially contradictory assertion (Abel is individuated through his institutional incorporation) betrays a more meaningful tension underlying the process of characterization in these passages. Abel's thoughts in themselves are not particularly distinctive; his is not an especially lively consciousness, if the value of Woolf's modernism lies in rendering that elusive entity; and indeed, many critics of *The Years* have pointed out that characters' thoughts and dialogue frequently trail off or go conspicuously unreported. But this inattention to the interesting consciousness of individuals (or the uninterestingness of their consciousness when revealed) is less a sign of aesthetic failure than an indication that the novel's investments lay elsewhere. With the price that Abel's coherence as an individual is always in question, because it seems as though he could recede at any time back into mere type, what at first seems like a contradiction—the co-presence of the individual and the institution in each other—is actually the tension that produces character.

In this first scene, the narration focuses on Abel only once he is alone, his companions physically absent or departing, "hurrying through the door" or "talk[ing] to another man" (5). From here, the trajectory of the process by which his individuality is developed is, in a sense, reversed. In the opening passages, putatively collective speech and description are narrowed until we gain a sense of the individual. Now, the individual that has emerged gains distinctive features that are only subsequently, but definitively, revealed to be products of an institutional context and role. Abel visits his mistress, Mira, and touches her neck "with the hand that had lost two fingers, rather lower down, where the neck joins the shoulders"; a page later, "the hand that had lost two fingers began to fumble rather lower down where the neck joins the shoulders" (8, 9). The uncanny repetition of the phrase, along with the disquieting detail of the lost fingers, raises a question that is not answered for several pages, when, at tea with his family, Abel's hand again "fumble[s]," and we learn that "[h]e had lost two fingers of the right hand in the Mutiny, and the muscles had shrunk so that the right hand resembled the claw of some aged bird" (13). The gap in an individual history is filled by collective history; physical trauma for Abel is revealed to be a product of the imperial trauma of the Mutiny.

Abel grows from an absence—one among any number of "men of his type" in this early scene (and indeed, one among many returned colonial officials in Woolf's oeuvre)—into a presence in the novel, an individual who relates to other individuals, through his accumulation of personal traits generated by an imperial, and institutional, training. But the process takes away as it gives; institutional incorporation is context-dependent, and the shared traits that allow for the expansion of individual character in one context reduce character to type in others. This technique can produce quite subtle effects: Abel is consistently referred to as "Colonel Abel Pargiter" or "Colonel Pargiter" in the club, but when the scene shifts to Mira's seedy flat and then to the Pargiter household, he is notably reduced to "the Colonel"—the reduction of proper name to functional title neatly illustrating how Abel is, curiously, most "human" when most fully incorporated into his formative context. The diminution of the name in the move to the domestic corresponds, moreover, to a diminution of Abel's personality:

> "Cut along," said the Colonel imperiously. Martin got up and went, drawing his hand reluctantly along the chairs and tables as if to delay his passage. He slammed the door rather sharply behind him. The Colonel rose and stood upright among them in his tightly-buttoned frock coat.
>
> "And I must be off too," he said. But he paused a moment, as if there were nothing particular for him to be off to. He stood there very erect among them, as if he wished to give some order, but could not at the moment think of any order to give. (15)

The misalignment of the domestic context with the Colonel's military bearing produces a sort of seizure of character; Abel is suspended between the "order" of the bureaucrat or commanding officer and the circumstances of the family home, where that form of order has little purchase. In overlaying the language of military command on the routine of domestic life, and perhaps having some fun with the irony of impotent Abel's "upright," "erect" posture, the passage quite clearly anticipates the equation and critique of militarism, patriarchy, and fascism that Woolf would undertake in *Three Guineas*.[38] My point, though, is less to draw attention to the social critique that scenes like this perform (a critique on which much criticism of the novel has focused) than to demonstrate how Woolf's characters come to life *as characters* through their relationship to the institutions that are implicated in politics. *The Years*, as London-centered as any of Woolf's novels, becomes imperial fiction not by addressing the politics of late empire thematically (though at times it does) but by incorporating the supranational institutions of the empire into formal processes of characterization. As Carl Sandburg wrote shortly after her death, Woolf in her writing created a "personal British Empire";[39] *The Years* confirms this idea more literally than Sandburg may have intended.

Professions for Women

Woolf constructs Abel and the other Pargiter men, such as her cousin Herbert, as being granted almost their very existence by the institutions of the British Empire. They are positive products of what Alex Woloch terms the novel's "character-system," differentiated from one another as they vie for attention in the narrative. Indeed, the longtime critical account of *The Years* as a failure may in part be a result of its remarkably egalitarian character-system. If, as Woloch argues, realist narrative is generated out of an *asymmetric* distribution of narrative attention, then it is easy to see why *The Years* is unable to tell a story: narrative attention is too *evenly* dispersed across what DuPlessis terms its "communal protagonist."[40] But this makes *The Years* all the more interesting for its exemplification of processes of institutional characterization, a field of character formation in which the actions, behaviors, and personal features that make fictional individuals legible in the first place also threaten those individuals' status as full-fledged characters. Their relationship not to other characters but to institutions pulls them incessantly from the distinction of one *versus* many to the uncertain status of one *among* many; that is, from distinctive individual to institutional type. Abel Pargiter is an early and relatively anodyne example of this process of emergence and incorporation at work in *The Years,* but this tension plays a role in the production of all its characters. And there is a division between negative and positive sides of this process, a division that generally maps onto gender difference. Edward, the eldest son, becomes an Oxford don; Morris becomes a lawyer; Martin joins the army. The Pargiter men and boys consistently take shape in the generative pull between individuation and incorporation; even young Martin, entering the house silently carrying books, speaks at tea only to announce his rank at the top of his class (12). Woolf's rendering of female characters, however, in acknowledgment of the section's late Victorian setting, generally relies on exclusion as a means of definition. As one character says in *The Pargiters,* women "are absolutely uneducated; they have received nothing from . . . the institutions of their country; they cannot practice professions, they are kept purely as slaves for the breeding of children."[41] Over and over, the novel presents situations in which female character is rendered fragmentary or amorphous; only by entering professional institutions, *The Years* suggests, can women and men be written as equals.

In the "1880" section, the exclusion of women from institutional life is most obvious as a thematic concern: it leads to a situation in which, as Woolf writes in *The Pargiters,* "[t]hey are young and healthy and have nothing to do but change the sheets at Whiteleys and peep behind the blinds at young men going to call next door" (28). But their exclusion, which the novel narrates in its plot, feeds back into a formal structure: locked in the house all day, the Pargiter women are constituted by claustrophobic family dynamics and petty domestic quarrels: "[T]here was a rustling in the hall and in came Eleanor. It was much to their relief, especially to Milly's. Thank goodness, there's Eleanor she thought, looking up—the soother, the maker-up of quarrels, the buffer between her and the intensities and strifes of family life. . . . Protect me, she thought, handing her a teacup, who am such a mousy, downtrodden, inefficient little chit, compared with Delia, who always gets her way, while I'm always snubbed by Papa, who was grumpy for some reason" (14). The three women are defined by their roles in a recurrent drama of familial discord: timid Milly, assertive "favorite" Delia, mediator Eleanor, all distributed around the central figure of the father. What are ostensibly Milly's thoughts are given sanction elsewhere by the narrator, but the distinctions drawn by domestic routine are erased and then restored by the proximity of the "social machine." "'I met old Burke at the Club,'" Abel says; "'asked me to bring one of you to dinner; Robin's back, on leave.' . . . Eleanor, sitting in her low chair, saw a curious look first on Milly's face, then on Delia's. She had an impression of hostility between them" (14–15).[42] Individual distinction is erased by Abel's "one of you," a phrase repeated in reference to the three women a page later. The women's distinctiveness is then restored by the "hostility" that their being lumped together generates in them: first Eleanor reappears, then Milly, then Delia. But their father's address to them as an undifferentiable set has the odd effect of stripping them of the characteristics that had defined them earlier, as though, in a satirical reflection of the conditions of the time, being drawn closer to the social machine de-constitutes those forms of female character that actually manage to make themselves felt.

Significantly, the passage alights on Eleanor as its focusing consciousness. Eleanor is the closest thing to a protagonist that *The Years* offers, though only in terms of how often she appears; her viewpoint is not especially privileged, nor do the events of her life seem more significant than those of any other character's, and for these reasons critics of the novel have had trouble defining her function in the novel with any consistency. Particularly in the early sections, though, she often serves as a relay between the novel's formal strategies of characterization and the inclusion of those strategies' effects at the level of theme. Shortly after the three Pargiter girls' miniature drama of emergence and erasure in the tea scene, Eleanor reflects that "[s]he wished people would not say, 'Bring one of your daughters.' She wished they would say 'Bring Eleanor,' or 'Bring Milly,' or 'Bring Delia,' instead of lumping them all together. Then there could be no question" (17)—a sort of metacommentary on the process of differentiation involved in the character-system. And this relay function is doubled when, as she is in conversation with her brother Morris, Eleanor's awareness of her own exclusion becomes the condition of Morris's elaboration. After he enters the novel as "a sound in the hall" (31), Morris's presence is expanded through the mechanism of Eleanor's questioning:

> He wrinkled his forehead. He was losing his boyish look, Eleanor thought. That was the worst of the Bar, everyone said; one had to wait. He was devilling for Sanders Curry; and it was dreary work, hanging about the courts all day, waiting.
> "How's old Curry?" she asked—old Curry had a temper.

"A bit liverish," said Morris grimly.
"And what have you been doing all day?" she asked.
"Nothing in particular," he replied.
"Still Evans *v.* Carter?"
"Yes," he said briefly.
"And who's going to win?" she asked.
"Carter, of course," he replied.

Why "of course" she wanted to ask? But she had said something silly the other day—something that showed that she had not been attending. She muddled things up; for example, what was the difference between Common Law and the other kind of law? She said nothing. . . .

"You'll be Lord Chancellor one of these days," she said. "I'm sure of it." He shook his head, smiling. . . . But even while she looked, a doubt came over him. Lord Chancellor, she had said. Ought she not to have said Lord Chief Justice? She never could remember which was which: and that was why he would not discuss Evans *v.* Carter with her. (31–32)

In an echo of Abel's eyes, "screwed up as though the glare of the East were in them," Morris's distinctive habit of wrinkling his forehead is tied to the bar, and then to the practices associated with it: the "dreary work" of "hanging about the courts all day, waiting." Equally important, though, is that the passage registers Eleanor's nascent consciousness of her own exclusion from the institutional world that constitutes Morris's being: lacking any formal education, she forgets, muddles, and as she does so becomes aware that a gap has opened between her and her brother, a gap that, although Woolf suggests that Victorian sexual ideology is its ultimate cause, is felt by Eleanor to be a product of Morris's access to the specialized knowledge of the legal profession: "When they met they never had time to talk as they used to talk—about things in general—they always talked about facts—little facts" (32).[43] Growing up, for Morris, involves a process of refinement that takes him from "things in general" to "little facts"; a winnowing away through school, university, and firm into a form of character, and a world, where his sister cannot follow.

This impression is deepened when Eleanor goes to the Law Courts with Morris's wife, Celia, to see him argue a case in the "1891" section, the novel's second. In what could be read as an ironic recognition of the hold institutions have over the construction of human character, she realizes that "the solemn sallow atmosphere forbade personalities," and she finds it difficult to pick him out in the "dark and crowded" space, where "men in wigs and gowns were getting up and sitting down and coming in and going out like a flock of birds settling here and there on a field" (102). Eleanor sees him, finally, and thinks "how odd he looked in his yellow wig"; but of course this is precisely the same yellow wig all the other barristers in the room wear, and a description that might be of Morris is also of the mass from which he emerges and into which he recedes: "They all looked like pictures, all the barristers looked emphatic, cut out, like eighteenth-century portraits hung upon a wall" (103). When he stands to speak, with "one hand on the edge of his gown," Eleanor thinks "how well she knew that gesture of Morris's.... But she did not know that other gesture—the way he flung his arm out. That belonged to his public life, his life in the Courts" (104). Here again, Woolf situates formal character between idiosyncrasy and institution: "[flinging] his arm out ... *belonged* to his public life, his life in the Courts." And in a sidelong affirmation of institutional durability, Sanders Curry, the lawyer for whom Morris had been devilling in "1880," is now the judge hearing the case. The machine keeps chugging along.

Despite these moments of irritation or resentment, Eleanor herself never develops the critical perspective that scenes like these offer the reader. She is an unreactive presence, as if the assumption of a more disruptive stance would jeopardize her role as the novel's relay point, registering the thematic and formal transactions of other characters, and as a unifying presence through many of the novel's temporally disparate sections. She involves herself with charitable work and a political committee (though we never discover exactly what its politics are), travels to Spain and India, has a "belief in science" (312), and thinks, near the end of her life, "I do not want to go back into my past ... I want the present" (318). At the same time, her niece Peggy imagines her, ambivalently, as a "portrait of a Victorian spinster" (316) who "believed with passion," even after the war, "in the things man had destroyed." Eleanor is part of "a wonderful generation ... believers" (314), and the novel suggests that her "belief" is what enables her to maintain her mediatory structural position in the novel. "Belief" here stands for what Steve Ellis describes as a set of "Victorian" elements that Woolf's writing generally affirms (and affirms, Ellis argues, *as* distinctly Victorian): "romance, beauty, lyricism, individuality, imagination"—what might be called a capacity for aesthetic experience.[44]

When she emerges from the Law Courts, "the uproar, the confusion, the space of the Strand came upon her with a shock of relief. She felt herself expand.... a rush, a stir, a turmoil of variegated life came racing towards her" (105). Her formal importance to the narrative cuts against Kathy Phillips's suggestion that "Eleanor's only partially awakened consciousness" and "insensitiv[ity]" to issues of class and imperialism make her merely an object of critique in a novel that "unsparingly documents monotony and injustice."[45] With Eleanor's belief and its attendant virtues comes a certain independence of perspective that, it is true, never makes the leap into critique, but this perspective is a thematic feature on which Eleanor's structural role depends.

As *The Years* progresses into the twentieth century, Woolf suggests that an independent perspective is all that remains of those virtues in a world grown less hospitable to belief. While Peggy's initial reflection on belief is prompted by Eleanor's anger at a picture in the evening paper of "a fat man [probably Mussolini] gesticulating" (313), the terms in which Eleanor articulates that anger ("Damned— ... Bully!" [313]) seem themselves to come from another time; while Peggy perceives that the sentiment is admirable, it also says little to an age, the 1930s, in which those "bullies" direct the fates of nations. Like the Teacher of Languages in Conrad's *Under Western Eyes*, Eleanor occupies a position from which events can be perceived but not influenced, and that position is marked as a Victorian holdover. But her consistent presence indexes the novel's historical trajectory, and in doing so runs counter to Ellis's broader argument, that "distinctions and contrasts between the Victorian and the modern" do not "animate or structure [*The Years*] as they do the earlier novels" (119). It is a modest victory for historical optimism, but a victory nonetheless, that at the novel's end Eleanor, a product of the Victorian patriarchal house, feels in the "Present Day" that she can be "happy in this world—happy with living people" (368).

The Functions of Exclusion

Still, monotony and injustice are important in the fates of the other Pargiter women, who, in positions less central to the novel's structure, exemplify the consequences of institutional exclusion. Minor female characters—particularly the sisters Rose, Delia, and Milly—compensate for this exclusion in ways that emerge early in the novel and develop across the decades of its plot. Rose will go on to become an activist for women's suffrage, go to prison "for throwing a brick" (219), and finally be decorated for wartime service, though Martin puts it differently: "She smashed [the King's] window . . . and then she helped him to smash other people's windows" (399). Delia, meanwhile, dreams of joining Charles Stewart Parnell's campaign for Irish home rule, but the inaccessibility of that desire is translated into elaborate fantasies about Parnell and ultimately, ironically, into marriage to an Anglo-Irish landowner, Patrick, "the most King-respecting, Empire-admiring of country gentlemen" (378).[46] As Thomas S. Davis puts it, in an extended reading of these characters' political "dreams," in both cases "what first appears to be a narrative of political awakening inverts into one of psychopathology."[47] For women lacking access to the normative institutional structures that increasingly dominate the social world, refuge in fantasy, whether political or sexual, serves as compensation but ultimately has unpredictable, ironic, and deforming effects on their lives.

Finally, Milly Pargiter's obsession with marriage, Woolf suggests, like Delia's obsession with a fantasy politics, is occasioned by a lack; but beyond their shared exclusion the two sisters are related by a set of interlocking ironies. While Delia's compensatory fantasies are ultimately associated with her dreamy insubstantiality and long periods of *absence* from the novel's plot, the obsequious Milly's obsession with marriage seems directly related to what eventually becomes an excessive physical *presence*. In her old age Milly is "voluminous in draperies proper to her sex and class. . . . In order to disguise her figure, veils with beads on them hung down over her arms. They were so fat that they reminded North of asparagus; pale asparagus tapering to a point. . . . He noticed how the rings were sunk in her fingers, as if the flesh had grown over them" (354). Milly is literally overrun by the features that distinguish her. Her husband, Hugh, appears first as "a vast bulk . . . chiefly white waistcoat, lined with black" (355); he is less a human being than an assemblage of the ornaments "proper to his sex and class." The entirety of North's conversation with Milly and Hugh (354–59) becomes phantasmagorical: from a mere waistcoat, Hugh becomes "an old elephant" (358); Milly has "unsheathed claws . . . fat little paws" (359); both are "amorphous bodies" with "long white tentacles" threatening to "suck [people] in." But these monstrosities sit side by side with a jarringly different set of images: as the couple discuss their children, North thinks, "[T]his is the steam roller that smooths;

obliterates; rounds into identity; rolls into balls.... Jimmy was in Uganda" (359). This imagery prefigures the "social machine" of "A Sketch of the Past," which "stamps and moulds" individuals and marks the men it produces as irreducibly institutional and imperial. And the language sits intertwined with the imagery of raw nature; children are "property," but also "flesh and blood, which they would protect with the unsheathed claws of the primeval swamp" (359). There is no suggestion here that, as we might expect, the orderly procession of modern "civilised" institutions stands apart from, or conceals, the violence of the natural order. Rather, there is a sense that no form of life can exist outside a relation to the institutional world, whether that relation takes the form of inclusion or exclusion. The monstrosity of the Gibbses does not represent instinct reasserting itself in a sort of Freudian allegory of civilization's discontents (though it is tempting to read it this way); instead, it gestures yet again to the fundamentally formative and deformative effects of the regular functioning of institutions. But *The Years* will go on to explore precisely how desires formed by institutional life might be transformative, as North and his sister Peggy respond implicitly to the question prompted by the Gibbses: "How then can we be civilised?" (359).

Sara Pargiter, cousin to Eleanor, Morris, and the other children of Abel Pargiter, takes this logic of institutional incorporation and exclusion to an extreme. Where the deformations of other excluded characters are primarily metaphorical, Sara is literally disfigured from the beginning: "She had been dropped when she was a baby; one shoulder was slightly higher than the other" (115). (Abel, despite his own missing fingers, is made "squeamish" by it.) It is as though Sara has begun life physically marked by "the machine into which [women's] rebellious bodies were inserted," as Woolf would write of herself in "A Sketch."[48] Sara's speech is repetitive and promiscuously allusive, and she often merely repeats what other characters have just said; she seems to be an alcoholic; and she is nasty and cynical in a seemingly unmotivated way. At a wartime dinner party interrupted by an air raid in "1917," Sara denounces war and proposes a toast to "the New World!" (277), but her antimilitarist politics are bound up with personal anger at her cousin North: "'Coward; hypocrite, with your switch in your hand; and your cap on head—' He seemed to quote from a letter that she had written him" (305). Despite the ambiguity of Sara's presentation, she is central to the critical history of *The Years*. Politically minded accounts of the novel have tended to read her as a truth-telling, if anarchic, feminist critic of the established order.[49]

Christine Froula's *Virginia Woolf and the Bloomsbury Avant-Garde* in particular redirects attention from Sara to her precursor in the novel's drafts, Elvira. Tracing diary entries that register the centrality of the Elvira/Sara character to Woolf's conception of her project, Froula illustrates how the "prophet Elvira . . . a prophetic consciousness in a society riding a wave of change" (241) became, in the course of the novel's composition, the ineffectual, incoherent Sara. Froula's broad argument about the novel is that Woolf initially imagined the "essay-novel" about "the sexual life of women" as a feminist foray into the public sphere; but as her notion of whom she would be speaking for and to shifted, the frankly political "talking cure" that *The Pargiters* promised turned into the "enigmatic allegory" and "talking symptoms" of *The Years*.[50] Woolf, "seemingly helpless against repression" (250), could not bring herself to say what she set out wishing to say with Elvira, and so the finished novel is less interesting than the nonexistent book about "the sexual life of women."[51] Yet the problems with Sara Pargiter need not be taken either as signs that the character herself occupies a space somehow external to the novel's genuine political and historical concerns, or as evidence of authorial repression and patriarchal victimization. Elvira may have been good polemic, but she was not good fiction, and not the figure Woolf ultimately settled on. Sara is less of a force thematically; that is, she is not a mouthpiece for a coherent critical sensibility, as Elvira promised to be. But more fundamentally, she embodies an outer limit to the novel's logic of institutional characterization.

In "1907," Sara (referred to in this scene by the diminutive "Sally") sits in her room, idly reading and waiting for her parents, Eugenie and Digby, and her sister, Maggie, to return from a party. (She has previously appeared only as a small child in "1891.") Although this scene, the only one in which we have access to Sara's thoughts, marks her real entry into the novel, it immediately takes the form of an exit; Sara, musing on scraps of George Berkeley's philosophy, thinks, "Nothing but thought, was it? . . . well, since it was impossible to read and impossible to sleep, she would let herself *be* thought. It was easier to act things than to think them. Legs, body, hands the whole of her must be laid out passively to take part in this universal process of thinking which the man said was the world living" (124). She finds that "it was impossible to act thought. She became something; a root, lying sunk in the earth; veins seemed to thread the cold mass; the tree put forth branches; the branches had leaves" (125). Failing to "become thought," she tries to read *Antigone*, until finally "a dark wing brushed her mind, leaving a pause, a blank space. . . . She was asleep"

(128). Sara's naïve attempt to enact the philosophy she has just read is not, perhaps, meant to be taken entirely seriously; but it is telling that her very entrance into the novel is itself an attempt at self-erasure. When Maggie comes in and wakes her up, Sara tries to recount what she has read in an effort to keep her sister in the room, but ends up only repeating, "What's 'I'? . . . What's 'I'?" (131–32). DuPlessis suggests that this moment of feminine "communion" "intimate[s] that the fluid ego boundaries of the pre-oedipal bond are one source for the communal protagonist."[52] Certainly Sara's questioning the status of her own subjectivity immediately suggests a different mode of characterization from that at work in Abel and the other Pargiter men, who emerge so unselfconsciously from the collective practices of institutional life; but given her subsequent development (or lack thereof), it is not clear that *The Years* offers an entirely positive evaluation of Sara. "What's 'I'?" shadows Sara throughout the novel, and the question is neither resolved nor rendered irrelevant.

In "1910," after a drawn-out and awkward lunch, Sara accompanies Rose to a political meeting; her account of it to Maggie offers a representative sample of her speech:

> "And what did you do with Rose?" said Maggie. She spoke absent-mindedly. Sara turned and glanced at her. Then she began to play again.
> "Stood on the bridge and looked into the water," she murmured.
> "Stood on the bridge and looked into the water," she hummed, in time to the music. "Running water; flowing water. May my bones turn to coral; and fish light their lanthorns; fish light their green lanthorns in my eyes." . . .
> "You went out with Rose," she said. "Where to?"
> Sara left the piano and stood in front of the fireplace.
> "We got into a bus and went to Holborn," she said. "And we walked along a street," she went on; "and suddenly," she jerked her hand out, "I felt a clap on my shoulder." "Damned liar!" said Rose, "and took me and flung me against a public house wall!"
> Maggie stitched on in silence.
> "You got into a bus and went to Holborn," she repeated mechanically after a time. "And then?" (177)

Sara moves almost seamlessly from singing at the piano to speaking in the course of this exchange; she often strains against the novel's realism, pulling toward a more lyrical, dreamlike, and allusive register (referring perhaps to *The Tempest*, for example, in the "may my bones turn to coral" passage). Her effect on language is thematized when North, reciting a poem to her later in the narrative, thinks, "The words going out into the room seemed like actual presences, hard and independent; yet as she was listening they were changed by their contact with her" (322). If this were all, if Sara simply lived in closer contact with aesthetic experience than her fellow Pargiters, she could be made sense of as a critic of dominant ways of seeing, as bearer of a distinctly feminine truth, or even as the "artist" figure in the only Woolf novel that lacks one. But as her story about her day with Rose continues, it becomes difficult to decipher which parts are entirely made up, which are exaggerated or distorted (and to what effect), and which are merely given a poetic twist. The lack of free indirect access to Sara means that we do not know what her attitude is, and our confusion is amplified by the fact that other characters—here, Maggie—are never presented to us as though *they* know, either; the odd understatement of Maggie's eventual conclusion that "there was something wrong with the story; something impossible" seems as misaligned with Sara's bizarre tale as the tale is with the ordinary prose of the novel. So, not only can we not tell what Sara should mean to *us*, we cannot tell what she means to other individuals *in the novel*. She is close to completely unconstrained in her speech, but the absence of constraint, predicated on her allergy to any form of institutional integration, does not register in the novel as freedom; rather, in an almost perfect negative example of institutional characterization, the absence of constraint is simply the absence of meaning. The formation of character comes to appear impossible in the absence of the institution.

Moreover, Sara actively refuses the forms of integration that generate coherence in other characters. In one of the most puzzling scenes in "Present Day," North, having recently returned to London after a long career in the military and running a ranch in Africa, sits with Sara in her room. To kill time before the party they plan to attend, North begins to recite Andrew Marvell's "The Garden," but he is interrupted by a noise in the hall. "'The Jew,' she murmured. . . . 'The Jew having a bath'" (322). Sara recounts how Abrahamson, the Jew with whom she shares the communal bathroom, works in a tallow factory and leaves a "line of grease" around the bathtub, the thought of which makes North "physically sick" (323). Sara says that she too has found it disgusting, and she tells a story about how, when she first found the grease in the tub, she was driven to seek proper employment as a means of escape: "I put on my hat and coat and rushed out in a rage. . . . And there were people passing. . . . And I said, 'Must I join your conspiracy? Stain the hand, the unstained hand,'—he could see her hand gleam as she waved it in the half-light of the sitting room, '—and sign on, and serve a master; all because of a Jew in my bath, all because of a Jew?'" (323). North repeatedly interrupts her lyrical recitation to request clarification, and she trails off remembering her words to the editor who interviews her for a job: "The Jew's in my bath, I said—the Jew . . . the Jew. . . ." (324). As in the long passage quoted above, neither we nor the other characters can be sure how to take Sara's tale; since she still lives in the boardinghouse with Abrahamson, it seems that she did not take the job at the newspaper. "How much of that was true?" North asks, but she doesn't reply, and the scene shifts to Delia's party.

Sara's anti-Semitism foregrounds the problems inherent in the notion that her characterization is motivated by Woolf's desire to present a critical, "outsider" perspective. Maren Linett, in an important reading of *The Years*, traces the history of this passage's composition and the critical response to it.[53] Linett points out that critics, starting from the assumption that at least by the 1930s and after twenty years of marriage to Leonard, Woolf was not anti-Semitic in any meaningful sense, have generally excused the anti-Semitic tone of the passage by arguing one of two things: that Sara's perspective is ironized and critiqued by Woolf; or that Sara's remaining in the flat despite her declared prejudice is intentional, a gesture of solidarity with workers and the excluded (as embodied by Abrahamson himself). Through an analysis of Woolf's letters and the drafts of this scene, Linett argues that *The Years* "makes of a specific reaction to a Jew . . . an abstracted collection of meanings supple enough to support the weight of multiple social and aesthetic concerns" (344). In the figure of the working-class Jew, according to Linett, Woolf confused the victims of political oppression with the oppressors, and thus the Jew first threatens Sara's autonomy and then becomes an index by which to judge her own independence: driven to seek employment by Abrahamson's presence, she ultimately will not "stain the hand," and so the only thing stronger than her dislike of the Jew is her drive for imaginative autonomy. Thus a complicated but persistent anti-Semitism exists side by side in Woolf's novel with a radical emphasis on the need for women to establish and maintain their autonomy.

Linett's broad point about Woolf's anti-Semitism is convincing and troubling, but there are two difficulties with this reading of *The Years* specifically. One involves the fact that even if Woolf is not critical of Sara's attitudes in this scene, Sara is established as a less valorized character for *other* reasons throughout the novel, as shown above. This leads directly into the second point, which is that Linett proceeds from the assumption that Woolf's concept of female creative autonomy is absolute, rather than predicated on access to the professions and to the institutions of modernity. Again, there are no Outsiders without a relationship to an inside, and in this sense Sara does not look forward in any constructive way to *Three Guineas*. Whatever the ideological implications of her character's attitude toward Abrahamson, her fissiparousness, her failure to cohere, resonates more broadly at the level of form. Sara is not even a full-fledged character in the sense that Woolf proposes in "Character in Fiction": in herself, she can reveal little of the "whole society" because she does not participate in it; she embodies the absence of the social, institutional aspects of character (substituting for rule-boundedness, habit, and meaningful action her talent for mimicry). North's question after her rambling account of her day is the only thing that can really be said of her: "How much of that was true?"

"Into the Future"

The Pargiter women's exclusion from the institutions of modern English life, in a world where life without a relation to those institutions has become unimaginable, produces in them only various frustrated forms of fantasy and desire. Milly finally identifies so thoroughly with patriarchal tradition that she is figuratively swallowed by it, while Delia, Rose, and Sara live the lives of what might be termed, to recall *Three Guineas*, Premature Outsiders: outsiders without access to an inside that would lend relative meaning to their outsiderdom. Their relation to institutional life is a negative one, but a relation nonetheless. This thematic is reflected in the deformations that mark these women throughout the novel. Anxiety and trauma feature prominently in their relationships to institutional life, and this anxiety is one of the dominant affects that Woolf would carry forward into her late work, especially in "A Sketch of the Past" (as we've seen) and *Between the Acts*. Recent revaluations by Paul Saint-Amour and Davis extend this assessment to *The Years* even as they further the case that the novel needs to be taken seriously as one of Woolf's major works. Saint-Amour, whose reading focuses on the air raid in "1917," allows that *The Years* "extends [*Mrs. Dalloway*'s] thinking about the reciprocal ties and alliances that may form among those who endure the charged futurity of modern warfare"; it "shows more interest in new coalitions of the living" than Woolf's earlier work. But the novel purchases these potentialities at the price of its characters living always under conditions of perpetual suspense; "the lattice of resilient social ties necessary to transcend war can only be formed in war . . . to think at all is to think in a raid."[54] Davis suggests, compellingly, that *The Years* reconfigures the genre of the historical novel, registering the sweep of historical events obliquely, in the everyday lives of characters, while dismantling the notions of historical *progress* that have traditionally been seen as constitutive of the genre since Lukács: "Woolf's characters do not progress but live out and repeat their family histories with disastrous consequences."[55]

I affirm Saint-Amour's sense that the novel is very much invested in new forms of connection that are more concrete than those imagined in Woolf's earlier works. And Davis's reading, across a range of late modernist works, of "everyday life as a scene where world-systemic distress attains legibility" (2) parallels my own emphasis on the ways that institutional collectivities are made manifest in the microlevel details of novelistic character. In the latter case, though, the scalar distension inherit in Davis's move from the minutiae of the everyday to the vastness of the world-system obscures how much of *The Years* is concerned with mid-range institutions such as those I have described already: military bureaucracy, the professions, the popular press. There may indeed have been little reason to be cheerful about the world-system in the thirties, but the closing acts of *The Years* are surprisingly optimistic at levels of organization further down the scale. Eleanor's niece Peggy and nephew North, the youngest generation of Pargiters, are central to "Present Day," the novel's closing section, which takes up the question of how to represent historical change "without death or violence" in the relationship between character and institution; here Woolf attempts to "shift the stress from present to future." North and Peggy offer perspective on the novel's other characters, if only because this longest section is largely given over to them, with Eleanor playing a secondary role. But unlike Eleanor, whose perspective takes up the bulk of earlier sections as Peggy's and North's do here, the two siblings are more than mediatory figures; in a more substantial way, they are the vehicles through which Woolf attempts to assimilate into the novel a fully institutionalized social world in which forms of freedom and change might nonetheless be possible.

Like Sara, Peggy appears first as a young girl in "1911"; when she appears again, in "Present Day," she happens to be thinking of Sara: "Sally sitting on the edge of a chair with a smudge on her face. What a fool, she thought bitterly, and a thrill ran down her thigh. Why was she bitter? For she prided herself upon being honest—she was a doctor—and that thrill she knew meant bitterness" (310). The aside "she was a doctor" suddenly brings Peggy into focus, and the habits of thought and perception that define her in this last section of the novel are directly linked to that institutional role, itself the product of a particular education and specialized knowledge of the body. Because she is "a doctor," Peggy knows that the "thrill" means "bitterness." The precise logic of this link aside, such moments of embodied feeling occur over and over in the episode. Told that her former teacher has praised her, "There, said Peggy, that's pleasure. The nerve down her spine seemed to tingle.... Each emotion touched a different nerve. A sneer rasped the thigh; pleasure thrilled the spine; and also affected the sight" (344). Perhaps most strikingly in a novel more notable for its oddly subdued tone and ambiguity of affect than for its moments of passion, Peggy is reconciled to her brother North, to whom she has been consciously cruel at an earlier moment in the party, through a moment of unspoken exaltation brought on by physical contact: "Her hand was still on his arm; she felt something hard and taut beneath the sleeve, and the touch of his flesh, bringing back to her the nearness of human beings and their distance, so that if one meant to help one hurt, yet they depended on each other, produced in her such a tumult of sensation that she could scarcely keep herself from crying out, North! North! North!" (377). Peggy's institutional formation feeds back into her personal relationships; at each moment of embodied feeling she is able to "examine it," leading to moments of critical appraisal of herself and others—a capacity that other characters in the novel lack. And she is relatively untroubled by questions of her independent subjectivity: in contrast to Sara's "What's 'I'?", Peggy says, "I'm a doctor" (343). What we might call a self-conscious sense of self would seem to be significant here; through it Peggy moves away from what Hermione Lee calls the rest of the novel's "case histories ... forms of frustrated and indecisive behavior" that "are products of a political system."[56]

And yet the promise of her contact with North is an exception, for Peggy's examinations of her feelings toward others usually serve only to deepen her cynical and resentful attitude. Her embodiment of the protocols of the medical profession becomes a social prop, ill-suiting her to the situations in which she finds herself: miserable at the party, she thinks, "What is the tip for this particular situation? . . . as if she were prescribing for a patient. Take notes, she added. Do them up in a bottle with a glossy green cover, she thought. Take notes and the pain goes. Take notes and the pain goes, she repeated to herself" (333). The attempt to apply the procedures of institutional life to a situation in which those procedures do not apply echoes Abel at the dinner table in 1880, wishing to "give some order"; the catechistic repetition of "take notes and the pain goes" suggests the danger of overidentification with one's role, which in turn evokes the tension between the individual character and the anonymous type. The awareness of the body that her education grants her threatens to define her; her "examinations" repeatedly reinforce the truth of the body's "spontaneous feelings." An obnoxious young man, she thinks, "can't help it, not with that nerve-drawn egotist's face" (342), which seems to get the relation between affect and body exactly backwards, as though for Peggy the testimony of the body determines the possibilities for human personality. Talking to an elderly uncle, she thinks: "Rest—rest—let me rest. How to deaden; how to cease to feel; that was the cry of the woman bearing children; to rest, to cease to be. In the Middle Ages, she thought, it was the cell; the monastery; now it's the laboratory; the professions; not to live; not to feel" (336–37). Here, Peggy's evocation of "the laboratory" recalls Chloe and Olivia, the fictional scientists in *A Room of One's Own*, who Woolf had imagined might mark the first tentative stirrings of women's independent creative consciousness. Peggy too is "brilliant" (344), but she is decidedly not those women. The narrator of *A Room* picks up "*Life's Adventure*, or some such title, by Mary Carmichael," and learns specifically that Chloe and Olivia share a laboratory, "like each other," and "were engaged in mincing liver, which is, it seems, a cure for pernicious anaemia."[57] In contrast to this scene of cheerful industry, mediated through an institutional context, Peggy is solitary and deeply unhappy, and we see nothing of her professional life. She tends to be critical of, if not cynical about, her profession and the people around her. Where Woolf imagines Olivia leaving the laboratory after a day's work to return to her children and family—a woman who has it all—here Peggy evokes the religion of the Middle Ages alongside modern science and business not to rehearse a feminist narrative of progress from the stifling cloister to the fresh air of educated professionalism but to draw an equivalence between institutions old and new, setting both in opposition to authentic bodily experience, the "liv[ing]" and "feel[ing]" that comes with "bearing children."

The "let me rest" passage turns on its head the liberal feminist critique that Woolf herself had long advocated, which, as Berman and Froula have both argued, involved a complex negotiation between restrictive embodiment and creative transcendence.[58] And unlike many of the more progressive or idealistic sentiments expressed in the novel, Peggy's critique of institutional life is not directly called into question; rather, the intensity and apparent truth-value of her own embodied experiences seem to affirm it. The passages are of obvious, perhaps predictable, critical interest: Why does one of the only professional women in Woolf's fiction resent her profession? What does Peggy's complaint tell us about the place of the body in Woolf's feminism? How might her strangely erotic interactions with her father and brother be read against the backdrop of Woolf's own experiences of incest?[59] These issues are not without significance, and *The Years* has typically been read in these thematic, historical, or biographical terms when it is read at all. But to stop there is to miss what is most significant about Peggy's place in the novel. If character is understood as merely individual, she is one more unhappy woman, as bitter perhaps as Sara and without the questionable consolations of marriage and family available to other Pargiter women. She seems to bear the full force of Woolf's observation in *Three Guineas* that "it seems as if there were no progress in the human race, but only repetition" (80). But if character is understood as essentially social and institutional, it is clear that Peggy's dissatisfaction is qualitatively different from that of other figures in the novel; the repetition is repetition with a difference. The habits, practices, and distinctive qualities that constitute Peggy as a character are generated not by her exclusion from modern institutional life but by her *inclusion* in it; as a character she emerges from the tension between incorporation and individuation.[60] She is both "a doctor" and the "exception," the "peculiar person," but her critical detachment reflects on this formal mechanism in a way that other characters do not. This signal feature of the novel—the inclusion of women in modern institutions—is felt less in *The Years*'s thematic concerns than in its formal structures of characterization, which are only intermittently dramatized within the plot. To put it another way: if we think that Peggy's dissatisfaction points to the impossibility of historical progress, we miss that her critical perspective is a product not of her exclusion from institutional life but of her incorporation into it. She, not Sara, is the novel's real Outsider, by virtue of this qualitative difference; her feelings in this scene are less significant than the structural position she is able to occupy, which enables the perspective that gives rise to those feelings. Woolf's optimism about professions for women is not unqualified, but at least in 1937, when she completed *The Years*, it was still quite real.

Woolf suggests that Peggy's position in the novel is both cause and effect of a historical shift. As James Naremore points out, the year 1919, when the professions were opened to women by the Sex Disqualification (Removal) Act, is of crucial importance in *Three Guineas* but is excluded from *The Years*: it stands for "an unstated boundary between old and new."[61] This historical moment is not represented in the novel but is incorporated by the very fact of Peggy's being a professional woman. Peggy's moments of critical detachment issue from within an institutional formation, suggesting that she too is subject to the "split" within herself of which Woolf wrote in "A Sketch," the "split" that grows from "perceptions, however slight and transient" that "gave [Woolf's] attitude . . . a queer twist" (154). Noting that "she was daily impressed by the ignorance of doctors" (312), Peggy begins to move beyond her professional cynicism and toward an explicit awareness of the limits of the medical institution of which she is a part. But explicit, constructive critique is not really the point here. Institutionally formed and bearing a critical sensibility (however slight and transient) that is not external to but predicated upon that institutional formation, Peggy instantiates the conditions of possibility for genuine institutional and social change.[62]

In *Mimesis*, Erich Auerbach argues that "the serious realism of modern times cannot represent man otherwise than as embedded in a total reality, political, social, and economic, which is concrete and constantly evolving."[63] *The Years* partakes of this realism by encoding modern institutions into character, creating imagined individuals who incorporate into the form of the novel social phenomena that *exceed* the individual, while remaining unnarratable except *through* the individual. Institutions "stamp" and "mould" characters who embody those institutions in a process of simultaneous individuation and incorporation, the generative tension between character and type. But the novel also extends this formal process to the supranational institutions of empire, making them positive presences in the narrative via their central role in the formation of character. Thus Woolf's realism presses against Fredric Jameson's well-known and much-disputed axiom that in an imperial world the formal and stylistic innovations of modernism compensate for literature's inability to grasp the totality of a system that is no longer national but global.[64] North Pargiter, who departs for the war after being mocked by Sara for his militarism, returns in "Present Day" as (significantly) an "outsider" (301, 306, 383) to what he sees as a world where people can only talk of "money and politics" (301). Like Abel in the beginning of the novel, North is "built" from traits acquired in the institutions of imperial governance and commerce; since leaving the army he has spent a number of years running an isolated farm in Africa. ("'And you, sir?' said the maid to North. . . . 'Captain Pargiter,' said North, touching his tie" [345].) Other characters refer to North repeatedly as a "farmer." Meeting his uncle Edward, now an Oxford don, he wryly observes, "Edward, the scholar, paid tribute to North, the soldier" (385); he thinks of his uncle as "stamped." But his twenty-five years on the periphery of empire have put him out of step with the metropolitan center. The novel dramatizes his vertiginous shift at the level of perception, in moments of almost Conradian "delayed decoding," ironically set in a central London that North thinks of as "the heart of darkness" (390): "But the cars behind him hooted persistently; they hooted and hooted. What at? he asked. Suddenly he realized that they were hooting at him. The light had changed; it was green now, he had been blocking the way. He started off with a violent jerk. He had not mastered the art of driving in London" (292). North is incapable of the "metropolitan perception" that Raymond Williams calls a precondition for the emergence of modernism. He finds himself falling back on his "stock phrase" (380), "money and politics," and the novel consistently relates this failure of perception back to "Africa," a word that, in relation to North, stands not just for the continent but for a whole complex of formative institutional experience.

But that experience, and the habits of thought and perception that it has bestowed on North, becomes the basis of an inchoate critical sensibility.[65] North insistently relates individual conduct to its institutional context. Listening to young men debate politics, he thinks, "That's Oxford, that's Harrow . . . recognising the tricks of speech that were taught at school and college." And he examines the normative basis for his own criticisms: "At their age, he thought, he had been in the trenches, he had seen men killed. But was that a good education? At their age, he thought, he had been alone on a farm sixty miles from the nearest white man, in control of a herd of sheep. But was that a good education?" (383). The passage ends with him thinking, of the Oxford and Harrow men, "If they want to reform the world . . . why not begin there, at the centre, with themselves?" (384). The sentiment could be taken as evasive, as displacing the issue of historical and institutional change onto personal behavior. But a more substantial reading would account for the fact that the novel's entire mode of characterization has worked up to this point to reveal the institutional and the individual as implicated in each other and would note that North, whatever his perspectival limits ("Damn the Jew!" he says to Sara; elsewhere he thinks, "Damn women . . . curse their little inquisitive minds" [375]), identifies this implication as the central issue. In a complex and image-laden passage, North effectively comments on the question of how the collective practices, habits, and rules of the institution could be constitutive of individual character:

> Not halls and reverberating megaphones; not marching in step after leaders, in herds, groups, societies caparisoned. No; to begin inwardly, and let the devil take the outer form. . . . Not black shirts, green shirts, red shirts—always posing in the public eye; that's all poppy-cock. Why not down barriers and simplify? But a world, he thought, that was all one jelly, one mass, would be a rice pudding world, a white counterpane world. To keep the emblems and tokens of North Pargiter . . . but at the same time spread out, make a new ripple in human consciousness, be the bubble and the stream, the stream and the bubble—myself and the world together—he raised his glass. Anonymously, he said, looking at the yellow liquid. But what do I mean, he wondered—I, to whom ceremonies are suspect, and religion's dead; who don't fit, as the man said, don't fit in anywhere? He paused. There was a glass in his hand; in his mind a sentence. And he wanted to make other sentences. But how can I, he thought . . . unless I know what's solid, what's true; in my life, in other people's lives? (389)

North's speculations speak to the central problem of the fully institutionalized social world to which Woolf addressed *The Years*, but they also speak to the means by which that problem is addressed in the form of the novel. What starts out as a paean to individualism is qualified and finally questioned as North works it through; rather than proposing an answer, the passage ends up presenting his awareness of dwelling within an irresolvable tension. The uninterrupted functioning of a complex of institutions, for North as for Peggy, ends up producing a mis-fit that is in part historically determined (by the conditions of late empire, embodied in the figure of the returned colonial administrator) and partly contingent; while less than ideal, it comes to look like the necessary if not sufficient grounds for the development of a new relationship between the individual and their institutional contexts. The "story" of *The Years*, it could be said, lies not in its haphazard accumulation of events across fifty-odd years but rather in the tale it tells of character itself. Peggy's and North's reflections on the circumstances of their lives in the "present day" of *The Years* might also be seen as reflections on the relationship between the concepts of character and institution.

The Years also stands alone among Woolf's late oeuvre in its embrace of institutional character. Of *The Waves*, her most avowedly "poetic" novel, she wrote in her diary that she had attempted to create "no characters," and in that novel the effects of the world's "invisible presences" on individual lives are evoked primarily in psychological rather than social terms. In the autobiographical fragments of "A Sketch," the previously dynamic relationship between individual and institution will come to seem static and deadening as the type comes to simply stand for the institution. Woolf began to view the institutional realm as essentially oppressive and would turn in *Between the Acts* to questions of culture, the nation, and more mystical forms of interpersonal connection and collective being. But of *The Years* she wrote, "Its different from the others of course: has I think more 'real' life in it; more blood & bone."[66] That "real life" was one in which the shared rules, practices, routines, and habits of institutions, in a world where "life" outside those institutions had become unimaginable, might foster and lend meaning to individual lives rather than suppressing them.

3

Institutional Picaresque

MULK RAJ ANAND FROM BLOOMSBURY TO BOMBAY

THE FIRST HALF of this book has theorized the ways in which two canonical representatives of modernist writing—Joseph Conrad and Virginia Woolf—narrate the relationships between individuals and institutions. At the heart of this theorization is institutional character, a formal device and a means by which these writers address ethical and political concerns. In Conrad's *The Inheritors*, *Nostromo*, and *Under Western Eyes*, anxiety about the effects of global finance, transit infrastructure, and telecommunications on individuals' capacity for heroic action is played out in the tension between form and content, between Conrad's reliance on institutions as the stuff out of which novelistic character is created and the negative assessments of these same institutions' dominance of the social world at the level of story. (In *Nostromo*, for example, the horror of the chief engineer's extreme managerial competence is that it corresponds to his utter flatness as a character.) Woolf's relationship to institutions is less conflicted. In *The Years* she imagines women's incorporation into the press, medical professions, and government as a condition of possibility both for legible female character in the novel and for social change over time. Only in re-engendered institutions, Woolf suggests, do modern individuals *gain* the capacity for considered, self-reflexive action; in *The Years*, the female characterization that is anarchic and fragmentary (and not incidentally, typically "modernist") in the failed journalist Sara Pargiter coheres in the critical professionalism of her doctor niece, Peggy.

Although their works offer divergent evaluations of these phenomena, character in both Conrad's and Woolf's novels finds a home in institutions, and characters acquire the capacity to act through their formation in those institutions. Moreover, the institutional character of *Nostromo* and *The Years* is a response to their authors' explicitly political concerns in adjacent texts like Conrad's "Autocracy and War" and Woolf's *Three Guineas*. One way these novels do so is by serving as repositories of what Merve Emre terms "embodied and socially mediated schemes of action . . . actions like speech, gesture, perception, and interaction that could be . . . performed by real people in historically consequential circumstances," narrating the means by which actual people, from the turn of the century through the 1930s, could fashion their own subjectivity through their relationships to institutions.[1] My point is not that readers did or do rely on these novels for this purpose but rather that in their works, Conrad and Woolf present ways of thinking about institutions, and about the social uses of literary form, that later writers and critics have taken up.

As modernism gave way to the international literary world of the postwar era, writers drew on institutional character to claim authority and shape their own careers. The work of Mulk Raj Anand (1905–2004), whose writing and career were both shaped by the genre I will term *institutional picaresque*, illustrates the sorts of tactics writers employed to make their way in the institutions of literature. Readers may be most familiar with Anand's novels of the 1930s, particularly *Untouchable* (1935) and *Coolie* (1936), which have become significant entries in the canon of global modernism.[2] Critics have attended to these works' leftist politics and Indian nationalism and to Anand's own story as an émigré to Bloomsbury, his connections to T. S. Eliot, E. M. Forster, and the Woolfs, and his work with George Orwell at the BBC.[3] Yet Anand labored prodigiously for nearly sixty years after decolonization and Indian independence, mainly as part of the Indian state's cultural apparatus. Anand's work demands practices of reading that are attentive both to literary form and to literature's practical uses in the maintenance of an authorial career—to the opportunities, one might say, that literary writing presents to develop a brand. And his fiction frequently imagines, if only in fleeting moments, the conditions of accountability, support, and amelioration that might be found in modern institutions. In his essays and political writing, especially in the 1940s, Anand returns repeatedly to consider the conditions and practices that might, as he put it, "bring about the institutions which may produce a new order."[4] His fiction was not only a report on those conditions and practices or a formal symptom of its historical moment: literary form was a resource on which Anand drew to make his way in the institutions of culture, from Punjab to Bloomsbury to Bombay. Taken as a whole, his long career is also a version of Anglophone modernism's own; in it we can trace across the decades the combinations of aesthetic experiment, public culture, and political commitment that originated with global avant-gardes, were disseminated through colonial education systems and cultural institutions, and both inspired and threatened postcolonial literary ventures. Anand was, in Simon Gikandi's words, a writer "whose political or cultural projects were enabled by modernism even when the ideologies of the latter . . . were at odds with decolonization."[5] The institutional picaresque that I suggest is the characteristic genre of Anand's fiction, in which rebellious outsiders ultimately rely on or shore up the durable institutions on which their existence depends, was also a strategy of authorial self-presentation that allowed him to preserve his position in an international literary culture.

Institutional Picaros

In June 1936 Anand received a letter from John Lehmann, then former (and future) managing editor of the Hogarth Press. Anand had been in England for more than ten years, having arrived from India (and a stint in prison for political activism) not long before the General Strike of 1926, and was at this point not an unaccomplished author. He had spent several years finishing a doctorate in philosophy at the University of London and had published two novels, *Untouchable* (1935) and *Coolie* (1936), two books on painting, and a study of contemporary Indian poets, and with Sajjad Zahir he had founded and composed the manifesto for the Progressive Writers' Association. Lehmann had read Anand's novella *Lament on the Death of a Master of Arts* and hoped to solicit fiction for his nascent magazine *New Writing*. While *Lament* was "of particular interest," Lehmann noted, the novella was not "good enough to represent" Anand's talent. "As you must have realized," he wrote, "I am aiming at collecting writing that is *realistic* as far as possible. . . . I hope you either have, or will do for us, something to stand up to THE COOLIE [*sic*], for we badly need an Indian writer."[6] The letter's enthusiasm for Anand's work seems to be contradicted by prompts it offers to further writing. Lehmann comments that the work should be *"realistic,"* which in the context of thirties Bloomsbury would connote "politically engaged" and "left"; at the same time, it should "represent *you*," while also being representatively Indian ("we badly need an *Indian* writer"). These demands were of course typical of the pressures placed on nonwhite writers writing for a white British audience in the period. Lehmann's insistence on "realism" from an Indian writer is entirely in keeping with Pascale Casanova's argument that "the political dependence of emerging literary spaces is signaled by the recourse to a functionalist aesthetic and ... the most conservative narrative, novelistic, and poetical forms."[7] To make headway from this peripheral position, Anand would have to approach *New Writing* highly conscious not only of his subject matter but of how his literary output was intertwined with the creation of an authorial persona and of the kinds of capital that he possessed as the sort of writer Lehmann understood him to be.

The story Anand produced in response, "The Barber's Trade Union," appeared that fall in the second issue of *New Writing*; it exemplifies the themes and formal devices that Anand would modulate and employ in varied genres across his career to innovate both in the "realism" of his fiction and in his representation of himself ("*you*") as a literary actor. The unnamed narrator of "The Barber's Trade Union," a version of the youthful Anand himself, recalls his childhood as a "high-caste boy" in a small village and tells the story of his best friend, Chandu, the low-caste son of a barber, who adopts a succession of mischievous schemes to elevate his own position and embarrass the village elite.[8] First, Chandu acquires "a white turban, a white rubber coat (a little too big for him, but nevertheless very splendid), a pair of pumps in which I could see my face reflected in clear silhouette, and ... a leather bag" (9).[9] Abused "in the foulest way," first by the village landlord and then by the moneylender, for wearing clothes above his station, Chandu then resolves to mount a one-man strike, purchasing "a Japanese bicycle" (10, 12) and riding it every day to a nearby town, where he makes money cutting hair and shaving the townspeople, beyond the reach of the village hierarchy. At the story's conclusion, when the landlord and the moneylender, mocked and reviled by the village peasantry and their own wives for their slovenly, unshaven appearance, attempt to hire a barber from another village, they discover that Chandu

> had conceived a new notion, newer than those he had ever thought of before.... [H]e had applied his brain to the scheme of opening a shop ... in partnership with his cousin, the barber of Verka, and with Dhunoo and the other barbers within a range of seven miles from his village.... [B]y that gift of the gab which he had, besides his other qualities of the head and the heart, he convinced them all that it was time that the elders

of the village came to them to be shaved rather than that they should dance attendance upon their lords and masters. (16)

A brief and comic story, "The Barber's Trade Union," while embracing Lehmann's call to be "Indian," detours around the indictment of colonialism that left-wing British intellectuals might have expected from "realistic" writing (an expectation met more directly by Orwell's "Killing an Elephant," first published in the same issue of *New Writing*). The story's target is not British rule in India, which appears not at all, but caste and the structure of the "traditional" Indian village. Indeed, Chandu's rebellion against the "lords and masters" is *enabled* by the consumer goods brought to India by imperial trade: the "Angrezi" clothes in which he imitates English authority, "in a beautiful heroic dress like the Padre sahib of the Mission School," and the "Japanese bicycle" that enables his "freedom of movement" (16, 10, 8). The story thus distances its author/narrator from mainstream Indian nationalism and its Gandhian fetishization of the village.

In his low origin, rebelliousness, physical mobility, and determination to subvert the dictates of caste, Chandu—that "low-caste devil" and "rogue," as the village pandit decries him—is best understood as a kind of picaro, a literary type of the "scheming social outlier" with origins in the Spanish Golden Age (11). As Rob Nixon points out, the picaro takes on a critical valence in the hands of colonial and postcolonial writers: "The picaro embodies everything the socially remote privileged classes, with their ornate rhetoric and social etiquette, seek to contain, repress, and eject."[10] At the story's opening, the unnamed narrator asserts his own social superiority and Chandu's abjection in a frank declaration of Chandu's inability to relate, or even understand, the narrative of which he is the protagonist: "Among the makers of modern India, Chandu, the barber boy of our village, has a place which will be denied him unless I press for the recognition of his contribution to history. Chandu's peculiar claim to recognition rested, to tell the truth, on an exploit of which he did not know the full significance" (7). Yet as Chandu's partner in crime, the narrator shares his status as a "rogue" (both are referred to as such by the village elite), becoming a vicarious picaro himself. And third, Chandu's story culminates in the establishment of an institution, an event that the story registers both in plot and narrative form. The penultimate paragraph effaces the particularities of the union's constituent members (Chandu, his cousin, the barber of Verka, Dhunoo, the other barbers) and incorporates them into a collective whole, which itself becomes the story's protagonist in its one-sentence final paragraph: "'Rajkot District Barber Brothers' Hairdressing and Shaving Saloon' has been followed by many other active trade unions of working men in our parts" (16).

"The Barber's Trade Union" is an institutional picaresque: the protagonist's irrepressible, rebellious nature leads him as if by accident into political assertion, which eventually takes embodied form in an institution: a set of norms (the refusal to "dance attendance") and a material structure (the "saloon" itself). Situated below the geopolitics of imperialism and nationalism, but refusing the stifling identitarianism of the local, Chandu and the other barbers arrive at a form of collective agency that the story valorizes in its closing lines. This investment in the genre of the picaresque and an appreciation of the power of institutions evidently allowed "The Barber's Trade Union" to navigate the conflicting demands both of Lehmann's letter and of the literary culture of England in the thirties with some success. Anand would publish more with *New Writing* and maintained a working relationship with Lehmann for decades, well past the point where Anand's connections with other figures of the British cultural Left of the 1930s had faded.

An institutional picaresque may seem like a contradiction in terms. What could be more unlike each other than the picaro's rambunctiousness—and the basically negative and critical charge of the picaresque genre—and the continuity and adherence to norms demanded by the institution? Yet despite being each other's obverse, the picaro and the institution are central figures of Anand's oeuvre as well as of his biography. Like that of other colonial intellectuals in twenties and thirties London, his own life took on a picaresque cast, as he traveled widely and made money writing what and where he could, though he eventually worked steadily for the BBC and maintained relationships with publishers. After his permanent return to India in 1945, Anand's international status as a nonaligned Cold War intellectual was enabled by the cultural institutions of the postcolonial state, of which he became an enthusiastic functionary. In 1946 Anand founded the journal *Marg*, which shaped modern Indian art and architecture and played a significant role in bringing Le Corbusier into the design and construction of the modernist capital of Punjab, Chandigarh. Anand also edited a remarkable collectively authored *Story of the Indian Post Office* in 1954. By the 1960s he was serving in numerous academic capacities: as chair of the Lalit Kala Akademi, as Tagore Professor of Literature and Fine Art at the University of Punjab, and as a professor at the Indian Institute of Advanced Study; he was a frequent attendee of the Commonwealth and Afro-Asian Writers' Conferences and regularly drew on connections to the Nehru/Gandhi family. Yet throughout his career he would present himself in terms identical to those of Chandhu and the other youthful male protagonists of his early novels: *Untouchable*'s Bakha, *Coolie*'s Munoo, Lalu of the *Sword and the Sickle* trilogy. His self-presentation as a rogue and outsider would persist and serve as a touchstone for the rest of his life, regardless of professional circumstance: at the height of his prestige in the cultural apparatus of the Indian state, in 1970, he was at pains to insist in a letter to the critic Saros Cowasjee, "It is not my anxiety to win the Sahitya Academy Award.... If I don't get the prize, I will be the only one of the four elder statesmen of 'Pigeon-Indian' who will not have received the award, and that will give you a very good point to show that I don't care a damn for the Establishment."[11]

Loud protestations of indifference like this one aside, Anand received the award two years later for his novel *Morning Face*. Perpetually positioning himself as an outsider's insider, Anand regularly evokes Chad Harbach's image of the creative writer in the university: "He's always lobbing his flaming bags of prose over the ivied gate late at night. Then in the morning he puts on a tie and walks through the gate and goes to his office."[12] This was the posture Anand assumed in his relationships to national identity and to the institutions of international writing, whether in Bloomsbury or Bombay, even when his position within those identities and institutions was relatively secure, as a way of maintaining that security through constant rhetorical agitation. Indeed, it was in this relentless crankiness and chafing at the establishment that Anand was perhaps most classically modernist.

Conversations in India

If Anand presented himself in England as an Indian rogue, he would later take precisely the opposite tack, presenting himself in India as a cosmopolitan Anglophile. In a November 1970 letter to Cowasjee, who was writing a book on Anand and attempting to bring a number of his works back into print, Anand reveals that he "wrote 20 pages of reminiscences of [Bonamy] Dobree, [T. S.] Eliot, and others," which might aid in Cowasjee's research.[13] This was the genesis of *Conversations in Bloomsbury*, often cited as a key account of Anand's relationships in the prewar British literary world.[14] Like "The Barber's Trade Union," *Conversations* emerged from a particular situation of writing. As Rosemary Marangoly George argues in her *Indian English and the Fiction of National Literature,* by the early 1970s, after the death of Prime Minister Jawaharlal Nehru, whose patronage he had relied on, "Anand's affiliation with the central government became more tenuous. There was a need to bolster his importance for the new generation of leadership" (130). *Conversations,* published in London in 1981, sought to perform this reputation enhancement by reinserting a particular version of Anand into a sanctified moment in Anglophone literary culture. Its date of publication, intentionally or not, allowed the memoir to ride the wave of Bloomsbury nostalgia (and debunking) that emerged in Britain in the seventies and eighties, kicked off in part by Quentin Bell's 1972 biography of his aunt Virginia Woolf. The presence of Anand's name alongside those of the major Bloomsbury figures may have helped boost his stock in the Anglophone literary world of India as well.

Conversations is a curious work. Over twenty short, disconnected episodes, Anand purports to recount conversations with various literary and cultural figures of late-twenties Bloomsbury, ranging from now canonical figures like the Woolfs, E. M. Forster, and Nancy Cunard to lesser-known academics and cultural workers like Eric Gill, Herbert Read, and Arthur Waley. (He also meets Bill Bland and Harry Tomkins, two Cockneys brought in straight from central casting.) Critics have drawn on it for information on Anand's activities in 1930s London, though *Conversations*'s value as a historical document seems questionable, given the staginess and detail of its scenes and dialogue and the fifty-five-year span between the events it recounts and its publication.[15] But it is the fictional qualities of *Conversations* that most interest me here. For example, after a contentious scene involving D. H. Lawrence, Eliot, John Middleton Murry, and Aldous Huxley in the second episode, "Lions and Shadows in the Sherry Party in Harold Monro's Bookshop," Anand writes, "Aldous Huxley felt differently from others, and even differed from himself of the days of his Jesting Pilate, because he had doubts about our benign white sahibs. All the others seemed to believe, more or less, in the 'Empire on which the sun never sets.' I, who had been to jail in the Gandhi movement, was fuming inside. I had left home because my pro-white-sahib father had beaten my mother for my going to jail. And I had learnt to be a rebel" (29).

The move this passage makes with its famous subject, claiming knowledge of Huxley's developing mind-set through faux-casual name-dropping of his works, is made over and over in *Conversations*, and it rarely succeeds in giving the feeling of intimacy or insight for which Anand appears to be reaching. Similarly, though, Anand repeatedly casts himself as an outsider and a rebel, someone who qualifies as a scoundrel and troublemaker in stuffy Bloomsbury. In the early episodes this role is most often taken by Anand's poet friend Nikhil Sen, who, in an echo of the structure of "The Barber's Trade Union," is figured as the more assertive and bolder of the two, with Anand following his lead. By the later episodes, though, Anand himself has taken over the role of picaro, through repeated (and self-aware) reference to his origin in a "craft family" as a qualification to discuss high art and through his self-characterization as a "naïve, unfashionable craftsman's son," a "peasant," and an "irrepressible Indian . . . always putting his foot in it" (107, 63, 105, 120). This is not a bildung story; it is not that Anand himself develops inwardly but rather that the contexts for his speech and his ability to externalize his roguish perspective change over the book's twenty episodes. (As Matthew Garrett points out, the picaro is "not just a character, the picaro is a situation.")[16]

Thus *Conversations* is best understood not as a memoir that might explain Anand's (or anyone else's) literary activities in Bloomsbury. Instead, it constitutes a flawed, awkward, but carefully constructed sort of autofiction, in which Anand, at the time of its composition a respected but marginal cultural functionary in the postcolonial republic of letters, remobilizes the picaresque as a way of demonstrating his connections to the cultural capital of Bloomsbury and the value of his persistent outsider status. It also illustrates the institutionalization of modernism as a source of cultural value in ways that require attention to how genres cross-pollinate and how literature and life are not as distinct as more temporally and spatially delimited accounts of modernism might suggest. His own *writing* was destined never to ascend into what Casanova famously terms "the world republic of letters," despite the forays Anand made against the constraints of national realism. Instead, Anand himself would draw vicariously on the canonicity and international brand of "Bloomsbury" to secure his career as a cultural worker inside and outside India.

Picaresque Postmortem

Anand leveraged his institutionalized anti-institutionalism for the last time in a satirical "Self-Obituary," written in 1999 and published after his death. By now a very senior figure of the postindependence Indian cultural scene, Anand offers autobiography in exaggerated, humorous, but perhaps by-now familiar terms:

> Someone christened him Muck Rake Anand. And that remains the best epitaph on him. . . . He was an incurable unregenerate leftist who, we believe, consistently wrote, spoke and worked for the despicable creed of socialism which has now been defeated on all fronts on this earth. . . . Knowing that he would be found out to be the empty windbag he was if he wrote in one of our own great languages, he began to bluff all innocent people abroad by writing in English and managed to pass off as a representative Indian writer. No fraud can outmatch that perpetuated by this charlatan. . . . The wretch always denied the charge that he had sold Indian local colour to the western world to great advantage to himself. . . . [H]e was frequently seen in the company of long-haired poets, writers, artists, actors and other such scum of the earth. The political sympathies of Anand were clear enough, but the clever plausible rogue that he was, he tried to disguise all his most sinister impulses and ideas behind the vague terms of what he called humanism. . . . He presumed once to write and produce plays. . . . Certain well-known figures of our dance world came under his influence. . . . He corrupted our art world by editing an Americanised magazine of art. His insistence on form in our sculpture and painting, diverted the emphasis from the deep religiosity of our artistic heritage to lewd surrealist abstractionism. This is an example of how one dirty fish can spoil the whole tank, so to speak.[17]

As Geeta Kapur puts it, "[Anand] narrativizes his 'origins' as an artist-intellectual from the vantage point of a runaway youth."[18] Once again, Anand tells the story of a "plausible clever rogue," a "charlatan" associated with the "scum of the earth," whose fraudulence leads him to a position of institutional authority, producing plays and dances and editing an "Americanised magazine." Anand analogizes the radical artist who gains access to cultural organizations to the "one dirty fish [that] can spoil the whole tank," a pungent but fitting metaphor for how institutions translate ostensibly individual action into collective effects, even if the results are smelly. But "Self-Obituary" is a political critique as much as it is a reassertion of Anand's picaresque authorial persona. The voice that attacks Anand in defense of "our great spiritual heritage" is that of the resurgent Hindu Right, which had only just begun its successful assault on Indian politics with the election of the National Democratic Alliance, headed by the Bharatiya Janata Party (BJP), in 1998 (xvi). Anand's career had involved him closely with the Indian National Congress, and its historic defeat by the BJP marked a watershed moment in Indian politics. In "Self-Obituary," Anand returns to picaresque tropes, trading on the reputation he developed by embodying those tropes in the service of the postcolonial state to satirize the ascendant political Right, fifty years after independence and sixty years after Chandu graced the pages of *New Writing*.

Anand's career was made possible by his affiliations with the Hogarth Press, the BBC, *Marg*, the universities where he taught, and the Indian state's cultural arm. His ability to successfully move among these institutions relied on and fed back into his writing, and he consistently deployed what I refer to as the institutional picaresque to make these moves. In "The Barber's Trade Union" Anand writes his way into the pages of leftwing British literary culture; with *Conversations in Bloomsbury* he seeks to reestablish his position as a literary and cultural authority in postcolonial India; and in "Self-Obituary" he mounts an intervention into Indian politics's neoliberal nineties on the basis of the reputation he had long worked to establish. Picaresque ultimately served Anand as a form of what Merve Emre terms *literary branding*, in which the postures and characterizations that readers like Lehmann expected from his fiction migrated into real-life strategies of self-promotion and institutional positioning.[19] Anand's output was prodigious and uneven, and critics have said relatively little about the work, both literary and administrative, that occupied him from the postwar period into the early years of the twenty-first century. Tracing his consistent but flexible use of a limited set of literary tropes in both his fiction and his authorial self-fashioning is an important way to account for Anand and writers like him, whose careers stretched from the high modernist moment in the imperial metropolis to the postwar era and beyond. Moreover, Anand's case demonstrates how theorizations of governmental and literary institutions that see institutions as external to or as the conditions of possibility for the production of modernist writing only tell half the story. Theories of institutions are in fact immanent to modernist writing, and Anand's work is exemplary in this regard. Seeing the affordances and limits of modernist thinking about institutions reveals the mutually shaping forces of literature and the institutions of literary production. And it provides insight as we follow the aesthetic energies of the modern from the age of empire (or the moment of high modernism) to decolonization (or the world of postwar international literature).

Coolie, the Critique of Culture, and the Promise of Continuity

Anand's self-presentation as picaro was one way he drew on fiction to secure his own standing as an individual within institutions of culture at midcentury. But as the final lines of "The Barber's Trade Union" suggest, his writing is also highly attentive to the ways that institutions are themselves actors—as Timothy Mitchell puts it, an institution is "both a domain and an abstract agent."[20] This double-sidedness of institutions—"both a domain and an abstract agent"—is key to what John Marx identifies as the Anglophone novel's capacity to "forecast a world after European imperialism by identifying problems with Empire's administrative strategies and by laying the conceptual foundation necessary to generate new schemes."[21] While the works discussed in the previous section speak to how Anand reworked his own career by writing in the picaresque, his novel *Coolie*, published in 1936, addresses public questions of governance and India's imperial inheritance. The extent to which *Coolie*, as institutional picaresque, is concerned with the institutions of British India and their future has remained somewhat obscured by readings that understand the novel primarily as a bildungsroman, as nationalist, or as working-class writing.

First published in England and banned in India until independence, *Coolie* was Anand's second novel. While his first, *Untouchable*, follows the events of a single day in the life of its introspective titular hero, *Coolie*'s plot expands both temporally and spatially, covering many months and thousands of miles in the life of its adolescent picaro, Munoo. Munoo, an orphan, is taken from his village in northern India by his uncle, a minor official at the Imperial Bank of India, to work as a servant in the home of a bank higher-up in the town of Sham Nagar. Beaten until he runs away, he flees by train to the small city of Daulatpur, where he finds work in a "pickle-making and essence-brewing factory" until its kindhearted owner, Prabha, is swindled by his business partner and forced to shut down.[22] Next, Munoo finds work doing odd jobs and hauling bags of grain, helping to support Prabha and his wife until they leave town. Taking to the rails again with a traveling circus, Munoo arrives in Bombay, finding work at a textile mill and befriending a worker, Hari, and his family. The novel's most complicated plot developments take place here: Munoo looks on as the leaders of a militant union outmaneuver their accommodationist rivals and call a strike that quickly runs aground on religious discord. In one of the more contingent plot turns in the novel, Munoo is struck by a car while fleeing the resulting riots. In the car is an emancipated Anglo-Indian woman, Mrs. Mainwaring, who takes him with her to the British hill station Simla, where he becomes her servant and rickshaw puller, contracts tuberculosis, and dies in the novel's last line.

Rejecting tradition and the domestic as stays against the depredations of imperial capitalism, *Coolie* turns to modern institutions for limited and circumscribed forms of accountability and fairness. The text is highly attentive to the tension between what George Lukács calls the novel's "biographical form" and the extended timescape of institutions, particularly in what Anand calls the "laws of political economy," mills, banks, unions, and public health services; and it exemplifies the global reach of a modernism that sought to give positive representation to the structures and effects of global empire. Yet like the other texts I have discussed, it also draws on Anand's own sense of himself as a literary producer and on his own background. As he writes in *Apology for Heroism*, first published in 1946 and revised multiple times over the next two decades, "Hinduism has been breaking up even in its caste aspect, through the coming of modern industry and the social and political ideas and institutions associated with it. So I grew up in a hotch-potch world of which I early began to perceive the inconsistencies" (29). In his mother's "pantheism," "vague and untrustworthy" (30), and her unquestioning adherence to ritual, he felt that he had seen the stifling effects of traditional practices, which he largely rejected as a resource for meaningful resistance to British rule. In his father's negation of those traditions, "through efficient service" (34) to the military, he perceived a secular alternative mode of social organization—the modern institutions of the empire—whose potential for systemic harm would nonetheless become to him increasingly clear and which, for those incorporated into it, offered but one "ideal" as "a gift from the benign Sarkar—to pass all examinations and to secure a good subordinate job in the pay of the government" (36). The broad opposition that his parents' lives figured for Anand, between tradition and modern bureaucracy, is reflected in the complexity of *Coolie*'s social world, and the novel's wide-ranging picaresque captures the whole of that world, "the muddle created by the impact of Europe" (36).

Coolie's plot links this relentless indictment of Indian society under British rule to the brief, difficult life of its central character, whose travels provide the narrative with occasions to observe the social spectrum of late colonial India and whose sufferings lend the novel its moral thrust. But *Coolie* leavens its critique with a pervasive sociological interest in everyday Indian life. At times this interest takes the form of didactic narration—"The usual length of the Simla rickshaw is nine feet, including the shaft, and the breadth is four feet. The weight is normally 260 to 360 lb" (262)—issuing from what Leela Gandhi somewhat less than enthusiastically calls Anand's "unflagging love of detail."[23] But this love of detail is equally embodied in the novel's drive to transpose the rhythms and vocabulary of the subcontinent's many regional languages into English prose, especially in bouts of elaborate cursing. Having gotten carried away playing with his employer's daughter in the house where he serves, Munoo is subjected to a tirade from Bibiji, the girl's mother:

> "I was only playing, Bibiji," said Munoo, anticipating a storm and seeking in vain to avert it.
> "Vay, you eater of your masters! May you die! May the vessel of your life never float in the sea of existence!" the tornado of abuse burst. "May you never rest in peace, neither you, nor your antecedents! That you should attack the honor of my child! Only a little child, too! You lustful young bull from the hills! . . . No respect! You spoiler of my salt! . . . How did we know we were taking on a snake in our house, who would turn treacherous after we had fed him with milk!" (57)

In *Coolie*, these transpositions are frequently deployed as comic relief, but this technique is also a product of Anand's desire to present the languages of a colonized society for an Anglophone metropolitan audience. *Coolie* suggests the political awkwardness of this practice—or perhaps tries to blunt that awkwardness—by staging moments of Munoo's own incomprehension of other regional languages within the diegesis, as when he arrives in Bombay and gazes at "the hieroglyphics of a language curious to him" (151), perhaps Marathi.[24] The novel demonstrates Anand's self-awareness in his deployment of what he would later call "Pigeon-Indian."

The youthful protagonist and a close attention to language as a site of authority and experiment have been the focus of compelling accounts of Anand's early career. Particularly relevant is that of Jessica Berman, who reads *Coolie* and James Joyce's *A Portrait of the Artist as a Young Man* together, arguing that both novels "embrace and rework the expectations of the bildungsroman . . . to challenge the genre's expectations for character and self-development and to shift the liberal, political model of the universal representative man that lies at its core."[25] Caught as they are in colonial settings that "interrupt not only the hero's development but also the temporal-spatial model of the nation that corresponds to it" (121), the protagonists of these works "can neither be absorbed in nor escape the social realm and so cannot accomplish the traditional project of *Bildung*" (122). Drawing on Hannah Arendt's concept of "enlarged thinking," Berman argues that Stephen Daedalus and Munoo, in part because of their inability to master through language their own subjectivity and the worlds they inhabit, become something more interesting than the homogenizing, traditional version of representative man: "a new version of the representative man as one who inhabits a number of subject positions and discourses at once without subsuming them into a common identity or language or becoming blind to their differences" (129). Part of this "alternative logic," Berman suggests, is a politicized attention to the play of language—"a power . . . that can exceed the bounds of authority" (133).

With regard to the latter, it is significant that *Coolie* specifically excludes the representation of untouchable—Dalit—experience.[26] As Sonali Pereira points out in a bravura reading of *Coolie*, "If in Anand's first published novel, *Untouchable*, he inscribes the topos of child labor within the narrative of caste, in this, his second novel, he makes a pronounced statement against liberal critics when he renegotiates the story in terms of global capitalism and theories of class—not caste."[27] Shouted at by a rude shopkeeper, Munoo thinks to himself, "I let him put me in my place as a coolie, but I was paying for the soda water and I am not an untouchable. I am a Hindu Kshatriya, a Rajput, a warrior" (157).[28] The irony here, of course, is that it is Munoo's "place as a coolie," a worker, that counts; caste, regional origin, religion, and the domestic are all proposed in the novel as sites of solidarity, but none meaningfully persist and most are unmasked as hollow or corrupt.

Untouchable is quite specific regarding the regional languages drawn into what Ben Conisbee Baer calls its linguistic "transvestism"—Punjabi, Hindi, Urdu. But while *Coolie*'s movement across the social whole of India brings onstage characters who speak a wider range of regional languages, their difference is less marked in the text and the apparatus pared down; the dialogue and interior states of all the novel's non-English characters are rendered in a roughly consistent style throughout.[29] Language in *Coolie* is decoupled from the political problematic of representing subaltern experience, and its markers in the text are smoothed over; it recedes as a primary concern. While Berman's suggestion that the collective speech of the Bombay workers who applaud the calling of a strike indicates "the political importance of a linguistic remainder . . . as the workers begin to take on force through their appropriation of a mode of meaning-making not within the purview of conventional systems of discursive power" is plausible as far as it goes, the logic of the remainder cuts both ways.[30] The workers' solidarity is destroyed a paragraph later by the very means that help constitute it, as agents of the factory bosses spread a rumor through the crowd that Muslims are kidnapping Hindu children. Anonymous and immune to both verification and debunking, rumor could be said to reside outside "the purview of conventional systems of discursive power," but here it serves the interests of power quite effectively. Anand's point is that the coolies' problem is not primarily linguistic, but institutional: they lack access to durable means of collective organization that would enable them to overcome the group prejudices that he presents as inhering in caste, class, ethnicity, or religion. Ultimately, the homogenized presentation of linguistic difference in *Coolie* helps to enable the novel's representation of life in the institutions of British rule, which frequently seek to efface difference in the service of institutional function (and as the novel will ultimately suggest, this isn't necessarily a bad thing). While *Untouchable*'s Bakha can only feel "a burning desire . . . to speak the *tish-mish, tish-mish* which the Tommies spoke," *Coolie*'s minor bank official Babu Nathoo Ram is pleased "to talk English to a Sahib, on an equal footing."[31]

Neither is *Coolie* quite assimilable to the tradition of the bildungsroman, even in that genre's critical or antidevelopmental modernist modes.[32] Certainly, Munoo's primary positive characteristic is what *Coolie*'s narrator calls "his old insouciance, his vigour, his zest for life, his fire—the fire that tingled in the cells of his body at all the sights and sounds about him" (49); and as Jerome Hamilton Buckley demonstrates, this fundamental energy and receptivity to the world are among the most recognizable characteristics of the classic youthful protagonist, who is as a rule "a child of some sensibility."[33] The problem with *Coolie* in regard to this tradition (even in its modernist incarnations) is that the novel does not so much critically invert or reconfigure the other standard tropes of the bildung plot as it flattens them out, laying bare their relative *inconsequentiality* in the novel's colonial situation. Orphaned Munoo's family life with his aunt and uncle in his provincial town is stifling, yes; but this does not seem to bother Munoo that much (and in any event, the crisscrossing forms of victimization—economic, caste-based, domestic—that appear in the village are only going to be writ large in the wider world). His schooling awakens certain potentialities, but it does not produce in him a burning desire to depart for the city; instead, "he had meant to go to town when he had passed all his examinations here and was ready to learn to make machines himself" (3). His initiations into sexual life are neither "debasing" nor "exalting" (Buckley, 17) but rather muddled and contradictory. And as Douglas Mao observes of the young Stephen Daedalus, it is difficult to tell whether Munoo's receptivity to the world is "unusual or typical," whether it issues from something special about Munoo or is simply a trait of youth in general (the novel's title, with its pull toward typicality, suggests the latter).[34]

But—and this is a key distinction—*Portrait*'s critical edge is to be found in how it directs the reader's attention, through very close free indirect narration, to Stephen's dawning awareness of the inadequacy of British-controlled Dublin to his development as an individual and artist. Anand's narrator, by contrast, disengages from Munoo for extended periods, differentiating his position quite clearly from the position of Joyce's; and these perspectival forays become progressively longer, such that by the fourth of the novel's five sections, in which Munoo takes a job at a Bombay mill, we are sifting among the perspectives of Munoo, his friend Lakshami, the mill's foreman, Jimmie Thomas, the mill's manager, Mr. Little, and the mill's chief investor. The novel's last section then devotes about a quarter of its pages to the perspectives of Munoo's Anglo-Indian boss, Mrs. Mainwaring, and her Indian admirer, Dr. Marchant. The narrator's attention to the protagonist is thus inversely correlated with the progress of the novel's plot, and the narrator's distance from Munoo produces opportunities for him to elaborate on the ways in which Munoo is, unfortunately, not going to learn about the forces that affect him: "He did not search for causes and effects. He did not know . . . that good health was nourished by the food which money bought" (36); "he knew nothing about directors and shareholders and threatening crises" (226). Munoo's limitations are, in a sense, prior to those of Stephen Daedalus; he is not provided with the opportunity to come to awareness of the circumstances that hold him down. And while *Portrait* concludes with Stephen prepared to fly away from Dublin, Munoo, while far more geographically mobile, ends his journey almost exactly where he started. Munoo is an energetic cipher; although his biography is the spine of *Coolie*'s narrative, his active but internally static subjectivity is not the novel's primary representational concern.

INDEED, MUNOO is better understood as continuous with Anand's broader cast of youthful rogues, including Chandu of "The Barber's Trade Union," Gangu of *Two Leaves and a Bud* (1937), Lalu of *The Village* (1939), *Across the Black Waters* (1939), and *The Sword and the Sickle* (1942), and of course Anand himself: as a picaro. J. A. Garrido Ardila offers a three-part definition of the picaresque genre: "(1) the narration of a life expounding the circumstances leading to a final situation; (2) the implicit satire of the novel that reflects the social bias of the author; (3) the picaro as protagonist."[35] This is a notably minimal definition, which I find attractive and fitting for Anand's work because of what it leaves out: the notion of individual development. Munoo moves through a series of "situations," but as I've suggested, the effects of those situations are more or less untethered from the cultivation of Munoo's internal subjectivity or the external arc of his biography (leading to his death). Claudio Guillén further delineates the situations of the picaresque as a "tangle," "an economic and social predicament of the most immediate and pressing nature (not a confrontation with absolute forces), an entanglement with the relative and the contemporaneous; and it leads to further situations or 'adventures.'"[36] The concreteness and everydayness of the picaro's entanglement is key, and the comparison with Stephen Daedalus, who hopes to forge in his soul the conscience of his race, is again instructive: Munoo just wants something to eat. He becomes entangled in a series of institutions as he makes his way up and down the subcontinent.

Coolie's demotion of bildung and linguistic experiment and its turn instead to institutional picaresque are in service of a wide-ranging exploration of the institutions of the late British Empire in India. This exploration involves minor characters, characters who embody institutions as collections of the shared traits, repeated actions, and norms of institutional life. *Coolie* aims to grasp the institutions of its world—the economic laws, cotton mills, banks, unions, and so on—as autonomous collective structures within a globe-spanning system, the better to delineate both their effects on individuals and the forms of amelioration and possibility that can be glimpsed, however fleetingly, within and between them. As Gail Day argues, in the Lukácsian tradition of realism theory the concept of totality "is surprisingly modest in what it performs; it simply demands that we consider the interrelations and interactions between different phenomena, that we relate the parts to the whole—and that we conceive these parts—the whole and all their relations—as mutable, as both materially constraining and subject to human actions."[37] These phenomena of constraint and enablement are, in *Coolie*, the institutions of empire; and the first conditions of *Coolie*'s institutional representation are the characterological insignificance of Munoo and the relative independence of the narrator, who, in the moments when he pulls away from Munoo to impress upon the reader the things that Munoo cannot know, goes on to explore the lives of the secondary characters Munoo encounters.

These effects are strikingly illustrated in a passage that exemplifies how the novel narrates collectivity. Having lost his pickle-factory job in the small provincial city of Daulatpur, Munoo seeks works as a day laborer. He and a group of other workers are told by "a merchant" to "come and lift the sacks in the godown and load Rahmat's bullock cart which is going to the railway station":

> FROM GOKAL CHAND, MOHAN LALL
> to
> RALLI BROTHERS, EXPORTERS, KARACHI
>
> Munoo read the blue Hindustani inscription on the sacks of grain. But he was too young to know the laws of political economy, especially as they govern the export of wheat from India to England. He only rolled the Ralli in his mouth with a taste for its melody and strangeness, as he had often rolled the words of his science primer in the old village days.
>
> All the coolies . . . had sat down to adjust their shoulders to the sacks which lay on the platform. And they arose, some shaking, some straining, some with ease, and began to walk away, bowed under the weight.
>
> Munoo had waited to see how to apply himself to the job. Having seen the others, he imitated their movements from the spitting on the hands to get a grip, to the heaving. (121–22)

The passage opens with the narrator closely aligned with Munoo's viewpoint; indeed, the "inscription" Munoo reads is set apart typographically, as though the reader were seeing it through Munoo's eyes. Yet Anand's narrator goes out of his way to remind us that Munoo is *unaware* of the broader consequences of the inscription; and tragically, as the novel goes on to show, he is never going to be old enough to learn.[38]

Instead, the narrator pushes off from Munoo to embark on a series of rapid expansions of scale, moving from the merchant whose warehouse has packed the grain, to the "bullock cart" and "railway" that will take it to the "exporter" in Karachi, and ultimately to the "laws of political economy" themselves. Though financial "laws" sound immutable and abstract, those that "govern the export of wheat from India to England" are, as the economic historian Paul Johnson establishes in his *Making the Market*, as much an active creation of Victorian policy as any of the more visible forms of imperial control, such as police forces and the military.[39] Here those laws are the context for the interplay among the corporation that exports the grain, the warehouses, carts, and state-constructed railway that store and transport it, and the individuals who interact with it, and they are finally embodied in the movements of "all the coolies," who undertake the physical labor of transferring the grain. The "spitting on the hands" and "heaving" that this labor requires are performed by the workers in slightly different ways—"some shaking, some straining, some with ease"—and by virtue of these variations the coolies are rendered as discrete individuals; prior to the issuance of the order, they are figured only as "a tide of seething humanity jostling in an ebb and flow of colorful cross purposes" (120), "wave after wave of men" (121). At the same time, this process is not purely individuating: the coolies go from a tide of humanity to a finite number of nonetheless basically interchangeable individuals—interchangeable not only with one another but presumably with any other coolies. The passage demonstrates how, from the railway to the export corporation to the laws of political economy, the institutions that imperial capitalism comprises demand particular actions of individuals, who, becoming characters through these actions, foreground those institutions in the narrative. This anticipates ideas that Anand would develop more directly in nonfictional forms during World War II; in *Apology for Heroism*, he would argue that under the conditions of late empire, "we find those continual alterations in the balance of power which leave wrecks of people behind as the fade-outs of history, shadows in the background of changing world forces" (102). The unusual reversal here—it is not "world forces" that move in the background, as one might expect, but individuals themselves, who recede as those "forces" take precedence—is given characterological expression in the coolies who are simultaneously evoked by, and "fade-out" into, the institutions of the imperial economy.

A further twist on this method appears when Munoo arrives at the Sir George White Mill in Bombay. He is confronted by a foreman, Jimmie Thomas, and objects to having to pay a commission for a job, to which another worker replies, "It is the same everywhere . . . the foreman . . . is the most important man in the factory." Munoo thinks, "Indeed . . . the Sahib must be an important man, but his clothes were greasy." Immersed here in Munoo's thoughts, the narrator pulls sharply away in the next sentence:

> [Munoo] did not know that the Sahib in greasy clothes was the virtual master of the factory, from the number of functions entrusted to him. He did not know that he was the employer's agent to engage workmen, the god on whose bounty the workmen depended for the security of their jobs once they had got them; that he was the man in charge, responsible for the supervision of the labourers while at work; that he was the chief mechanic who, with other mechanics, helped keep the machines in running order; that he was the technical teacher of the workers; that he was the intermediary between the employer and the worker (it was through him that the employer signified any change he wished to communicate to the workers); that because of all this he charged every worker in the factory a price for the gift of a job, a price which went up if there were more men about than there were vacancies to fill; and that, incidentally, he ran a moneylender's business; that lastly he was a landlord who owned hundreds of straw huts in the neighbourhood and rented them out to the coolies at a profit. (175)

The passage opens with a typical narratorial assertion of Munoo's inability to understand what we readers are about to be told, and given Anand's "love of detail" it is tempting to overlook the passage as merely a didactic aside that disrupts the flow of the narrative. But even as they offer sociological detail, passages like this one play an important role in *Coolie*'s construction of institutional character.

Two pages prior, Jimmie Thomas is given a name and a blustering physical presence. Here, though, the name is effaced, distancing the description from the individual in order to describe the practices and institutionally dictated behaviors that constitute the position of "the foreman"—which is "the same everywhere." The foreman is a particular species of type. There are potentially many foremen, although not an infinite number, all of whom share—are foremen by virtue of—the practices described here. Some of these practices are officially sanctioned by the cotton mill (engaging, training, and supervising workers, fixing machines, setting regulations), and others become associated with it by virtue of the destructive incentives it creates (commissions, loan-sharking, slum-lording), but these typical actions are not, in any case, drawn simply from the social world at large (as would be the case for classic types like the miser or the clown). They are characteristic of an institution: the mill.

This arrangement of demands and opportunities allied to a material structure figures the institution itself. The institution becomes the stuff of character, and the character Jimmie Thomas, as an assemblage of practices shared by many other foremen, comes to embody the institution in narrative. He is an employee of the mill, but in the sense that all the features of the character are generated from a sort of template of shared practices that make up the institution itself, he *is* the mill. As Aaron Kunin puts it, "When Graziano [in *The Merchant of Venice*] speaks as the fool, he becomes a spokesperson; he speaks for all fools."[40] But Jimmie Thomas, I want to suggest, doesn't speak for all foremen as much as he speaks for the factory. Furthermore, the passage in which Jimmie's characteristic traits are established embeds types within types, producing a template of actual and potential traits tied to institutional roles. In an effervescence of titles Jimmie becomes "foreman," "Sahib," "agent," "god," "man in charge," "mechanic," "teacher," "intermediary," "moneylender," and finally "landlord."[41] His potential is exhausted by these roles; or it might be more accurate to say that Jimmie as an individual capable of particular acts is simply a product of these roles. Nothing he will do in the course of the novel will exceed the frameworks for action presented in this passage, and the narrator's sustained attention to his actions rather than to his thoughts suggests the irrelevance of his internal life to his institutional roles. Jimmie Thomas becomes a vector of the mill's ability to structure the social world in myriad ways—both official and unofficial, formal and informal—producing individuals who embody it as characters.[42]

Jimmie Thomas is an especially striking instance of the institutional minor character in *Coolie*, but while the group of institutional traits that coalesce around him produce the whole of his character, the reverse is not the case. That is, the novel returns repeatedly to the seeming inexhaustibility of the mill's productive capacity. In thematic terms, the mill perpetuates itself by turning cotton into textiles; in formal terms, and like the novel's other institutions, it represents itself by turning sets of actions and incentives into individuals. The novel tracks Munoo's first day on the job, with his and his friends' morning routine punctuated by the sound of three whistles: "The third and final whistle greeted them a few yards from the factory, as they walked with the swarm of other coolies.... Occasionally one of the many coolies muttered a hoarse curse as he splashed the dirty water of a puddle over his bare legs, or lost his hold on the earth; or 'Ram Ram,' said a pious old coolie greeting another; or a young coolie peevishly nudged a comrade who was not agile. For the progress of this swarm was slow, very slow" (183). Linking this description to the earlier "laws of political economy" passage, where they appear as a "tide" or "wave," the workers are first figured here not as persons but as a "swarm." Indistinct actions appear, untethered to particular individuals: muttering *or* losing hold on the earth, greeting *or* nudging, performed by "one of many" or by an "old coolie" or a "young coolie." The group's presence and actions, though, are evoked by the factory whistle, and they grow increasingly differentiated as they approach "the door of the shed which led into the factory." Munoo "follow[s] Hari," then notes that "the other workers did not seem to notice the cramped spaces of the factory, except Hari's wife and her children. All the other coolies filed past as if they lived and ate and slept and *had their being there*" (183, italics mine). The "as if" is almost facetious here, since the coolies are indeed dependent on the closed economy of the mill for their food and housing, so the final sentence makes exaggeratedly literal how the coolies' emergence on the page is produced by an institutional logic: the mill is where they "have their being." In a real sense that is captured in the novel by this process of individuation and characterization, the workers, like Jimmie Thomas, become perceptible—come into being—as a function of the institutional structure.

Envisioned this way, as a source of being itself, the mill becomes horrifying for reasons that exceed the practical facts of the atrocious conditions inside. But while *Coolie* anatomizes the institutions of British control as a means of laying bare their vast capacity for exploitation and immiseration, it also registers in fleeting moments the potential for accountability and fairness that inheres in the concept of the modern institution. Jimmie Thomas threatens Munoo with violence for vacating an uninhabitable hut without receiving prior approval, but another worker steps in saying, "Leave them, Sahib" (200):

> "You are insulting a superior," said the foreman. "Are you in your senses?"
> "Sahib or no Sahib," Ratan returned, "you may be a foreman, but you have no right to beat the mill employees!"
> "I will charge the full rent for the month," said the foreman, relenting. (201)

Anonymizing the position's occupant, this exchange foregrounds Ratan's appeal to Jimmie Thomas's position as foreman, not to his sympathy as a moral individual, to stop the beating. Jimmie Thomas's interior life and biography ("sometime mechanic in a Lancashire mill" [172]), for example, are irrelevant to this exchange, because what counts is the broadly accessible protocols of the mill (accessible enough that the coolies are aware of them) and the position of foreman. While the role of foreman in the institutional structure of the mill enables certain forms of action (training workers, engaging in graft), it constrains others (beating the employees), and on this basis, at least in this episode, the "huge," "greasy" foreman relents. But of course there is a trap built in: Jimmie Thomas relents by shifting from a course of action not sanctioned by the institution—beating the employees—to one that is—gouging them on rent. Indeed, his relenting only makes the overall extractive function of the mill more effective since, as the novel dramatizes elsewhere, the coolies' employment amounts to indentured servitude by means of debt: pay is cut for production errors, loans are advanced at usurious rates, access to food and clothing is restricted to the company's own price-gouging stores, and the rent is more than they can afford. A fleeting moment of amelioration that *Coolie* accesses through its attention to institutional character is thus folded back into the novel's indictment of late colonial Indian society.

The insight generated by passages like these—that the institutional character tends toward type because of the institution's relative indifference to the particulars of character outside the bounds of institutional protocols—is expanded, and complicated, from the novel's beginning by way of its first significant minor character: Munoo's uncle, "Daya Ram, the Chaprasi of the Imperial Bank of India" (4). Daya Ram emerges over the course of several pages. He is first seen taking "big military strides, in his gold-brocaded coat and white turban, along the circuitous hill road constructed by the Angrezi Sarkar, of which he felt himself to be the symbol" (5). Here, the scale of the narration expands unevenly, moving in one sentence from Daya Ram's disciplined strides, to the bank uniform he wears, to the road he walks on, built (presumably with financing from his bank) by the imperial state he feels he now symbolizes. The passages suggest that Daya Ram's "imperious" behavior has little to do with innate personality—indeed, he "wants to soften and be kind" but "irritably ... stiffens his ... body" (5). Moving from disposition to bodily comportment to dress to infrastructure to symbolism, the sentence maps how the character named Daya Ram embodies the Imperial Bank as "the Chaprasi."[43]

Like Jimmie Thomas, Daya Ram is a special incarnation of type. As Alex Woloch writes, "How do you represent ten people who share the same living conditions, or ten thousand people who all belong to the same social class? You can find common traits and conjure up a single individual who exemplifies much more widespread characteristics."[44] The type thus presents an individual who stands in for a general social category. The problem, Woloch argues, is that "this dialectic between the particular and the general ... does not necessarily account for the underlying multiplicity of the larger group of people. Between a particular individual and a general social category is a mass of discrete persons" (250). The institution is one form of social arrangement that falls into this space between the particular individual and the general social category. Jimmie Thomas is one among a large but not infinite number of foremen; similarly, Daya Ram among Imperial Bank officials (similarly too the coolies whose employment shifts their figuration from a "seething tide" to a finite though indefinite number of individuals). These characters are institutional types, standing not for a general category but for a historically delimited institution comprising "discrete persons." Institutional character thus ties types to the historical conditions of those types' emergence, which is to say, to the increased visibility of institutions themselves as actors and contexts for action in the world of late empire.

As Woloch suggests, and as I have aimed to demonstrate in slightly different terms in the case of Jimmie Thomas, the typical character is "ontologically unstable": "On the one hand, he is pressed into that static fusion of the particular and the general. . . . On the other hand, he is drowned out by the actual plurality of individuals who compose this social group" (250). *Coolie* registers both the formal and social consequences of this instability, illustrating the shared nature of institutional characteristics. When Daya Ram arrives at the bank, he meets Pir Din, the bank's "head peon," in "the gold-braided coat which he, too, wore" (9). Both lackeys are affiliated with the sub-accountant Babu Nathoo Mal, who wears "a pyramidal kulah of red velvet" and distinctive "black boots" (11), which in turn tie him to "the burra Sahib" of the bank, in his "strange brown boots" (12). Daya Ram is a poor high-caste Hindu; Pir Din is a "Muhammadan" with a "fiery, henna-dyed beard" (9); the Babu is an educated man with "forty thousand shares in the Allahabad Bank . . . a trusted ally of the government which owned most of the banks" (37); while the burra Sahib is, of course, an Englishman. These figures are rendered in increasingly abstract terms as the narrator moves up the institutional hierarchy: where Daya Ram is given a name and a personality, the "burra Sahib" appears only as "a grim apparition" in "strange boots." So each figure is connected to the others vertically, one might say, by their place in the bank's chain of command, but they are also linked horizontally by the narrator's attention to the common features of their costume and bearing. The traits that initially individuate Daya Ram dissolve outward into the larger, but not infinite, group of "discrete individuals" who make up the bank, situating those individuals within the common life of the institution. Through a process of differentiation and effacement, the features that are emblematic of the bank threaten to overwhelm the features of caste, economic class, ethnicity, and religion that determine inequalities of power in the broader social world of the novel.

Partha Chatterjee, in an influential formulation, argues that anticolonial nationalist thought typically separated "material" from "spiritual" concerns, conceding imperial dominance in the first but using the second as an incubator in which to grow a national identity distinct from that of the colonizing power.[45] But as I have already noted, Anand joins these two spheres in rejecting them; as he would write, "My hatred of imperialism was bound up also with my disgust for the cruelty and hypocrisy of Indian feudal life."[46] Examples of Anand's unmasking of traditional forms abound in the novel. The pastoral life of the village, valorized by Anand's putative sometime mentor Gandhi, turns out to rest on a foundation of economic violence; orphan Munoo thinks of how "the landlord had seized his father's five acres of land. . . . [H]is father had died a slow death of bitterness and disappointment and left his mother a penniless beggar, to support a young brother-in-law and a child in arms" (2–3). (And in the village, moreover, exploitation is personal; the landlord is the father of Munoo's playmate Jay Singh.) Munoo's brief sojourn as a disciple at a shrine ends with his abrupt departure when he discovers that the supposedly chaste yogi assists in "the births of 'sons of God' to the wives of the merchant class" (135)—by having sex with the young women. And a third example comes in the complicated climax to Munoo's employment in the Bombay cotton mill. Here, the fiery speech delivered by a leader of the militant Red Star Union culminates with the assembled crowd reciting a charter, ending with the demand, "We want our organizations to be recognized by law" (234). Almost immediately, this moment of unity is shattered: "a screaming crescendo of pain shot into the air through the edge of the crowd": "Kidnapped! . . . Kidnapped by the Pathans! . . . These bullying, swaggering Muslims are kidnapping Hindu children" (234). While the rumor turns out to be false, and serves the interests of the mill ownership (the rally becomes a riot, and the impending strike dissolves into sectarian violence and a military crackdown), the novel goes to noticeable lengths to emphasize that the rumor's success is largely a product of prejudices associated with what Anand calls "Indian feudal life." The ground for the rumor about "Pathan" kidnappers is prepared by the union leader himself, who asks the crowd, "How many of you have not been pounced upon by the Pathan warder and moneylender outside the mill gates and even inside, on pay day?" (233)—the only portion of his speech that does not appeal to specifically class concerns. Roaming the city in the aftermath of the riots, Munoo overhears Hindu activists and a Muslim dignitary offer contradictory accounts of the violence, competing narratives that the narrator, so quick to intervene elsewhere, does not attempt to reconcile, as though there would be no point.

Similarly, the novel systematically evokes visions of a reparative domestic sphere only to shatter them, though here the key concept is gender rather than ethnicity, caste, or religion. Orphaned from the beginning, Munoo acquires surrogate families at each stage of his journey—or more specifically, surrogate mothers, female characters being confined entirely to the domestic, with one key exception. Absent from the narrative's modern institutions, women appear in these domestic contexts as by turns threatening and smothering, bad mothers in the guise of good, or vice versa (which amounts to the same thing here), and circumstances conspire to expel Munoo from each family situation. Bibiji, wife of Munoo's first boss, is likened to "not a woman but a collection of blandishments" (12), either silent or "shriek[ing] continuously" (13). Parbati, wife of the pickle-factory owner, "soothes the unbearable agony in his limbs with kind words such as his mother used to utter: 'May I be your sacrifice! May I die for you! May I suffer instead of you!' . . . She would lie down by him and take him into her arms while he was tossing himself from side to side, restless and weak, and he would fall sound asleep, drugged into a stupor by the warmth that radiated from her comfortable body, intoxicated by the wonderful tenderness that was in the smell of her body" (94–95). Mrs. Mainwaring, the dissolute Anglo-Indian woman into whose employ Munoo falls at novel's end, alternately gives him manicures and works him literally to death. He "stirs the chords of her being in a strangely disturbing fashion," and while it is not clear that her desire is acted upon, Munoo's death is figured as an almost sexualized exhaustion: night after night after night he pulls her around in a rickshaw until he drops.[47]

The contingency of Munoo's demise is striking. Readers might expect Munoo's death to come at the hands of, say, an industrial accident, thus putting a final twist on the novel's critique of global capital, but despite his tribulations, Munoo is strong and in good health at the end of the fourth section, after the riots. He is then struck by Mrs. Mainwaring's car in an accident that is, if anything, a result of his innate capacity for aesthetic absorption (he is "[standing] dazed" in the middle of a hill road staring down at the sparkling city when the car rounds a corner and hits him [248]). This accident is the proximate cause of his subsequent ill health, which, combined with overwork, leaves him susceptible to consumption; but this is merely implied in the text. The lack of a tight connection between Munoo's death and the circumstances of his life is surprising if we assume with many of its critics that the novel's sole interest is in a moral critique tied to Munoo's bildung. It makes more sense, though, in the context of a narrative that in formal terms is more interested in finding ways to represent imperial institutions and that frequently performs its critique by staging violent encounters between competing ways of ordering collective life, as in the riots.

In any case, neither traditional social structures, nor religion, nor the domestic sphere, however problematically rendered, ultimately offers a basis for renovating Indian society, or even a shelter from the violence of that society, in *Coolie*.⁴⁸ The village presents the oppressions of the wider world in more personal terms; religious leaders are corrupt; families expel Munoo or smother him.⁴⁹ But neither can it be said that the brief moments of accountability and equality proffered by bank, factory, and union play an overtly redemptive role in individual lives. Instead, institutions' capacity in the novel to produce character while effacing its particularities most often creates what the psychologist Ashis Nandy terms "intimate enemies."⁵⁰ For example, in a fantastically awkward scene where Babu Nathoo Mal invites a fellow bank employee (named, naturally, Mr. England) to his home, hoping "to get him to write a recommendation before he was influenced by all the other English officers in the club and began to hate all Indians" (37). Nathoo Mal is horrified when his rasgulas and gulab jaman cause Mr. England to "recoil" in the sweltering heat; England, meanwhile, expects his host's home to "be like the house of 'Abdul Kerim, the Hindoo', in that Hollywood film called *The Swami's Curse*" (39). The predictable failure of the meeting through its misunderstandings, and the reassertion of hierarchy that results, is only heightened by the assumptions of commonality produced in both men by a shared professional framework. As B. B. Misra's *The Bureaucracy in India* shows in historical terms, the expansion of secular institutions in late colonial India through the era of independence, while creating economic opportunities for certain marginalized groups, did not erase distinctions of caste, class, or religion; instead, it more often reified them, creating what Misra terms "vested interests in backwardness."⁵¹ *Coolie* could be termed an institutional picaresque not only for its methods of characterization but also for the way that it arranges and plays the institutions of its narrative off one another, inviting us to discriminate among them in much the same way that a novel of ideas embodies and dramatizes antagonistic systems of thought.⁵² If this is the case, though, *Coolie*'s apparent disenchantment with both traditional and modern institutions makes it difficult to assess where its commitments lie beyond pity for its central character.

Coolie weaves together two different levels of narrative: Munoo's picaresque journey is the occasion for the novel's exploration of institutions, but in its exploration of institutions—in the level of its narrative that is relatively independent of Munoo's unhappy trajectory—*Coolie* gestures toward an unlikely source of value, one that is suggested primarily by the formal mechanics of institutional character themselves. The mode of character at work in Daya Ram, Jimmie Thomas, and the anonymous coolies' embodiment of the protocols of the bank, mill, or "laws of political economy" ultimately serves to make institutions as such visible in the novel; to narrate them; to give them an aesthetic home. I want to suggest that precisely because these characters are unindividuated or positively unappealing, what *Coolie*'s institutional narrative captures is what Walter Benn Michaels, following Bertolt Brecht and the photography of Viktoria Binschtok, calls "the beauty of a social problem": "If . . . we think what matters about our relation to the unemployed is our ability to feel their pain, we're making a mistake. And if we think that political art should provide identification rather than 'beauty,' we're making it again. Rather, to feel the beauty of the problem is precisely *not* to feel the pathos of the suffering produced by the problem; it's instead to feel the structure that makes the problem."[53] On one level, *Coolie* clearly does want to make its readers attend to the pathos of the suffering of individuals like Munoo, but it short-circuits that individualized pathos by emphasizing Munoo's lack of alternatives (the contingency of his death reinforces this; it could have happened no matter what) and his attenuated picaresque subjectivity. Minimizing the tropes of the critical bildung narrative, developing its wide-ranging narratorial perspective, and embodying the institutions of the imperial economy in character, the novel redirects our attention from the individual to institutional structures.

In moving Munoo among the bank, factory, union, and public health service, *Coolie* allegorizes a history of institutions in British India that the political scientist Leo J. Blanken describes as operating on a spectrum ranging "from plunder to public goods."[54] But the novel, anticipating Anand's later nonfiction writing, also embeds in its form an ideal account of how institutions *might* function and how public goods might be turned from a technology of imperial rule to a means of liberation. When the features that individuate Daya Ram are shown to circulate promiscuously among the other individuals who make up the bank, regardless of external features of individual identity, the bank's simultaneous production and effacement of character suggests that the successful occupation of a particular institutional role might theoretically be independent of personal traits that are irrelevant to the performance of that role, even if this is not actually borne out in the narrative. When the workers appeal to Jimmie Thomas's position as foreman to stop a beating, rather than to the individual himself as a moral actor, it suggests that if institutional protocols are publicly shared, they offer a means of holding institutional authority accountable on its own terms.

A literary-critical tradition particularly alert to subversive or counter-hegemonic textual elements might read these moments of institutional fairness and accountability in terms of what Michel de Certeau calls "tactics," a term Rebecca Walkowitz defines as "makeshift cultural maneuvers that bring moments of innovation into rigid social disciplines."[55] In *Cosmopolitan Style*, Walkowitz shows how such tactics are central to modernist fiction, "emphasiz[ing] the connections between private acts or opportunities and institutional systems" (27). But what is crucial to such moments in *Coolie* is precisely the *public* and shared nature of the actions that character comprises, and their predication on a logic *internal* to the institutional system. These passages in *Coolie* gesture not to moments of individual ingenuity in twisting or deforming institutional demands but to the ideal functioning of the institution itself. In this *Coolie* is best read as a work of what Anna Kornbluh terms *political formalism*: "a speculative projection of hypothetical social space, where 'social space' signals the medium of collective life."[56] As Kornbluh writes, "Realism's exploration of the city, governmentality, labor, and law affirms *that there is* institution, but does not inherently affirm any particular institution or form thereof" (54). Unlike *Coolie*'s fleeting evocations of domestic comfort or cultural affinity, the novel's projections of collective life evoke—though they do not dramatize at length—the idea that fairness and accountability might inhere in durable institutions that would render issues of identity relatively indifferent.

Where *Coolie* gestures toward a source of value, then, is in the novel's formal embrace of a concept of the institution that looks very much like the utilitarian social structure as envisioned by Jeremy Bentham, who, Frances Ferguson suggests, "attacked what we would think of as identity groups by arguing that social structures did not need to seek to know more about the character of the individuals that people them, and by arguing against the notion that there were any particular kinds of actions that could be seen as organizing character."[57] "Utilitarian social structures," Ferguson writes, "were developed to be environments that would elicit actions from individuals by making persons visible to one another, by creating artificial groupings that made individuals feel their 'propinquity' in time and space" (3–4). *Coolie* repeatedly indexes the failure of the institutions of British India to offer this type of visibility, and often does so in literal terms, as in the interplay of looks and refusals to look as Munoo encounters members of the bank hierarchy: meeting the Babu, he "dare[s] not raise his head to look at the person he addressed" (10); the burra Sahib is only "the apparition of a man" at whom Munoo "dare[s] not look" (11, 12).[58] But it also attends to the practical application of such visibility, as in the scene of collective discrimination at the union rally held in response to the decision of the mill management to put the factories on "short work" (228). The crowd of workers is made up of "all these dwellers of the slums, the feeble new-born babes, the naked children with distended stomachs, the youths disfigured by smallpox and sores and hookworm, the men who were old without ever having been young, the women whose bellies were always protuberant with the weight of the unborn, the aged who hobbled about slobbering down the sides of their mouths and stinking" (229). The crowd becomes the collective agent of a kind of rough-and-ready democracy; first, they hear a long-winded speech from Lalla Onkar Nath, "President of the All India Trade Union Federation" (231), whose arguments for negotiation and an understanding of the common interest of the workers and owners are ill-received: "'What about the strike?' someone shouted. 'What is the Union going to do about the order for short work?'" (231). In the face of the workers' skepticism, Nath is silenced by Sauda, of "the Red Flag Union," who argues compellingly for an immediate strike, is approved by the crowd ("'That is right! That is the right talk!' some voices shouted" [232]), and leads them in reciting a list of demands. It is not clear whether the crowd has chosen correctly; despite Lalla Onkar Nath's expression of "sardonic contempt" (230), his argument is not self-evidently wrong, and the riots break out before the strike can be implemented. But the crowd of downtrodden coolies is given an opportunity to choose between two courses of collective action, presented in a situation in which the identities of the arguments' proponents are not determinative—indeed, one of the founders of the Red Flag Union is not himself from India but is noted as "a fellow called Jackson, from Manchester" (224). The rally becomes a public enactment of the mechanisms at the heart of the novel's account of institutional character. The strike never gets off the ground because it lacks an institutional context that would enable it to take durable form and overcome the pull of other forms of collective organization, such as religion and caste.

The question of how to evaluate competing forms of collectivity is central to the political writing to which Anand soon turned. In 1942, Anand published *Letters on India*, with an adversarial introduction by Leonard Woolf. *Letters* is arranged as a series of eighteen (imagined) exchanges between Anand and "Tom Brown," an English factory worker and union member. Excerpts from Tom's letters appear first, followed by Anand's essayistic replies. *Letters* begins by addressing the development of contemporary proposals for Indian self-government, then ranges over the entire history of British colonialism and nationalist response, building to an argument for socialism and immediate Indian independence. In his *Apology for Heroism*, which would appear a few years later, Anand characterizes the challenge facing India not, surprisingly, as one of overturning an existent system but as "a renaissance [and] an enormous reformation" (111), and *Letters* places alongside its call for revolution a sustained attention to the institutional history of the Indian state and economy. In letter 14, Anand writes,

> Now, throughout these letters, I have tried to show the workings of the laws of cause and effect, specially in history. It is not that men borrow each other's ideas and graft them on to their localities, but that one fact in history begets another. What I mean may be concretely put this way: it is not British ideas of this, that or the other thing, which have created the Indian national movement, but the British Government as an historical force which, by introducing a system of railways, post and telegraphs and establishing a central bureaucracy, created the conditions for a movement of protest against the inadequacy of this machine of Government and of its financial, political and cultural stranglehold on the people of India. The ideology of the protest movement developed out of this struggle.[59]

This passage articulates a stance toward empire's institutions that refuses the language of rupture. It detaches India's modern institutions of railway, post, telegraphs, and bureaucracy from the power that constituted them—"the British Government as an historical force"—and in doing so envisions those institutions as durable but autonomous, by their nature not necessarily beholden to particular interests, and capable of "creat[ing] the conditions for a movement of protest" against their own "inadequacy." Kristin Bluemel suggests that "Anand's nonfiction presents more thoroughly, consistently radical heroes than his fiction, in part because his autobiographical narratives are freed from the constraints of modernism" (93), and Anand himself refers to what he calls the "assertiveness... of my [nonfiction] formulations, against the tentative insights shown in my novels."[60] As Bluemel suggests, the genealogy of Anand's modernism is not that of "the stream of consciousness novel" (60); *Coolie*'s radicalism inheres not in its propositional content but in its attempt to trace out the beauty of its social problems at the level of form, and the potential buried within those problems. If *Letters* "asserts" a revolutionary institutional politics, *Coolie*, to a greater extent even than the other novels of Anand's early career, does something qualitatively different, making visible in character the experiential basis of that politics as its characters emerge and dissolve, "shadows in the obscure background" of institutional totality.

"Today, we are situated in the midst of a total world," Anand writes in *Apology for Heroism*, "and what happens to one country happens to another" (168). The institutions figured by *Coolie*—factory, union, bank, public health—are imperial forms, products of a system in which "India has been made into a suburb of London, New York, or Chicago, politically, economically, and culturally."[61] From India's "suburban" vantage, *Coolie*, like the other works I have discussed, does not aim to register late empire in negative Jamesonian terms but works rather as what Jed Esty and Colleen Lye term *peripheral realism*, aimed at "the remapping of the world-system as a positive, if partial and mediated, object of representation."[62] As Rosemary Marangoly George puts it, "The 'many freedoms' that Anand championed encompassed scales that were both larger and smaller than the struggle for national liberty."[63] In her *Realism in the Twentieth-Century Indian Novel*, Ulka Anjaria includes Anand in a lineage of South Asian writers who "rather than imitating earlier genres and styles ... actively redefined them, producing a mode that, although I have called it realism here, might equally be called modernism to account for its sheer innovativeness, its self-reflexivity, and its skepticism of naïve mimesis."[64] If *Coolie* draws our attention repeatedly to the ways that the novel can represent institutional life (and represent collectivity more generally), it also encourages us to consider different arrangements of the lineages of modernism and Anglophone writing.

Writing Like an Institution

Institutional picaresque, I've suggested, also provided Anand with strategies for making a career for himself in Britain and in Indian state institutions after independence. Anand immersed himself in two collective endeavors after his return to India: the art and architecture magazine *Marg* and a state-sponsored project to produce a volume titled *Story of the Indian Post Office*. Having consistently cast himself as an outsider's insider, a rogue, an "irrepressible Indian," Anand nonetheless proved himself at home in the relative anonymity of these cultural organizations.

The beginning of this chapter traced some of the places that Anand's institutional picaresque took him, from Bloomsbury in the 1920s and 1930s to the liberalization of the Indian economy in the 1990s and the rise of the Hindu Right. In 1945, though, with World War II over, Anand departed London for Bombay. He was forty-one years old, and he had finished all the work that initially made him a figure of significance to twenty-first-century modernist studies: the early novels, especially *Untouchable* and *Coolie;* his work with the All-India Progressive Writers' Union, and his involvement with the BBC. Bombay represents the first day of the rest of his life, a life that Anglophone scholarship has addressed only fleetingly. He would spend the next sixty years in Bombay. Although Anand has been canonized as a transnational modernist figure, he remains an example of a writer whose works by and large have failed to transcend their national origins to qualify as world literature. Western audiences—with the possible exceptions of discerning Britons in the 1930s and 1940s and scholars of the new modernist studies today—do not come to Anand's works expecting (in Gloria Fisk's terms) to find a bridge to another culture.[65] Indeed, they don't come to his works at all. Anand's late career exemplifies how an international modernism and Left politics were institutionalized in the project of building and legitimating the postcolonial Indian state, a project that at times carried utopian promise but was also massively bureaucratic. While Anand continued to write and publish novels, they reached a national audience rather than a global one (though his older works continued to be reprinted in Britain and the United States from time to time).[66] The insight his later career provides into the longer career of modernism itself has less to do with literature than with architecture, design, and the creation of a *national* "Indian" culture and heritage. The primary vehicle for that work was the magazine *Marg*.

In *Coolie*, Munoo's friend Ratan tells him a story about a heroic strike at "the Tata steel works at Jamshedpur" (201). A dozen years after that novel's publication, Anand persuaded J. R. D. Tata, head of the Tata & Sons conglomerate, to provide office space and funding and to commit to buy advertising for a magazine of art and architecture. Anand joined the sisters Anil and Minette De Silva, an illustrator and architect, respectively, who had also spent time in London, and the architect Otto Koenigsberger, a Berliner who had fled Nazi Germany in the 1930s. Koenigsberger had already served as chief architect of Mysore state and drawn up plans for the city of Bangalore, and he would go on to work as India's chief of housing under Nehru. The first issue of *Marg* was published in October 1946. The audience it courted was in cosmopolitan, heavily English-speaking, bohemian Bombay, quite distant from the anti-imperialist leftist circles of Anand's earlier life. Tata himself was the richest man in India, head of the subcontinent's largest industrial conglomerate, and something of a playboy, and he intervened freely in editorial and hiring issues. The magazine they produced is a product of that world: richly illustrated—though also priced cheaply, thanks to Tata's subsidy—*Marg* channeled its enthusiasm for the New India and for independence into an exuberant consumerism, laced with an optimistic sense of social responsibility. In its first volume, contributions from internationally known architects like Frank Lloyd Wright, Le Corbusier, and Richard Neutra appear alongside reviews of gallery shows, historical surveys of Indian sculpture and visual art, plans for rural housing and the Tata factory town of Jamshedpur, book reviews, and ads for international brands such as Buick, Chevrolet, and Carrier air-conditioning.[67] *Marg* was a collective undertaking, but its various elements, including its editorial stance, advertisements, layout, and graphic design, were remarkably consistent early on in using images to construct an aspirational national character for independent India and a particular kind of Indian consumer-citizen. In its early issues, its most striking illustrations juxtapose images of Indian heritage (sculpture, art, monumental architecture) to modern technology, a leap into a progressive future that draws on a classical past.

Marg's first issue opened with an editorial by Anand arguing for "the possibilities of a planned society." As he writes, "Planning . . . does not mean what it is superficially supposed to mean, a mechanized, regimented society. On the contrary, planning is like dreaming—dreaming of a new world. And in that sense economic and political planning becomes an essential ancillary to the planning of villages, towns and cities, the centres of human culture, where men and women congregate in small or large communities, to live the good life."[68] In both content and design the editorial operates by drawing evocative pairings and contrasts. Its equation of "planning" with "dreaming," making technocracy something ludic, utopian, or spiritual, anticipates Jawaharlal Nehru's announcement a year later at the Bhakra-Nangal Dams that dams would be "the temples of new India."[69] "Political planning" serves the timeless values of "human culture" and "the good life." The layout frames a progressive, modernizing argument with a graphic of temple architecture, a layout that is repeated in future issues.

Later in this same editorial, Anand writes that "[i]n India, where there has been no widespread building for two hundred years, we are not talking of reconstruction but of construction. . . . [A]s we love our past we have also begun to love our future" (6)—imagining a break with the immediate past but a deep channel to the culture's ancient roots. Even the journal's title, *Marg,* contains a juxtaposition of ancient past and progressive present: *marg* is a Sanskrit word meaning "pathway" but also served as an acronym for "Modern Architecture Research Group." Yet this is a particularly ersatz kind of past, with Sanskrit and "Indianness" erasing historical distinctions of caste, region, and religion just as English and Hindi were erasing them at the late colonial moment of the editorial's publication. This instantaneous juxtaposition of classical past and chaotic present faintly evokes T. S. Eliot's "mythic method" and the kind of high modernist classicism that Anand had encountered in Europe twenty years earlier (a classicism that also wanted to ignore the past two hundred years). But there is also something vaguely absurd behind Anand's suggestion that in actual housing policy India could ignore the past two hundred years of its history and infrastructure. This indifference to actual *processes* of development, and (in contrast to *Letters on India*) to the institutional continuities between the Raj and postcolonial India, becomes very clear when we note that *Marg* published nothing acknowledging independence and partition in the late summer and fall of 1947. The closest it seems to have come was six months later, in its second issue of 1948, when the magazine memorialized Gandhi after his assassination. Anand's editorial for the issue, titled "Letter to an Englishman," addresses "the last secretary of state for India" on the matter of an art exhibition.[70]

Given this lacuna in the journal's coverage, it is unsurprising that just as Anand found himself isolated from the British cultural Left for his proletarian nationalism, he quickly found himself isolated from the Indian cultural Left for his elite cosmopolitanism. *Marg*'s enthusiasm for the New India was in fact an elision of politics; it was to be a magazine of a particular class fraction of independent India rather than of the Indian Left. *Marg* as an organization would go on to play an important role in some high-profile architectural undertakings in India, most notably Le Corbusier's design for Chandigarh. Nonetheless, in 1963 Anand reprinted "Architecture and You" with a note that the journal had "failed" in its mission to develop a truly indigenous modern architecture and a style for modern India—a task that, on the terms *Marg* itself set, was probably not attainable.

Marg is well known and still published today, remaining an important venue for developments in Indian art and design. A less well known undertaking of Anand's was initiated in the early 1950s, evidently at the behest of the Indian government: a collectively authored *Story of the Indian Post Office*, for which Anand served as editor in chief. The result was a two-hundred-page volume, published in 1954 with a foreword by Nehru, a preface by Jagiwan Ram, the minister of communications, and opening acknowledgments by Anand. It is an impressive book, giving the history of the Indian post office and its predecessor institutions from the distant past through Mughal and British rule to national independence, heavily illustrated in black and white and with a number of glossy color plates, with portraits of ministers, government buildings, and Indian stamps. Anand's name is the only one to appear on the cover. In his acknowledgments, he immediately links the project to the status of newly independent India: "Apart from the fascination of the study of an institution which we all take for granted, there is to be derived from this book a great deal of factual information, which is important at this stage of our preoccupation with nation-building. . . . If the names of . . . contributors do not appear on the title page, it is only because of the tradition of anonymity of an institution whose motto is 'SERVICE BEFORE SELF.'"[71] *Story of the Indian Post Office* thus instantiates something like the dream of an ideal institution that appears only fleetingly in *Coolie*, one in which particulars of individual identity are minimized in the service of institutionalized goals. Nor were those goals insignificant: as Chinmay Tumbe points out, the Indian Post Office was and continues to be one of the largest financial entities in South Asia: "The financial history of modern India remains incomplete without integrating the Post Office as a key institutional actor in the narrative."[72]

In the above passage, the many contributors to *Story of the Indian Post Office* are effaced and given a new, collective identity in the slogan "SERVICE BEFORE SELF," an identity that is a non-identity. Interestingly, passages in the volume's introduction, authored by Anand, on the institutional continuities from British to independent India turn out to be cribbed nearly word for word from *Letters on India:* "The British introduced a unitary administration in the country and made possible the development of public works, of trade and commerce and other social institutions. And, with the railway and telegraph systems, a revolution was brought about."[73] Literary form functions as a set of resources for characterizing oneself. In his work for the Post Office, Anand came to occupy a real-world institution in a manner much like that of the minor characters of *Coolie;* once there, he reproduced his own theorizations of how that process might work. One can imagine Anand having a good chuckle at seeing this pointed out: "No fraud can outmatch that perpetuated by this charlatan," as his "Self-Obituary" would read.

In 2004, *Marg* issued a volume in honor of Anand's one hundredth birthday. In it, the painter Gulammohammed Sheikh writes, "Mulk and *Marg* are so inseparably intertwined in my memory that I find it impossible to speak of one without the other. So many years after his active editorship ceased it is still difficult to imagine *Marg* without Mulk. His vision is present both in the spirit and substance of *Marg* today despite the changes it has gone through. *Marg* in that sense is not just a journal inasmuch as it has a persona, molded by Mulk; so writing about it means writing about two old friends."[74] Sheikh's rhetoric is affectionate and sentimental, but the passage also gives, in a way, a rigorous account of one form of relationship between individual cultural workers like Anand and institutions like *Marg*—or the BBC, or the Post Office, or, for that matter, between character and institution in the modernist novel. It's in these spaces that we can find the concrete history of modernism, institutional character, and empire, and it is often—as Anand finally shows—not quite what we might expect.

4
Elizabeth Bowen
WAR, WELFARE, AND THE INSTITUTIONAL IMPERSONAL

ELIZABETH BOWEN appears in historical perspective as an untimely writer: her life and her work seem often to have been suspended not only between disparate places but also between disparate senses of time. The same age as the twentieth century, as she put it, she was born in the precise historical moment in which the term *Anglo-Irish* attained maximal significance, between the beginning of the decline of the Protestant landowning class it designated (who had once thought of themselves simply as Irish) and the founding of the Irish Free State, in which that class lost its historical justification entirely. She was an only child and the heir to her family's Big House, Bowen's Court, and her first seven years were divided between summers at the house in County Cork and winters in Dublin. Her father, Robert, was the first Bowen to take up a profession, becoming a lawyer to generate the income that gentlemanly farming no longer could in Ireland; the breakdowns he suffered led his wife and daughter to move to England at the suggestion of his doctors when Bowen was seven. As she admitted in a 1950 interview with Jocelyn Brooke, she was a writer "whose interest lies chiefly in a sense of place," and on leaving Ireland she discovered the coastal landscape of Kent, which, along with London and Bowen's Court itself, would inform the imaginary geography of her writing throughout her career.[1] She spent the war years in Kent and at Bowen's Court, attended art school in London, and married Alan Cameron, a successful administrator with the British Board of Education, in 1923. In the same year she published her first book of short stories, *Encounters*. She came too late to make the scene of high modernism, and her friendships with figures like Virginia Woolf (with whom she became close) came years later—she would refer to them as "the great elder group, to me, the people in Bloomsbury." Her own generation she considered to include Henry Green, Graham Greene, Rosamond Lehmann, Evelyn Waugh, and the Oxford coterie of Isaiah Berlin, Maurice Bowra, and Cyril Connelly.² In 1930 her father died and she inherited Bowen's Court, which had remained intact through the Troubles, when many of the nearby houses were burned.

Bowen spent World War II writing short stories, volunteering as an air raid precautions warden in her London neighborhood of Regent's Park, and working for the British Ministry of Information producing reports on the political situation in neutral Ireland, to whose leadership her literary reputation and background gave her access.³ She also began an affair with the Canadian diplomat Charles Ritchie that continued, in one form or another, for the rest of her life, though she remained happily married. She and Alan Cameron intended to move to Bowen's Court to live there full-time in 1952, but his death in the same year placed her in reduced financial circumstances, and she was soon driven out of Ireland again, across early Cold War Europe as a journalist and to a number of American universities as a sought-after teacher of writing. She died in 1973, having sold Bowen's Court and seen it dismantled and having returned late in life to a small house in Hythe, Kent.

Thus, a set of places, with their own distinct temporal rhythms, overlap in her life and work: agrarian Anglo-Ireland, where, she wrote, "I know of no house . . . in which, while the present seems to be there forever, the past is not pervadingly felt"; suburban Kent, where she lived throughout her childhood and which gave her the variously inflected Edwardian villas of her novels, with names like Waikiki, Cathay, and Holme Dene; London, especially in wartime, which was, as Victoria Glendinning writes, "her noon" (177); the Continent in the early Cold War, characterized by rapid travel and bureaucratic delay; and America, where she spent academic semesters affiliated with creative-writing programs and English departments. Unlike the canonically enshrined modernists of the preceding generation, though, Bowen was perennially displaced, less from a desire to occupy a center of culture and aesthetic innovation than from a dilemma of belonging that was built into Anglo-Irish identity. Owning an Irish estate, she said, was "something between a *raison d'être* and a predicament," and she suggested that she felt most at home at the midpoint of the ferry journey across the Irish Sea. But the ways in which Bowen's cosmopolitan mobility and untimeliness issue from a foundation in Anglo-Ireland make that context an especially generative one; it enables all the others, is the one that her own work most extensively interrogates and relies upon, and infiltrates the formal features of her literary writing at its most engaged, contemporary, and political—particularly that writing addressed to World War II—in ways that have not been fully appreciated. Her two long works of the 1940s, *Bowen's Court* and *The Heat of the Day*, bracket the important middle period of her career and illustrate a unique confluence in Bowen's literary writing of Anglo-Irish institutionalism and the enabling conditions of wartime. In the historical moment just before the emergence of the postwar welfare state, these offered a stay against what she called "the dire period of Personal Life."[4]

For the modernists of Paul Fussell's *The Great War and Modern Memory*—a study that remains fundamental to any understanding of the literature of World War I—the war was a rupture in history and in the history of literary style, and rupture would seem to be the antithesis of the concept of the institution that I have traced in previous chapters.[5] As Hugh Heclo puts it, to think in terms of institutions is to attend to the "faithful reception" of inherited ideas; to the "infusions of value" that accepted practices offer; and to the "lengthened time horizons," in which the life of the institution exceeds the life of any particular individual who might partake in it.[6] The Great War ostensibly put an end to what Fussell terms "a coherent stream of time running from past through present to future" (21). Yet war is a recurrent presence in the literary genealogy I have traced thus far. In the Costaguana of Conrad's *Nostromo*, society's normal condition is war, understood not as a clash between nation-states but as civil conflict between material interests in an imperial world-system. While Woolf's works of the 1920s, such as *Mrs. Dalloway* and *To the Lighthouse*, incorporate the rupture of the Great War, in *The Years* the "soldier" North Pargiter returns to London not with shell shock but with a desire to find different forms of collective life: "to keep the emblems and tokens of North Pargiter . . . but at the same time spread out."[7]

In these works, war is figured not as the eruptive other of modern institutions but as something like institutions' unpredictable accompanist or familiar. War becomes a collective condition in which the accepted practices, habits, and values of institutional life are thrown into relief, modulated, and themselves re-infused with meaning, for better or for worse. As Elizabeth Bowen would write in *Bowen's Court*, "The values with which I set out—my own values—did, at least to my own feeling, remain constant: they were accentuated rather than changed by war" (453).[8] For Bowen's characters, war is in part a form of time itself, as in her novel of World War II, *The Heat of the Day*: "that 'time being' which war had made the very being of time. Wartime. . . . this tideless, hypnotic, futureless day-to-day."⁹ In a 1950 essay titled "The Bend Back," on the uses of the past in literature, Bowen acknowledges that the Great War might once have been best understood as rupture, writing that "confidence was broken by 1914. . . . After 1918, the artist, by general assent, took up the attitude of the critical exile, the psychologically displaced person."¹⁰ But as the twentieth century went on, the Great War became merely "one war that War as we now know it encloses in its immense To-day" (*Bowen's Court*, 437). Modernism, the literature of the Great War, "was to remain a literature of sensation only—cerebrally brilliant but skin-deep, ultimately bodiless in that it lacked soul." "Between the world's two wars," Bowen writes, "that literature ran its course"; it failed to "root down deeply in the imagination . . . mystery, loyalty, tenderness shriveled under its ray" ("Bend Back," 54). Bowen's demand for a literature attentive to "roots" and "loyalty" could "be met only by recourse to life in the past" (55).

The "time being" of war became for Bowen a portal through which "life in the past" could be enlisted to inform the representation of the present—in particular, of the experience of World War II.¹¹ Bowen viewed herself as descended from a people who had approached life in terms of collective perpetuation rather than individual achievement, what Barbara Brothers calls "the Anglo-Irish tradition of a circumscribed family life within the history of which a social order was preserved that transcended the individual's experience of time."¹² Critics have most frequently found Anglo-Ireland in Bowen's work in the figure of the Big House, and in what she calls "the order, the form of life, the tradition" that accompanies it.¹³ As a material structure joined to a set of persistent practices, relatively indifferent to the specifics of the individuals who occupy it, the Big House emerges in Bowen's family history, *Bowen's Court*, and in related essays as the embodiment of Bowen's concept of the institution. Bowen finds in the institutional life of Anglo-Ireland a conservative spirit of impersonality and style, expressed in her literary writing through a distinct attention to the "stream of time running from past through present to future." The unique hybridity of the Anglo-Irish—always, in their history, already pulled between England and Ireland, between state power and civil society, and between the historical roles of European aristocracy and settler-colonial bourgeoisie—both enables this stylish and impersonal concept of the institution and makes it surprisingly exportable in fiction to quite foreign contexts, including the technocratic, cosmopolitan setting of World War II London, where it is reconstituted in the shadowy complex of institutions that make up the wartime state. Whether linked to the Big House or to the intelligence service, Bowen's unusual forms of character come to fruition not in a desire to capture the precise workings of the institution in narrative but rather in a commitment to exploring the forms of behavior—beautiful, stylish, courageous, exciting—to which politics is largely incidental and that are enabled by the impersonality of institutional life. Bowen's novel *The Heat of the Day*, written during the war and published in 1948, depicts a world in which human relationships are mediated entirely through wartime institutions—institutions that, because of the atmosphere of secrecy that pervades the novel's plot and setting and infiltrates the very rhythms of its prose, come to seem nonetheless impossible to describe with any specificity. What I will term the novel's *crypto-institutionalism* figures the Anglo-Irish ancien régime in literary form, grafting Bowen's institutional aesthetic of style and impersonality onto a hypermodern wartime milieu to produce highly abstract forms of character. The aristocratic history from which she drew this concept of institutional life as style and impersonality also generates a limit to that concept, in Bowen's encounters with the postwar welfare state. But her late career finds Bowen reconstituting Anglo-Ireland in yet another highly bureaucratized institutional setting: the American university English department in the 1950s and 1960s. "Not disrespectful or hostile to institutions," she writes in an unpublished essay, "women do none the less feel free to examine them."[14]

Bowen's Court and Anglo-Irish Impersonality

Bowen's Court is easily Bowen's longest work, suggestive of its ambitiousness. Jonathan Cape, Bowen's regular publisher, refused to publish this work of history and biography during wartime because of its "controversial" treatment of the Ireland-England relationship—a testament to how that relationship remained, in 1942, permeated by the past.[15] *Bowen's Court* traces 350 years in the life of a family and 200 in the life of a house, both products of the complex history of the Anglo-Irish Ascendancy. The "English," in the form of French-speaking subjects of Henry II, had been in Ireland since the twelfth century, when they arrived as soldiers at the invitation of certain Gaelic kings; these "Old English," as those who stayed would come to be called, largely retained Catholicism after the Reformation along with a nonetheless persistent sense of being set apart from the Gaelic (and Catholic) Irish. With Protestant settlement in the early seventeenth century, tensions arose between Old English and Protestant "New English" arrivals, leading to the Ulster Rebellion of 1641. Old English and native Irish nobles, acting, they claimed, as loyal subjects of Charles I (i.e., as Irish Catholics claiming fealty to a Protestant English king), sought to overthrow the Protestant lords of the Ulster plantation. Cromwell's armies would arrive in 1649 and crush them decisively. The lands of the Catholic lords who had led the rebellion were given over to Protestant officers who had accompanied Cromwell and to the financiers who had backed his army. This created a wealthy Protestant landowning class sitting atop a not inconsiderable population of ordinary Protestant settlers, native converts to Protestantism, and the mass of native Catholic Irish. This Protestant Ascendancy reached the apex of its cultural, political, and economic power in the eighteenth century, peaking with the Irish Parliament and the Constitution of 1782. This Irish nation was a Protestant nation, nominally self-governing and loyal to the Crown; Catholics were excluded from the establishment. The Act of Union in 1800 dissolved the Irish Parliament, brought English troops to the country on a permanent basis, and put Irish governance in the hands of the British Parliament, giving the lie to the notion that Irish parliamentarians had represented a whole Irish nation rather than a mere "English garrison."[16] Structurally isolated, retaining economic power but with dwindling political capital, Anglo-Irish landowners as a class declined slowly throughout the nineteenth century, until the nationalist historian Standish O'Grady could describe them in 1901, in memorable if perhaps not wholly just terms, as "rotting from the land in the most dismal farce-tragedy of all time, without one brave deed, without one brave word."[17] With the founding of the Irish Free State in 1922, seventeen years before Bowen began writing *Bowen's Court*, their obsolescence was assured.

Even this brief overview of Anglo-Ireland suggests the many crossed allegiances and hyphenated designations that would come to be built into Anglo-Irish self-understanding. *Bowen's Court* traces this history, from Cromwell onward, as it was lived by the Bowens themselves, though the significance of the individual Bowens ultimately lies in their role as a relay between the collective life of Anglo-Ireland and the house in which its values are instantiated. As Bowen writes, "If I did not show what went to make the Bowens, from the time of their first coming to Ireland, I should fail to show what went to make Bowen's Court" (32). Family patriarchs are lent somewhat tongue-in-cheek dynastic titles: from Colonel Bowen (Henry I), who came to Ireland from Wales, to Henry III, who finished building Bowen's Court in 1776, to Bowen's own father, Henry VI (Johns and Roberts also appear).[18] Strictly speaking, the term *Anglo-Irish* itself could refer to either Catholics or Protestants who came to Ireland from England over a period of hundreds of years. In this respect, that Bowen treats her family as typically Anglo-Irish is itself significant, as the term silently contracts in her use to treat the specific class-fraction that is at the center of the story she tells: W. B. Yeats's "hard-riding country gentlemen," descendants of the Protestants who came with Cromwell and became significant landowners, acquiring wealth but who, having taken over the land, "had still no *idea* of living to integrate them."[19] In Bowen's account, the need to construct an "idea of living" drove the Anglo-Irish to develop a particularly sustaining and valuable notion of the institution.

The construction of that idea begins, in Bowen's account, ignominiously. "For some time," she writes, "many Cromwellians remained squatters, busied with the accumulation of wealth but living . . . in patched-up ruins, in the tedium and squalor of poor whites" (87). Colonel Bowen came to Ireland alone, leaving the children of his second marriage, along with his third wife and the children of that marriage, in Wales; when his wife attempted to visit him, he sent her back. He lived "in the small semiruinous castle just across the Farahy stream; just *off*—by the width of the water—his own lands" (74). In the only gothic flourish in an account that largely rejects the gothic conventions of the standard Big House narrative, Bowen tells the story of "the Apparition" as recorded in Richard Baxter's *Worlds of Spirits* (1691): Colonel Bowen, having acquired a reputation as "an absolute Atheist, denying Heaven or Hell, God or Devil" (43), appeared (while still alive in Ireland) to his wife back in Wales as a ghastly apparition, blaspheming and smelling "of a Carcase some-while dead" (45). His son John I and the two succeeding generations, having through strenuous application put the living-dead tendencies of the Colonel behind them, occupied small houses built in or around Kilbolane Castle, miles from the Bowen lands, with the Nicholls family, into which John I had married and to whom he became heavily indebted. Only with Henry III, the eventual builder of Bowen's Court, does the institutionalization of the Anglo-Irish come into focus.

Henry III was "the first Irish Bowen to come to full bloom" (145). He was not, Bowen is at pains to stress, an intellectual man; he had no formal education besides tutors as a child. "I detect in his nature," she writes, "a mixture of pride and timidity. . . . He would not stand as a stranger at anyone's—no, not at King George's—door. He posed himself here in Mallow, in the rich positiveness of a provincial society" (145). This "positiveness" was largely the absence of self-doubt; in the 1750s Anglo-Ireland was "at the vital, growing, magnetic stage: it enjoyed not only material but real psychological dominance" (130). It "took itself for granted; there was no need, yet, to say, 'We are the people!' . . . they *were* the people" (though as Bowen notes, "the poor had to flatter to live—and, even so, most of them barely lived at all") (131). In this period of Anglo-Irish hegemony, the edge had come off religion; wealthier Catholics integrated or conformed, and just enough of the intellectual ferment taking place on the Continent filtered through to places like Mallow, County Cork, to make possible the belief "that God was not after one the *whole* time" (131). Books were present, as part of a gentleman's home furnishings, but probably were not read, according to Bowen; horses, entertaining, and large numbers of servants were the primary expenses. Henry III could excel through his "flair for living, his innate stylishness, and his love of the grand":

> The pleasures of the mind, the arts, discourse were all denied to Henry III—one can hardly say denied, for he never demanded them. His destiny was, to be a *beau* in Mallow society, a liberal landowner, the builder of Bowen's Court. Did he miss much? He lived his life to the full. . . . Henry, a preeminently social figure, lived in a Philistine, snobbish, limited and on the whole pretty graceless society. But he got somewhere, and lived to die in his drawing-room surrounded by hosts of children and the esteem of what looked like a lasting order. (124–25)

This is the peak of Bowen's Anglo-Ireland: "Philistine," "snobbish," "limited," and "graceless," redeemed primarily by "hosts of children" and the concept of "a lasting order." As the passage continues, though, this seemingly mixed judgment is refined as it is brought into relation with the present, in one of the few explicit linkages between the history presented in *Bowen's Court* and the moment of its composition: by contrast with that "limited" world, Bowen asks, "to what did our fine feelings, our regard for the arts, our intimacies, our inspiring conversations, our wish to be clear of the bonds of sex and class and nationality, our wish to try to be fair to every one bring us? To 1939" (125). The ambiguous tone of this conclusion, and its questionable validity, should not obscure the curious movement of the passage as a whole.[20] The subject of each sentence is a "he," but the passage is silent about Henry III's motives, desires, thoughts, or feelings, presenting him instead in terms of the roles he occupies: beau, landowner, builder, social figure. Constructing the society of Henry III's time by subtracting from his subjectivity, the passage then contrasts its positive appraisal of this totally externalized personality with the evident failure of a modernity overstuffed with "feelings," "regard," "intimacies," "conversations," and "wishes." In doing so it begins to offer a frame for Bowen's institutional thinking in *Bowen's Court*.

One way that the passage sets up *Bowen's Court* is by indexing the value of the Anglo-Irish idea of living, arguing that this value has little to do with anything that might be called Anglo-Irish *culture*. By contrast, Yeats, their most prominent reimaginer, mounts a case for Anglo-Irish greatness on the strength of Anglo-Irish literary and philosophical production. As Bernard McKenna points out, "For Yeats, cultural nationalism had the potential to unite the nation under the leadership of the Anglo-Irish."[21] In his introduction to Joseph Hone and Mario Rossi's *Bishop Berkeley*, Yeats writes: "Born in such a community, Berkeley with his belief in perception, that abstract ideas are mere words, Swift with his love of perfect nature, of the Houynhnms, his disbelief in Newton's system, and every sort of machine, Goldsmith and his delight in the particulars of common life that shocked his contemporaries, Burke with his conviction that all States not grown slowly like a forest tree are tyrannies, found in England the opposite that stung their own thought into expression and made it lucid."[22] Yeats's account is strongly "cultural" in both primary senses of the term: Ireland as "a community" (Eliot and Raymond Williams's sense of "culture as a whole way of life")[23] produces writers whose works are "genius"—high culture, the best that has been thought and said.

The Irish eighteenth century thus birthed a culture uniquely suited to producing culture: "Its mind"—that of Ireland itself—"became so clear that it changed the world" (411). Seamus Deane points out that "this particular version of eighteenth-century literary and intellectual history is manifestly absurd. . . . Yeats misreads Berkeley and Swift, makes Goldsmith appear far more eccentric and controversial than he actually was, attributes to England a role in Burke's thought which really belongs to France." As Deane suggests, Yeats's construction of an Anglo-Irish culture is an exercise less in history than in Romantic aesthetics, "making history palatable by imaging it as a version of the personality."[24] But this only makes clearer that Yeats is engaged in a project of national justification via the assertion of aesthetic value that has become ever more recognizable in the wake of postcolonial studies and debates around world literature, even if, in Yeats's case, the partiality of the justification is especially obvious. Yeats's cultural Romanticism thus throws into relief Bowen's indifference to Anglo-Irish intellectual production and her emphasis instead on what is enabled by that society's "Philistinism," "snobbishness," and "limits." As Neil Corcoran notes, Bowen repeatedly asserts the importance of a "style of living" and yet "very strangely, virtually no instances of Anglo-Irish cultural, as opposed to purely social, achievement, are ever adduced."[25] Bowen says almost nothing about the art, philosophy, or literature of the Anglo-Irish, and while Corcoran gestures toward the strangeness of this fact, the passage above suggests that more than simple omission is at work; the continuous "lasting order" that is the fruit of Anglo-Ireland is possible not despite but *because of* that society's "limited" ambit.[26] Later in *Bowen's Court*, Bowen suggests that Victorian Anglo-Ireland "looked for culture everywhere but inside her home shores," commenting that, for example, "the Gaelic League seemed no more than a bizarre activity on the part of the son of a clergyman" (399). And the conclusion of the above passage emphasizes culture's inadequacy to the task of sustaining a "lasting order" through the caustic irony of Bowen's shift to the present, in which "our" modern cosmopolitan culture has brought us inexorably "to 1939."

Sharon Cameron suggests that "representations of impersonality suspend, eclipse, and even destroy the idea of the person as such."[27] If the literature of Yeats's great men allows him to imagine history as culture and thus as a version of the personality, the typicality of Henry III allows Bowen to find in history an institutionalized form of *impersonality*.[28] In her 1940 essay "The Big House," composed as she was writing *Bowen's Court*, Bowen writes, "The idea from which these houses sprang was, before everything, a social one. . . . What is fine about the social idea is that it means the subjugation of the personal to the impersonal" (29). Bowen sketches these impersonal values as "wit, knowledge, sympathy or personal beauty"—"the best (everyone) had" (29); Victoria Glendinning sums up Bowen's impersonal "social idea" as "stylishness, vanity, discipline, energy, lack of cant, independence, courage" (201). In *Bowen's Court* Bowen explicitly contrasts these values and the impersonality developed by the Anglo-Irish in the eighteenth century with the "Personal Life" that succeeds it: with the Act of Union in 1800, "[s]ociety . . . was on the decline; it was breaking up. . . . [T]he main healthy abstract was gone. And with this break-up of society there set in the dire period we are not yet out of, the dire period of Personal Life" (*Bowen's Court*, 259).

Accordingly, *Bowen's Court* is less concerned with the personalities of Bowen's forebears than it might at first seem. While chapters are headed by the names of Bowen patriarchs, their pseudo-monarchical titles produce the effect of differentiation without distinction: names (Henry I, John I, Henry II, etc.) become indicators of mere chronology rather than of unique persons. Recurring descriptive phrases—Henry I is "the Colonel," Henry III is "the Builder" (32, 125)—reinforce this typicality rather than adding characterological depth. Bowen emphasizes that capturing the individual psychologies of her ancestors is not her aim: "I accepted the ignorance, set up by time and death, that divided my ancestors' conscious lives from mine. In the writing of this book, sheer information would not have taken me very much of the way—only a little displaced by my researches, the greater part of that ignorance still remains: it is natural" (452). And at times Bowen doubly distances herself from the rendering of interior states by relying not just on typical description but on *other authors'* typical description: "Henry (III)," she writes, "was in no sense 'an original': his traits of mind, his notions, his ways of living were so much those of his class that I think I can do no better than quote from Arthur Young's rather tart note . . . on the Irish country gentry" (170). Once quoted, Young's "tart note" only adds another layer of remove, as it confines itself to the cost of food in Ireland, horses and servants, and table manners. In the case of Henry V, Bowen writes, "His career at Trinity College, Dublin, is outside my power to pursue"; instead, she posits that his experience of Dublin was analogous to that of "Miss Edgeworth's Lord Colambre" (281), citing several paragraphs from *The Absentee* to this effect.[29] Through titles, types, and literary pastiche, *Bowen's Court* hollows out the representation of the creative individual personality and dispenses with the forms of culture associated with it by Yeats in favor of an account of the construction of an impersonal "idea of living" composed of shared values and embodied in the infrastructure of the Big House.

Indeed, *Bowen's Court* is at times quite explicit about this attempt to reconceive the Anglo-Irish legacy. A thematic emphasis on the absence of human agency throughout *Bowen's Court* combines with the prominence of types and citationality, displacing the individual Bowens themselves from the center of the account and setting up an opposition between conscious activity and the unconscious action of an institution being realized in a material structure. As Maud Ellmann writes, "Everything in Bowen's prose conspires to efface the human subject."[30] Henry III's attributes include his "flair for living" and "love of the grand," but Bowen maintains that "Henry the big boy, the naïve chatterer, the coaxing, loving and rather childish husband was not present in the building of Bowen's Court. The stern and cold force of his unconscious nature perpetuated itself in stone as the house went up. . . . He was more than building a home, he was setting a pattern" (169). The traits attributed to Henry as an individual are removed from consideration of how the house was made; only the impersonal aspects of his "unconscious nature," features that are "so much those of his class," inform the "pattern." Bowen emphasizes that "a Bowen, in the first place, made Bowen's Court. Since then, with a rather alarming sureness, Bowen's Court has made all the succeeding Bowens" (32); but neither is this first Bowen revealed to be an independent agent. Instead, Henry III, like "all the succeeding Bowens," is himself an expression of the impersonal and unconscious effects of the practices, habits, and values of the Anglo-Irish institution.

In her 1964 afterword to the second edition of *Bowen's Court*—itself an important document that justifies Bowen's method, traces the history of the house through Bowen's ownership, and recounts its ultimate demise—she revisits and elaborates on the relationship between her ancestors and the historical institution she seeks to narrate:

> What runs on most through a family living in one place is a continuous, semi-physical dream. Above this dream-level lives show their tips, their little conscious formations of will and thought. With the end of each generation, the lives that submerged here were absorbed again. . . .
>
> It is the involuntary, or spontaneous, aspect that interests me most. Having looked back at [the Bowens] steadily, I begin to notice, if I cannot define, the pattern they unconsciously went to make. And I can see that that pattern has its relation to the outside more definite pattern of history.
>
> The Bowens' relation to history was an unconscious one. . . . Their assertions, their compliances, their refusals as men and women went, year by year, generation by generation, to give history direction, as well as

colour and stuff. Each of the family, in their different ways, were more than their time's products; they were its agents. (451–52)

This passage offers a progressively deepening account of the relationship between the individual and institutional life. It first asserts the aristocratic vision of continuity underlying the ideal of "a family living in one place," reaffirming the primacy of the "unconscious" collective relationship to history over the individual lives whose significance Bowen minimizes by terming them "little conscious formations of will and thought." The passage then turns to the "pattern" that is most notably embodied in Henry III's construction of the house, an event resulting less from Henry III's distinctive personality than from his typification of the features of his class and "the pattern of history," setting up the specificity of the context in which the Bowens' "assertions," "compliances," and "refusals" take place and acquire substance—"colour" and "stuff." This is the language of institutional character, capturing the ways that the institution constrains individual action but at the same time lends it meaning. *Bowen's Court* does not imagine a world devoid of important individuals, of course, nor does it conceive of the "pattern" established by institutional life as static, but it insists on the relative insignificance, over time, of the details of personality, and it presents institutional change as a product of choices made within the bounds of the institution itself. Hence the precision of Bowen's language in the final sentence of the passage, which does not oppose absolute freedom to absolute constraint, but does something subtler: to be more than a "product" of one's time, Bowen suggests, is to be its "agent"—a term that implies both a capacity for action ("agency") and external constraint (one is the agent *of* some other entity). Bowen thus acknowledges the constraints on individual expression imposed by institutional life even as institutions become something more than vehicles of social control; they become the place where the social is produced. One's being an agent is particularly resonant in *The Heat of the Day*, whose characters are indeed all secret agents. In *Bowen's Court*, though, Bowen's rendering of her ancestors as time's agents serves to put a fine point on the extent to which the text constantly works to emphasize the impersonal, collective, and institutional components of character.

The architectural embodiment of the Anglo-Irish institution, for Bowen, is the Big House. She notes "the rule that I have tried, in this book, to keep—the rule of not leaving Bowen's Court for more than a page or two" (392), and unlike the Bowens themselves, Bowen's Court itself is drawn with a high degree of clarity. The first chapter of *Bowen's Court* is largely given over to careful description of the house itself, beginning with the countryside and neighboring towns and growing more focused as it presents the exterior of the house, the various gardens and outbuildings, and a room-by-room account of the layout and furnishings: "Bowen's Court, finished in 1776, is a high bare Italianate house. It was intended to form a complete square, but the north-east corner is missing. Indoors, the plan is simple; the rooms are large, lofty and few. The house stands three stories high, with, below, a basement sunk in an area. Outside the front door a terrace, supported on an unseen arch, bridges the area; from this terrace the steps descend to the gravel sweep" (21). Bowen emphasizes the simplicity and formality of Bowen's Court throughout the passages devoted to it, and the clarity of description in this section contrasts with the vagueness of the language used to discuss individuals. This ordered, transparent writing seems to reflect the form of the house itself and the values institutionalized there, as if conditioned by its subject in the way that the house's inhabitants are conditioned by it: "One must accustom oneself, wherever one settles down, to much space behind one's back, much height over one's head. There are no nooks. Oddly, perhaps, the effect of this is not restless; it is compelling and calm. Steady behavior of *some* sort, even formality, is enjoined by every line of the house" (26).

In "The Bend Back," Bowen writes that "the reader, led into an unfamiliar region of time, must have a key to his whereabouts slipped to him—as unostentatiously as possible" (56), and in this context the intentional lucidity of Bowen's description becomes an extension of style into the past, an attempt to embody in the prose itself the "social idea" of the historical moment of the house's completion. But this clarity has a more immediate, contemporary import as well. "I want Bowen's Court to be taken as existing, and to be seen as clearly as possible" (32), writes Bowen, insisting, in a notably direct tone, on the centrality of the house's continued existence and juxtaposing a prose style that seeks to embody historical formality to an emphasis on the present significance of the object of description. Thus the passage anticipates the later comparison of Henry III's "Philistine" society with "1939," bringing not only disparate times but also disparate senses of temporality—the stylish, impersonal institution that transcends the individual experience of time; the "time being" of war—into close proximity. The past is not called upon to sit in judgment of the present, but to inhabit the present, in the enduring figure of the house, in a way that vivifies both.

Ultimately, though, the formalism of Bowen's institutional thinking is such that she envisions the practices and values that she valorizes as persisting even past the lifetime of the house that had seemed so central to them. This, at least, is the suggestion of the afterword to *Bowen's Court*, which tells how, facing financial ruin, Bowen sold the house in 1959 to a neighboring farmer, who ultimately tore it down. In the last lines, addressing the reader directly, Bowen writes: "Knowing, as you now do, that the house is no longer there, you may wonder why I have left my opening chapter, the room-to-room description of Bowen's Court, in the present tense. I can only say that *I* saw no reason to transpose it into the past. There is a sort of perpetuity about livingness, and it is part of the character of Bowen's Court to be, in sometimes its silent way, very much alive" (459). In part this passage reflects the impermanence that overtook the once reassuringly solid Big Houses, hundreds of which were destroyed in the Irish Civil War. Earlier in the text, Bowen recounts that after the burning of three neighboring houses in the spring of 1921, "I . . . taught myself to imagine Bowen's Court in flames" (440), but in the event, the house's end turns out to be less traumatic; it simply "is no longer there."[31] But the above goes further: not only is the trauma of destruction effaced but it is as though the house had not been destroyed at all, as Bowen's (perhaps faux-naïve) declaration begins to suggest: "*I* saw no reason to transpose it into the past." The house is "very much alive," and the final sentences suggest that the significance of Bowen's Court, and of *Bowen's Court*, lies not in the physical structure of the house, so carefully delineated hundreds of pages (and twenty years) previous, but in the house's "livingness," a nonce term that evokes the Anglo-Irish "form of life" that the text records and theorizes.

Bowen's afterword is itself a reading of the body text of *Bowen's Court* that emphasizes the impersonal and shared aspects of the "social idea" that finds expression in Anglo-Irish collective life as embodied in the Big House. It offers a retrospective comment, twenty-two years after the book's initial publication, on the relationship between the immaterial, formal features of the Anglo-Irish institution—impersonality, style, courage, wit—and the physical reality of Bowen's Court. Critics have tended to run these two components of Bowen's social vision together, treating the house and the institutional form of life that Bowen grounds in it as essentially one presence in her work. As Vera Kreilkamp asserts, in an influential reading, "The emblematic Anglo-Irish Big House, or diminished versions of it, hovers before her characters, yet repeatedly fails them."[32] But in bringing the biography of the house to an end, the afterword to *Bowen's Court* suggests a quite different understanding. As its closing sentences note that the house "is no longer there" even as they insist on the "perpetuity" of its "livingness," they work to disarticulate the immaterial aspects of the institution from their primary physical embodiment. To suggest, as Ellmann does, that "in *Bowen's Court*, architecture shapes personality" (66) is to overlook part of the story; infrastructure is not the whole of the institution, and to the extent that the Big House is for Bowen a vehicle for a set of practices, habits, and values, these last lines suggest that it is not the only possible vehicle. Bowen's Court itself, after all, might be termed sufficient but not necessary to the stylish, impersonal form of life whose development *Bowen's Court* traces around and into it.[33] The Big House and domestic spaces indebted to it appear throughout Bowen's fiction, giving rise to a recurrent critical tendency to read *Bowen's Court* and Bowen's novel of the Troubles, *The Last September*, as the two texts that most overtly reflect on the fate of the Big House as a historical fact.[34] But the afterlife of Anglo-Irish impersonality, I will argue, structures and informs more deeply *The Heat of the Day*, a novel about "a time when all homes were threatened" (*Bowen's Court*, 454).

Institutional Style in *The Heat of the Day*

For Stella Rodney, Bowen's heroine in *The Heat of the Day*, the coming of war is "an opportunity to make a break, to free herself of her house, to come to London to work" (24). Stella married and divorced young; her ex-husband died soon after, and her only child is now, in September of 1942, in the army. But she has fashioned a new life for herself:

> In the years between the wars she had travelled, had for intervals lived abroad: she now qualified by knowing two or three languages, two or three countries, well—having had some idea what she might most usefully do she had, still better, known whom to ask to support her application to do it. She had in her background relations, connections and at least former friends. She was now therefore employed, in an organisation better called Y.X.D., in secret, exacting, not unimportant work, to which the

European position since 1940 gave ever-increasing point. The habit of guardedness was growing on her, as on many other people, reinforcing what was in her an existing bent: she never had asked much, from dislike of being in turn asked. Or, could that have been circumstance?— for by temperament she was communicative and fluctuating. Generous and spirited, to a fault not unfeeling, she was not wholly admirable; but who is? (24–25)

The passage concludes the novel's introduction to Stella, which, for several paragraphs, proceeds in straightforward descriptive prose, beginning with her physical appearance and concluding with these notes on her recent history and current occupation. "Younger by a year or two than the century," she has a "charming" face, "grey" eyes, and a "pale, fine, soft" complexion, made "striking" only by a single lock of white hair "springing back from her forehead" (23–24). Highlighting her world's difference from that of *Bowen's Court,* the cited passage opens by noting that Stella has "freed herself of her house"; what she has replaced it with, as the passage progresses, becomes increasingly difficult to define, and in contrast to her physical description, components of Stella's character are confidently asserted by Bowen's narrator only to fall into generalization or to be withdrawn. She "now qualified by knowing two or three languages, two or three countries, well," but we are not told—nor will we be, in the course of the narrative—exactly what she is qualified for or what languages and countries she knows. Likewise, "what she might most usefully do" and "whom she might ask" will remain largely empty categories, defined, respectively, as "secret, exacting, not unimportant work" and "relations, connections" and the peculiar category of "at least former friends." The narrator's near-passive-aggressive evasiveness aside, we are told that Stella works for "an organisation better called Y.X.D." (but better than what?), and the pseudonymous abbreviation and the secrecy of her work there implicate Y.X.D. in the production of the first positive characteristic attributed to her: her "guardedness."[35] Yet again, a lack of clarity persists: the "organisation" either "reinforces" an "existing bent" or fully generates her guardedness over against her preexistent "communicative and fluctuating" nature.

The knotted prose of the passage, then, finally yields an assurance that Stella's guardedness is in some way a product of the anonymous institution Y.X.D., which distributes this trait across the individuals of which it is composed. But this purely formal assurance is combined with total ambiguity with regard to her innate "temperament": prior to this, did she "never ask much" or was she "communicative and fluctuating"? The novel will never resolve this question. Nor does guardedness itself make Stella particularly distinctive: it "was growing on her, as on many other people." Thus, what purports to be a sketch of an individual undoes itself as it is drawn. It first offers empty placeholders for Stella's background, job, and relationships: she speaks "languages," has visited "countries," knows three indistinct categories of people, and is "employed, in . . . work." It then devolves into the outright contradictions and double negatives that Jacqueline Rose identifies in Bowen as producing characterological traits "with one hand, and then tak[ing] them back syntactically with the other."[36] Offering one account, the narrator suddenly offers the opposite with "Or . . . ?"; in a slightly different way, Stella is "[g]enerous and spirited, to a fault not unfeeling," but these qualities are then rendered contiguous rather than in tension, with her being "not wholly admirable."

Ultimately, I want to suggest here that *Bowen's Court* and *The Heat of the Day* form a unified project that occupied Bowen through the 1940s.[37] Stella may be freed from her house, but these suggestive passages echo *Bowen's Court* in at least two ways, while looking forward to the earlier text's 1964 afterword. They recall *Bowen's Court* at the level of style by condensing into a few paragraphs the shift from deliberate, transparent descriptive sentences to contradictory and syntactically self-consuming constructions that in *Bowen's Court* span many pages, beginning with clarity in rendering the house itself and concluding in the appended afterword with the abstruse formulation of a "perpetuity about livingness." More specifically, the passages recall how character works in *Bowen's Court*, where traits that initially appear to be qualities of, for example, Henry III as a distinct person are in actuality aspects of the Anglo-Irish social idea. As the contradictions and double negatives accumulate in *The Heat of the Day*'s description of Stella, the passage directs our attention back to the "organisation" Y.X.D., the proximate cause of her and others' guardedness. But whereas in *Bowen's Court* the Big House is presented at length as a concrete material structure that serves as a vehicle for the cultivation of impersonal values, Y.X.D. remains undefined and abstract. That it is a wartime institution of the British state there is no doubt, but its secrecy and importance, embodied in the "guardedness" of its constituent individuals, are all that can be known about it. Even its name is not its own: the apparently random letters Y.X.D. could stand in for any of the three-character designations that proliferated in the institutional landscape of World War II Britain (SIS, SOE, MI5, RAF)—indeed, this is the point. Y.X.D. comes to stand in the novel less for a particular institution than for the entire complex of more or less shadowy departments and bureaus that structured wartime life in London for all who remained there as participants in the war effort. These institutions appear in *The Heat of the Day* as names at most. Their anonymity reverberates through characters who are defined by roles in institutions that themselves cannot be described, either by the characters or by the novel's narrator, and whose relationships are mediated by the institutions that form them. What Bowen termed her *"present-day* historical novel" accordingly shuns any sustained concern with politics or the internal workings of these crypto-institutions, exploring instead the impersonal forms of relationship that they enable. The potential to live life at a certain "pitch" (in Bowen's term), figured centrally in the Big House in *Bowen's Court,* is here dispersed across a field of anonymous institutions; in *The Heat of the Day,* as Stella's son Roderick repeats, "everything depends on so much else" (48, 56).

As it establishes the coordinates of character in the novel, Bowen's crypto-institutionalism becomes the condition for the events of its central plot. As the novel opens, Stella is two years into a love affair with Robert Kelway, who, left with an "uncertain knee" after being wounded at Dunkirk, has come to London to work at "the War Office" (97). Much as in the description of Stella herself, their relationship's beginnings are narrated in such a way as to produce the impression of relationality with as little of the content of the relation as possible. The lovers' first meeting, at the height of the Blitz, is "in a bar or club—afterwards they could never remember which" (103). Their first words to each other are overpowered by the "cataracting roar" of a bomb falling on a nearby building: "It was the demolition of an entire moment. . . . What they *had* both been saying, or been on the point of saying, neither of them ever now were to know. . . . What they next said, what they said instead, they forgot: there are questions which if not asked at the start are not asked later; so those they never did ask" (104). It is as though the "demolition" of "the moment" consists in scattering what had been its possible constituent parts across sentences: what they had been saying, what they had been about to say, what they next said, what they said instead, the questions they could have asked—all are evoked but then erased from the text. This erasure, both thematized and enacted by the narrator, enables what would be a momentary impression—"a flash of promise, a background of mystery" (103)—to become the governing atmosphere of Stella and Robert's affair. "It was a characteristic of that life in the moment and for the moment's sake," Bowen writes, "that one knew people well without knowing much about them: vacuum as to future was offset by vacuum as to past; life-stories were shed as so much superfluous weight" (103). If there is the "promise" of new kinds of intimacy in the idea of casting off one's life story as "superfluous weight," there is also the possibility of danger, or "mystery," in the notion that one could "know people well without knowing much about them." The novel's plot traces out this promise and danger.

The promise of impersonal love is the other side of the terror of the Blitz. *The Heat of the Day* delineates how the threat to life from German bombs and the demands placed on each individual by incorporation into the British war machine create a "particular conjunction of life and death" (100). It was a "heady," "sweet autumn"; against the "tenseness of evening. . . . [Y]ou felt more and more called upon to observe the daytime as a pure and curious holiday from fear" (98). "Never had any season been more felt," Bowen writes; "one bought the poetic sense of it with the sense of death." Descriptive terms accumulate to evoke a mood: *heady, sweet, tense, poetic*. This mood runs up against the continual pressure of regulated, institutional work: "In offices, factories, ministries, shops, kitchens the hot yellow sands of each afternoon ran out slowly; fatigue was the one reality" (99). With proximity to the dead increasing with each night's casualties, "[t]he wall between the living and the living became less solid. . . . In that September transparency people became transparent" (99–100). The sustained tension of wartime life and the circumstances of evacuated London perform what Bowen in "The Big House" calls "the subjugation of the personal," producing as compensation "an easy and unsuspicious intercourse, to which everyone brought the best they had":

> To be at work built her up, and when not at work she was being gay in company whose mood was at the pitch of her own—society became lovable; it had the temperament of the stayers-on in London. The existence, surrounded by one another, of these people she nightly saw was fluid, easy, holding inside itself a sort of ideality of pleasure. . . . This was the new society of one kind of wealth, resilience, living how it liked—people whom the climate of danger suited, who began, even, all to look a

little alike, as they might in the sun, snows and altitude of the same sports station, or browning along the same beach in the South of France. The very temper of pleasures lay in their chanciness, in the canvaslike impermanence of their settings, in their being off-time. . . . Faces came and went. There was a diffused gallantry in the atmosphere, an unmarriedness: it came to be rumoured about the country, among the self-banished, the uneasy, the put-upon and the safe, that everybody in London was in love—which was true, if not in the sense the country meant. (102–3)

"Built up" by work, Stella finds that people have become "transparent" or have begun "all to look a little alike"; rather than lending heightened definition to individual personalities, wartime makes individuals interchangeable ("Faces came and went"). If the interchangeability of persons is sobering to contemplate in the face of mass death, it nonetheless frees its subjects from personal concern into a "diffused gallantry." The anonymity and impersonality of institutions, individuals, and social intercourse opens a space for ephemerality, for "living how it liked," for a new kind of "love"—in short, for the development of a style of living.[38] While Heather Bryant Jordan argues that in *The Heat of the Day* "a world at war . . . invades and poisons the love affair between the central figures," these passages suggest the opposite—that the impersonal world actually makes possible what occurs between Stella and Robert: "the continuous narrative of love . . . kept gaining substance, shadow, consistency from the imperfectly known and the not-said" (108); that narrative builds on the impersonality at its heart.[39] Stella and Robert's story, a product of the crypto-institutional setting of wartime, has a precedent in literary history: in *Bowen's Court* the Big House, "like Flaubert's ideal book about nothing . . . sustains itself on itself by the inner force of its style" (21), while the love affair in *The Heat of the Day*, "like the ideal book about nothing, stayed itself on itself by its inner force" (97).

While the novel's love story could not take the form it does without the mediation of London's anonymous institutions, this same logic of anonymity brings it under threat. The central crisis of *The Heat of the Day* is initiated by Harrison, a vague but unpleasant figure who, through an apparently chance meeting, insinuates himself into Stella's life. As the novel opens, he has impressed upon Stella the necessity of his meeting with her at her flat, where he delivers an accusation and offers her a bargain. Robert Kelway, Harrison says, is a spy passing secrets to the enemy. Harrison is part of the agency charged with patrolling such activity; in fact, he himself is in charge of monitoring Robert, and he has the power to determine whether Robert will be arrested or allowed to remain free. "A lot could happen to him," he says, "at any moment—which would be too bad, eh? As against which, it might not. If you and I could arrange things, things might be arranged" (34–35). Through such empty oppositions and tautologies, it emerges that if Stella breaks with Robert and takes up with Harrison, Harrison in turn will not have Robert arrested. As Stella says, "You propose that by becoming your mistress I buy out a man, in whom I have an interest, who is by your showing dangerous to the country" (41). Harrison is less definite: he wants "[y]ou to give me a break. Me to come here, be here, in and out of here, on and off—at the same time, always. To be in your life, as they call it—your life, just as it is" (31). "Is it so odd I should want a place of my own?" he asks (34).

Harrison's blackmail opens the time frame in which the bulk of *The Heat of the Day* takes place, on "the first Sunday of September 1942" (4). The novel's chronology can be baffling—it looks back at various points, with only fleeting indicators of the shifts, to autumn 1940 and May 1942 before concluding in February 1944, during the "Little Blitz"—and the disorientation this creates serves as ample illustration of how the time of war could become a "tideless, hypnotic, futureless day-to-day" (109). Thus it is jarring to realize the precision with which Bowen pins the story's central events to a specific period of just over two months, concluding with "the Allied landings in North Africa" (November 8, 1942) and "the Sunday set for victorious bell-ringing" (presumably November 15) (327). For Stella, the novel's present is a period of Hamlet-like indecision, brought on by Harrison's unproven but confidently asserted mastery of the situation. If she tells Robert that he is suspected, Harrison says, those watching him will know that he has been informed and he will be brought in: "I've never yet known a man not change his behavior once he's known he's watched; it's exactly changes like that that are being watched for" (37). On the other hand, if Stella, who is "not a woman who does not know where to go" (41), should turn Harrison in, she can bring him down, but she will have brought Robert down with him, as it will be assumed by "a number of people" (42) that Robert has been told as well. If all these conditions are true, she is trapped; if they are not, as she repeatedly tells herself, she should turn Harrison in. But Stella hedges.

In the course of this standoff, the irony of Harrison's desire for "a place of my own" becomes clear: Harrison is everywhere. The catch-22 he presents to Stella relies on a level of surveillance that no individual could possibly be capable of, and yet he comes to appear to be the singular, uncannily acute agent of that surveillance. When Stella travels to Robert's family home, a dreadful Edwardian villa in the Home Counties that the Kelways call Holme Dene, Harrison immediately knows where she has been, appearing on her doorstep as she returns from, as he puts it, going "to look at the first place where the rot could start" (144). In rationed London, he always has an excess of matches and flashlight batteries, suggesting that he does in fact occupy the high-level role that he implies he does (140–41). And he repeatedly offers unimpeachable accounts of how he has proceeded in framing his plot that nonetheless give nothing in particular away. All these factors combine to justify Stella's hesitation, but Harrison's identity—at least his identity insofar as he is the counterspy he claims to be—is confirmed when he reveals to Stella that he knows the exact moment in which she finally *has* told Robert: "That night you got back from Ireland" (260). Indeed, after returning from a trip to Ireland, Stella has confronted Robert with Harrison's accusation, only to have it denied (210–12). Told now that, as predicted, Robert's behavior has changed, Stella realizes that Harrison has been telling the truth; she implicitly offers Harrison what he initially demanded as ransom, but he refuses. Late the same night, Stella again confronts Robert, who admits that he is a German spy. Convinced that her apartment is being watched and that his time is running short, he insists on making an escape across the rooftops, despite his bad knee. As Stella closes the door behind him and returns to her apartment, "[i]n the street below, not so much a step as the semi-stumble of someone after long standing shifting his position could be, for the first time by her, heard" (326). These are the last words of the chapter, and they indicate that Robert has in fact been tailed; but in a resolution delayed across the chapter break, he dies in a "fall or leap from the roof" (327).

Each turn of the plot around Robert, Stella, and Harrison thus hinges on the novel's crypto-institutional logic. Compelled by their work at Y.X.D. and the War Office to be silent about so much, Stella and Robert can have only an imperfect knowledge of each other—as Harrison says, "He's, as you know, at the War Office—that's probably all you do know" (35)—much as that same silence, adopted by the narrator, allows the reader only an imperfect knowledge of them; this is what lends their relationship its "promise" and "mystery." But just as impersonality enables new forms of love, it also enables new forms of treachery. As Stella says to Harrison, "If it only were that you loved me, I could do no worse than not love you back; but there has been something worse—somehow you've distorted love" (156). Stella and Robert's love relies on unspoken assumptions based on the merely formal knowledge that they have of each other's character, assumptions about trustworthiness that, in time of war, they never have to interrogate and that issue from the institutions they occupy. Harrison "distorts" this situation by both inhabiting it himself and turning its logic against Stella by invoking the institution of which he is a part: "You've bludgeoned me with your perpetual 'we'—your 'we' is my 'they,'" she says, exasperated (41). Harrison's effect on the plot is predicated on his being part of that "we," the intelligence agency; Stella's hesitation, on the impossibility of knowing for sure whether he is. His seeming omnipresence and omniscience are the conditions for his threats being credible, and despite these qualities' unlikeliness, they turn out to be real—as far as the plot is concerned, Harrison appears to be everywhere and know everything—to be the intelligence agency incarnate. From Stella's viewpoint, "he was as a character 'impossible'—each time they met, for instance, he showed no shred or trace of having been continuous since they last met. . . . [T]he uninterestingly right state of what he wore seemed less to argue physical care—brushing, pressing, changes of linen—than a physical going into abeyance, just as he was, with everything he had on him, between appearances" (155). Harrison is, as *Bowen's Court* suggests it is possible to be, not only the intelligence agency's product but also its agent. As with Conrad's chief engineer, his being is entirely contiguous with the outlines of his "inhuman" institutional home, the intelligence agency, and Stella experiences his attentions as those of an institution rather than of an individual: "His concentration on her was made more oppressive by his failure to have or let her give him any possible place in the human scene" (155). As Ellmann puts it, "He is 'a character "impossible"' because he represents a switchboard rather than a personality, a link to a vast invisible bureaucracy" (168). Ellmann suggests that Robert is also impossible in this sense, "a spy-ring rather than a single spy" (168), but even this does not go far enough. Stella too is "impossible"; all these characters and their connections depend on links to some "vast invisible bureaucracy"—invisible to them and to us, even as its presence is the condition for the narrative itself.

Thus, when we have seen how crypto-institutionalism "thin[s] the wall between the living and the living," it comes as no surprise to see this dynamic "distorted" too. While part of the "pleasure" of wartime London is that "people . . . began, even, all to look a little alike," Stella is disturbed to realize that in hedging and delaying she has begun to turn into Harrison. "You succeed in making a spy of me," she tells him (152). The second time Harrison appears at Stella's apartment, they find themselves standing next to each other looking out over the city: "two persons speechlessly at a window became as anonymous as the city they overlooked. These two, though fated to speak again, could be felt to be depersonalized speakers in a drama" (154). As Stella hesitates to bring her situation with Robert to a crisis, she and Harrison develop their own strange intimacy. He fetches her a glass of milk (145); she asks him to post a package that she has brought for a relative of Robert's (147). Presuppositions about who one might trust (a lover) or not trust (a blackmailer) undergo a slow reversal. Desire for the impersonal lover depends on imperfect knowledge, while the blackmailer holds out the possibility of certitude with regard to at least one question: whether or not he can follow through on his threat. Their inversion is condensed and completed when Robert confirms that he has been a spy throughout his affair with Stella: "It seemed to her it was Robert who had been the Harrison" (310). And predictably enough, at the end of the novel it is also Harrison who has been the Robert: "I don't know your other, your Christian name," Stella says. "What's wrong with it—what is it?" "Robert," he replies (362). Their last words in this exchange, conducted during the "Little Blitz" of February 1944, hold open the possibility that, after all, the terms Harrison originally requested will be fulfilled: Stella, though now engaged to a distant cousin, asks him to stay; he seems to refuse, but the scene closes with "Harrison looking at his watch. 'Or would you rather I stayed till the All Clear?'" (363).

Stella's becoming a "spy," and the exchange of places between Harrison and Robert Kelway, are only two instances of the games *The Heat of the Day* plays with names and doubling: the novel features two Victors, two Roberts, a Roderick Rodney, and a Louie Lewis. At one point, Harrison is called "Robertson" (354), while Roderick is told he looks "more like yourself" wearing Robert's bathrobe (49) and is referred to as "Robert" (89). Neil Corcoran refers to this replication of characters and traits as Bowen's "*doppelganger* effect" (180) and points out the "Irish watermark" on the novel's doublings, which recall the interchangeable names of Bowen patriarchs in *Bowen's Court* and the fact that had Bowen herself been born a boy, she would have been named Robert.[40] Andrew Bennett and Nicholas

Royle argue that through its doublings and mergers the novel mounts an "explicitly historical" "affirmation of the undecidability of identity" as a condition of the emergence of the political.[41] There certainly is an Anglo-Irish "watermark" on *The Heat of the Day*, but as I have sought to emphasize, the novel's Anglo-Irishness inheres less in its thematic or biographical echoes of that history than in its characterological investment in impersonality, which Bowen locates in Anglo-Ireland in *Bowen's Court* but redeploys here, pushing it to ends that look very different from those of the social idea developed in the Big House. If Anglo-Ireland's failure to keep up the social idea led to the descent into mere "personal life"—the production of selves overstuffed with nothing of significance—in wartime the threat runs in the opposite direction, to the destruction of selves, and not necessarily by bombing. In one of the novel's few explicit references to a particular institution, Stella "fear[s] that the Army was out to obliterate Roderick. In the course of a process, a being processed, she could do nothing to stop, her son might possibly disappear" (50). Likewise, while the institutional impersonality of *The Heat of the Day* is certainly historical, as Bennett and Royle argue, it is the product of two quite specific histories—of Anglo-Ireland and wartime London—colliding in the text, and it is difficult to find anything there that would amount to a straightforward affirmation of its crypto-institutionalism, which, as I have argued, ultimately produces both the promise of style and impersonality and the danger or "distortion" attendant on the unavoidability of wartime secrecy.

Bowen's crypto-institutionalism incorporates none of the political meaning of, for example, Mulk Raj Anand's institutional picaresque, which finds the promise of amelioration and accountability in the way that institutions might theoretically render many details of individual identity irrelevant. Indeed, it is precisely the institutional position Harrison occupies that renders him unaccountable (to any other character in the novel, at least), and the one directly narrated scene of institutional accountability, Stella's deposition in the coroner's court after Robert's death, has no bearing on the novel's plot. The deposition is presented as a monologue: "I cannot say, I'm afraid; I did not notice. . . . No, I do not remember drinking more heavily than usual. . . . As far as I know, absolutely clear: I remember everything" (341). Stella never has to deny knowledge of Robert's spying, as it is in no one's interest to mention it, and the narration reinforces institutional anonymity by placing ellipses where the voice of the institution's representative would be. Stella herself never learns the truth, as "the silence from behind the scenes never broke" (340), and she leaves the court "with one kind of reputation, that of being a good witness" (344), only to have a different reputation circulated in the press, that of being "the woman friend in the luxury flat" (340). There are hints here of a greater danger than that of having one's identity destroyed; worse, perhaps, is to have it stolen and disseminated in an unrecognizable form through unaccountable institutions.

If, by this point, the impersonal social idea of Anglo-Irish institutional life seems, as does Stella, to have "come loose" from its "moorings" (125), those moorings remain in the novel in residual form through Mount Morris, a Big House that Roderick has inherited. Its owner, Stella's cousin Francis Morris, is dead when the novel begins; his wife, Nettie, has for many years lived in a small, quiet mental hospital. Cousin Francis's funeral is where Stella and Harrison first meet—Harrison knows Cousin Francis, a political dilettante, through unnamed machinations related to Irish neutrality. Stella spent her honeymoon at Mount Morris, and it has been left to Roderick, though he never met Cousin Francis, "in the hope that he may care in his own way to carry on the old tradition" (95). The house is important for Roderick, who, long pegged as "one of the dreamy ones who get by somehow" (53), is given purpose and definition by his inheritance: without his having seen it, the house becomes for him "a habitat" (97). Bowen writes that "the house came out to meet his growing capacity for attachment.... The house, nonhuman, became the hub of his imaginary life" (52). Initially an unpromising soldier, under the influence of this imagined Mount Morris he, "having bestirred himself, obtained his commission in the autumn of 1943" (339). And his first visit to the house, walking the grounds at night, leaves him "deeply stirred" (350): "The place had concentrated upon Roderick its being: this was the hour of the never-before—gone were virgin dreams with anything they had had of himself in them, anything they had had of the picturesque, sweet, easy, strident. He was left possessed, oppressed, and in awe. He heard the pulse in his temple beating into the pillow; he was followed by the sound of his own footsteps over his own land. The consummation woke in him, for the first time, the concept and fearful idea of death, his" (352). As the house "concentrated upon Roderick its being," it recalls Bowen's Court, which, "with a rather alarming sureness . . . has made all the succeeding Bowens." The exaltation of inheritance leads him to the "idea of death, his," and with it an awareness that he might live for something that transcends his individual existence. In this way Mount Morris becomes a refuge from the depredations of wartime and "personal life." This effect is heightened by Mount Morris's juxtaposition to the Kelway family house, Holme Dene, which the Kelways put up for sale as soon as it was built. Holme Dene is surrounded by garden gnomes, lawn furniture, and "vegetables of the politer kind" (115). Robert's mother, "Muttikins," his sister Ernestine, and her children speak to each other in baby talk and fawn over pets: "I often think," Ernestine piously intones, "that if Hitler could have looked into that dog's eyes, the story might have been very different" (137). Here, architecture and character *are* directly implicated in each other, and the shallowness of the house's sham Tudor design both expresses and shapes the falsity of its inhabitants. *The Heat of the Day* links Robert's Quislingism directly to his search for a way out of the house's "swastika-arms of passage leading to nothing" (289) and the "class without a middle" (307) into which he was born.[42]

Against Holme Dene's fraudulence, the apparent authenticity of Roderick's possession of and by Mount Morris and the organic resonance of "his own footsteps over his own land" can seem like a reanimation of Bowen's Anglo-Irish social idea in the location from whence it originally came. Many readers of the novel have found this problematic. Vera Kreilkamp suggests that while Bowen's *The Last September* (1929) offers a subversive view of the Big House that acknowledges the violence of its colonial history, the later novel steps back from this critical stance into a complacent conservatism. As Kreilkamp argues, "In *The Heat of the Day*, where Bowen's revulsion against contemporary society engenders a powerful nostalgia, her hierarchy of values often slides into a familiar Yeatsian worship of social lineage and inherited property" (162). This seems a fair assessment only if we take the figure of the Big House as the sole embodiment of the Anglo-Irish ideal in Bowen's fiction, and if we see her as participating alongside Yeats in a cultural revitalization of that ideal.

As I have argued, though, Anglo-Ireland's social idea migrates in *The Heat of the Day* to the crypto-institutional field of wartime London, a move enabled by Bowen's refusal of Yeats's cultural nationalism in favor of an impersonal account of Anglo-Irish institutional life. Accordingly, Bowen's portrayal of Mount Morris is more equivocal than Kreilkamp's reading credits. The house is empty except for the caretaker, Donovan, and his two daughters; nothing "social" happens there anymore.

Roderick, though actualized by his inheritance, finds that its terms resist interpretation: "Does he mean, that I'm free to care in any way I like, so long as it's *the* tradition I carry on; or, that so long as I care in the same way he did, I'm free to mean by 'tradition' anything I like?" (95). And Stella, visiting the house to begin settling its affairs in Roderick's absence, holds up a lamp to see her face in the drawing-room mirror and "became for a moment immortal as a portrait. Momentarily she was the lady of the house" (193). From this imaginative vantage she briefly feels the suffering that accompanied the decline of the Anglo-Irish ideal, especially for women: "After all, was it not chiefly here in this room and under this illusion that Cousin Nettie Morris—and who now knew how many more before her?—had been pressed back, hour by hour, by the hours themselves, into cloudland? Ladies had gone not quite mad, not quite even that, from in vain listening for meaning in the loudening ticking of the clock" (193). Stella herself "turned away from" the house's "judgement," unable to imagine herself trapped as Mount Morris's previous female inhabitants had been. When she puts the lamp down, the reflection vanishes, and she thinks, "that was that" (194), acknowledging with a gesture that that form of life, which in its decline had become so constrictive, is gone. What remains is a thread of potential: "There was still to be seen what came of Cousin Francis's egotistic creative boldness with regard to the future, of his requisitioning for that purpose of Roderick" (194). Far from conservative nostalgia, these passages acknowledge that the social idea that once fueled life at Mount Morris, for better and for worse, has departed; like character itself in *The Heat of the Day*, the Big House is evoked only to be emptied out.[43] The last gasp of Anglo-Irish "egotistic creative boldness," with its echoes of Henry Bowen, the Builder, is enough to hand the house on; but the ambiguity of Cousin Francis's will, which so puzzles Roderick, speaks to the empty future to which that passing-on opens. The novel gives no hint as to whether Roderick will survive the Allied invasion of Europe that marks the end of the narrative, or what will become of the house if he does. But the stylish and impersonal form of life that flourished there centuries before has fled elsewhere.

From Wartime to the Program Era

Bowen began her career migrating from civil-war-scarred Ireland to Bloomsbury in the 1920s; she would end it as a writer of international repute, regularly traveling to the United States to teach and lecture in the English departments of a dozen or so universities. *The Heat of the Day* concludes the key period in that career—"her noon," the wartime 1940s. Many of the short stories that Bowen published during the war read like studies in miniature of the structures and themes that Bowen explores at length in the novel. "Careless Talk," only four pages long, depicts almost entirely through dialogue a lunch meeting between Joanna, exiled to the countryside, and her friends Mary Dash, Edward, and Ponsonby. Having presented Mary with three delicate eggs, unobtainable in the city, Joanna is bewildered by the rush of conversation among the other three and finds herself with nothing to contribute to the high-octane exchange of names and insider references in which they engage. "These days everything's frightfully interesting," Mary says. "Joanna, you must be feeling completely dazed."[44] The narrator of "Green Holly," a ghost story set in a country house converted for wartime use, enacts a literalized version of crypto-institutionalism: the three main characters "were Experts—in what, the censor would not permit me to say."[45] Both stories briefly put institutional character and the excitement of wartime that Bowen captures through it to comic use.

More interestingly, Bowen's short story "The Happy Autumn Fields" links the London of the Blitz to Victorian Anglo-Ireland. The narrative opens in the nineteenth century in a Big House where Sarah and her sister Henrietta await the arrival of Sarah's suitor, Eugene, whose presence threatens the bond between the two sisters. Suddenly the scene shifts to a bombed-out house in wartime London, where a sleeper named Mary wakes up, distraught to find that she is herself and not the Sarah she was in the dream. Before falling asleep, she had found a box of letters and family heirlooms that seem to have prompted her dream. Her fiancé, Travis, encourages her to get up and leave the house, but she goes back to sleep, becoming Sarah again. Henrietta accuses Eugene, who has not declared his love for Sarah, of "making something terrible happen" (683), and the inhabitants of the drawing room turn to Sarah, when another bomb strikes near the house in London and Mary awakes for good, in tears. "How are we to live without natures?" she asks Travis. "So much flowed through people; so little flows through us. All we can do is imitate love or sorrow" (684). But Mary's sense that she is descended from Sarah is wrong; Travis has read the letters while she slept, he says, and discovered that Sarah and Henrietta remained unmarried, while Eugene died young in a fall from his horse. The letter's author, Travis says, "wonders, and will always wonder, what made the horse shy in those empty fields" (685).

Maud Ellmann argues that this story, showing as it does that tragedy could strike without reason in the seemingly golden past as much as in the wartime present, functions as a commentary on the insufficiency of the Anglo-Irish ethos. As she argues, "Mary projects on to the past her fantasies of plenitude and equipoise," but "the horse that throws its rider in the empty field proves that terror can rise up without a bomb.... [T]he literature of [wartime] can no longer rely on the old certainties of time or place" (172). Thus "The Happy Autumn Fields" would echo the emptying out of the Big House that I have argued is enacted in *The Heat of the Day*. But Ellmann does not note another, minor presence in the wartime scene of the story. Asked by Mary who is playing a piano in an exploded house down the street, Travis replies, "Oh, one of the furniture movers in Number Six. I didn't count the jacquerie; of course *they're* in possession—unsupervised, teeming, having a high old time.... You know there's a workman downstairs lying on your blue sofa looking for pictures in one of your French books?" (677). The workmen are pointed out, but they play no role in the drama unfolding in Mary's dream or between Mary and Travis. Present but unaffected by the ostensible main thread of the narrative, they "don't count." But keeping in mind the story's near allegorization of the concerns of *The Heat of the Day*, the "jacquerie" of "The Happy Autumn Fields" also reflect the situation of the novel's final subplot, that of Louie Lewis and her friend Connie.

Louie speaks in the novel's first dialogue, trying to attach herself to Harrison as he sits thinking in Regent's Park, and the novel closes two years later on her, holding up her newborn son to watch as three swans pass overhead, "disappearing in the direction of the West" (372). At its beginning Louie's husband, Tom, is in India; her parents have been killed by a bomb in the Battle of Britain. In the course of the novel Louie goes to work in a factory, briefly befriends Stella in a restaurant on the night that she learns of Robert's betrayal, gets pregnant in an anonymous encounter, and learns of Tom's death; her child will be named Thomas Victor, combining the names, coincidentally, of her and Stella's dead husbands. Louie is, as Hermione Lee puts it, "lonely, naively promiscuous, weepy and silly" (183), though as Lee argues, she embodies the part of England "left out of count by Robert's ideology—the unconscious natural will to survive and produce life" (184). More than this, though, Louie and Connie—Louie's friend and neighbor, an air raid precautions warden eternally dressed in "dark-blue official slacks," with a "postbox mouth" (163) taken straight from Dickens—don't "count," just as the workmen of "The Happy Autumn Fields" don't count. They are in but not of the novel's institutional world, essentially comic, and all too personal. Louie herself is physically constituted by the newspapers:

> But it was from the articles in the papers that the real build-up, the alimentation came. Louie, after a week or two on the diet, discovered that she *had* got a point of view, and not only *a* point of view but the right one. . . . Was she not a worker, a soldier's lonely wife, a war orphan, a pedestrian, a Londoner, a home and animal-lover, a thinking democrat, a movie-goer, a woman of Britain, a letter-writer, a fuel-saver and a housewife? . . . Louie now felt bad only about any part of herself which in any way did not fit into the papers' picture: she could not have survived their disapproval. (168–69)

Louie comes to recognize herself through the "alimentation" of her newspaper "diet"; without it "she could not have survived." Her dependency on a less figurative form of institutional sustenance is reinforced at the novel's end, when, taken in hand by the wartime state, she gives birth to her son and "departed from the very door of the hospital into abeyance in a Midland county" (371). Crypto-institutional form, which linked *The Heat of the Day* to Bowen's Anglo-Irish ideal, does not operate here; the deleterious effects of the Civil Defence Service, the health service, and the media on individual character are rendered with stark clarity. Absent too is the sheen of style and gallantry that settles on the characters of the novel's central plot line. Louie and Connie thus point beyond the novel to the postwar period, registering Bowen's skepticism about the legacy of wartime in the welfare state.

Not long after the war ended, Bowen wrote to her friend William Plomer: "I have adored England since 1940 because of the stylishness Mr. Churchill gave it, but I've always felt, 'When Mr. Churchill goes, I go.' I can't stick all these middle-class Labour wets with their Old London School of Economics ties and their women. Scratch any of those cuties and you find the governess."[46] Given the disdain for the avatars of state planning that drips from these lines, it may seem puzzling that Bowen's wartime novel is so invested in a crypto-institutional style whose ultimate referent, though occluded, is the state—especially given the historical continuity between the wartime expansion of government and its increased reach in the era of the welfare state. Why was the state in the first context electrifying—what was "stylish" about Churchill?—and in the second deadening? Bowen's apparent affirmation across her literary writing of both the Big House *and* the intelligence service as homes for a social idea and her fixation on Churchill's "style" suggest an evaluation of all the institutions in her writing less in terms of their ability to foster collective change or justice (or even to preserve tradition) and more for the opportunities they afford individuals to develop impersonal, stylish, exciting, and gallant ways of living.

The basic conservatism of this sensibility does not object to state power as such. What elicited from Bowen "the authentic rhetoric of reaction" (Glendinning's terms), and what she found impossible to assimilate to an institutional imagination formed by the Anglo-Irish social idea, was institutions' simply providing concrete social goods rather than opportunities for individuals to live at a heightened "pitch." Perhaps because her concept of the institution was based in the maintenance of the Anglo-Irish elite, a small fraction at their peak, Bowen presents a markedly different evaluation of the role of the state from that of her close friend Isaiah Berlin, who broadly favored welfare reforms precisely because they promised to deliver positive liberties to an increasing population.[47] Thus Bowen could find the postwar welfare state stultifying, while writing enthusiastically, on a journalistic assignment in postwar Germany, of the single-mindedness and determination of German students, enabled by the state-run universities. Those universities' administrative structure and social role she delves into in great detail in a 1954 essay titled "Without Coffee, Cigarettes, or Feeling," which reaches a crescendo with the follow points: "Young Germany, and most of all its students, has what maybe the young of the democracies lack just now—a vast, commanding, and to them noble incentive. Everything that they do counts; everything they give themselves to matters. True, one is only young once, and some of what should be youth's pleasures are passing by them. But is it not one's ideals which make life worthwhile and, by doing so, keep one happy? *Their* ideal is single—it is recovery."[48] Elsewhere, she writes that "in spite of these deprivations, 'life' as one understands it does spring up. . . . In each place, the students *could* be felt to be a community, within which existed sympathies and attractions, shared points of view and exchanged secrets" (94). Visiting the state-run university, Bowen rediscovers in the hard-pressed German students both the suppression of personality and the richness of collective life that she had previously located in Anglo-Ireland and wartime London.

Bowen's sympathy for the German students, and for their schools, may have grown out of her own experiences in the expanding postwar world of international literary culture. The ethos of Anglo-Irish impersonality that she developed in her work of the 1940s found another institutional home in the later decades of her life: the American university.[49] In late 1950, her American publisher, Blanche Knopf, arranged for Bowen to visit and lecture at a number of colleges and universities. From a base in New York, she spent several months crisscrossing the United States, meeting students and faculty and establishing contacts at a wide range of schools. This initial trip involved visits to Williams, Amherst, and Reed College and the universities of Kansas, Washington, Illinois, and Oregon. She spent weeks and sometimes months at a time in the United States over the next decade and a half, delivering lectures on multiple occasions at Stanford and the University of Chicago and spending time at Berkeley, the University of Wisconsin, the University of Pennsylvania, and Bryn Mawr. Few of these arrangements were full-semester teaching positions, but Bowen's presence in US English departments was substantial enough that in 1963, when Knopf planned to nominate Bowen for the Nobel Prize in Literature, she wrote to faculty and chairs of the departments that had hosted Bowen to solicit letters of support.[50] Bowen frequently cultivated friendships with young men; Glendinning notes that she did so particularly in her final visit to Princeton, where she taught for the fall semester of 1969.[51]

Bowen's enthusiasm for American campuses might be surprising. She wrote to Charles Ritchie upon her arrival at Wisconsin in the spring of 1958:

> It's a bouncy exhilarating existence, and the vast size of the place and the thousands of streaming figures in constant motion are *un*-claustrophobic. There's a strange blend of extreme friendliness and total uncuriosity which suits me. I *do* see the point of the Middle West. I have been several times enough to acclimatize. Its complete self-centredness and self-sufficiency, its immense remoteness in space *and* ideas from anywhere else is the outstanding thing....

> The university itself is a Pentecostal mixture of races. The students I work with in my 3 classes are of extremely various kinds. They are good-humoured and good-looking, but chiefly I'm glad to say, as that's to the point, *clever:* quick on the uptake....
>
> In fact, this *is* quite a university. My two chums so far are 2 New Englanders called Mr Presson and Mr Forker, who like going out drinking and going to the movies: we have had several pleasant evenings around the town....[52]

Nothing, one would think, could be further from Henry III's house in County Cork than US higher education in the heyday of the "multiversity."[53] Yet Bowen's language in her letters from Wisconsin—and other schools where she spoke or was on the faculty—is imbued with the same deep valuation of variety, freedom, and style that she carried out of Anglo-Ireland to London in the forties. The university is "*un*-claustrophobic," with a recognizably impersonal blend of "extreme friendliness" and "total uncuriosity"; Bowen's joy at finding cleverness, humor, and good looks among her students is palpable. Bowen assesses institutions, and institutional character, positively when they enable these forms of pleasure and excitement. The novels she produced gave her entrée, along with innumerable other writers, into the large institutions of culture in the postwar era, which supported her continued embrace of those values of style and pleasure for the remainder of her career. Bowen's concept of the institution thus evades politics—despite her own engagement in the political life of her time—by conceiving of institutions in essentially aesthetic terms. The ersatz aristocratic formation that produced these insights and aesthetic innovations, though, also produces in Bowen's work (and outlook) an opposition to the kinds of collective change promoted by an activist state in peacetime. Indeed, Bowen seems not to have thought of the welfare state as an institution at all, at least not in the sense in which she thought of Anglo-Ireland, the wartime state, or the American university as institutions that produce character and ways of living. Bowen's aestheticization of institutions might warn us to beware of our own presuppositions as we seek to formulate theories of institutional life adequate to its complexity today—to find ways not only of bringing to light the collective commitments of institutions but also of affirming them.

CONCLUSION

The Institution as Promise and Limit

OVER THE course of this book, I have argued that to fully understand the modernist novel we must learn to read its representation of institutions. Doing so requires renewing and broadening our attention to the concept of character—to see it as an aspect of literary form through which the social world is represented but also, secondarily, as a repertoire of strategies and modes of presentation on which writers themselves have drawn to forge their own careers. Character in the works I have examined here is institutional: it inheres in individuals but also in the large collective structures within which individuals exist and move. As I have suggested, this understanding of character deprivileges the development of the individual and thus deprivileges as well the tropes of "biographical form" and the bildungsroman.[1] Works like *Nostromo*, *The Years*, *Coolie*, and *The Heat of the Day* largely reject the satisfying closures of biographical form, and when they turn inward they tend not to find an exceptional consciousness or unique perceptual schemes. Instead, they reveal individuals' constitutive involvement in collective life.

By revealing character in the modernist novel as more social than we might have imagined, my aim here has also been to reconnect twentieth-century modernism to the realist impulse to which the history of the novel persists in seeing modernism as opposed. I follow Joseph Cleary and others in taking the modernist novel, and the imperial contexts from which it issued, as in part a "sublation" of national realisms.[2] Working from literary form to historiography, reasserting the modernist novel's continuities with its predecessors also allows us to reconsider the non-literary histories with which literature is engaged and to perceive the less progressive, more varied story of the twentieth century woven through the overlapping plot lines and institutional characters of these novels.

While this book takes an expansive understanding of modernism as given, there is also value in considering more strictly defined accounts of modernist style and periodization in evaluating what institutional character's legacy in the present might be. That legacy is especially pertinent given that in light of late-twentieth- and twenty-first-century developments in media and digital technology the idea of the institution might seem reduced against, say, the idea of the *network*. David James and Urmila Seshagiri have argued for a more definitional account, arguing for a "rigorous periodization" of modernism's origins and gesturing to the significance in contemporary fiction of writers who "style their twenty-first-century literary innovations as explicit engagements with the innovations of early-twentieth-century writing."[3] This book opened with the work of E. M. Forster, so it might be fitting to close with the work of the most Forsterian of contemporary novelists, Zadie Smith. Smith's 2006 *On Beauty* riffs on Forster's *Howards End*; *NW*, from 2012, pays extensive homage to the fragmentation, narrative games, and interiority of Joyce and Woolf; and her agenda-setting 2007 essay "Two Paths for the Novel"—one of the most significant critical statements of the aughts—calls for a reconsideration of modernist and avant-garde writing. Smith's writing is among the best places to begin to find modernist narrative's legacy in the present.

Less noted than the ways that Smith's writing engages with modernist styles, though, is the way that her novels circle around and return repeatedly to one particular institution: the university. This might seem surprising, since only *On Beauty* takes a campus as its primary setting. That novel's Wellington College is of a type immediately recognizable to US American readers, if actually inhabited by a much more limited number of them (though many of *those* are readers of Smith's novels): elite, northeastern, ivy-covered, and largely white. Wellington is an institution that keeps people *out*—because of their race, their class background, or what its dean of humanities delicately calls "the educational situation of economically disadvantaged young people." But it is also not always clear why one would want to get *in*. *On Beauty* is a campus satire: subtle, at times affectionate, but frequently razor sharp. On the one hand, as the epigraph to the novel's second section intones, "A university is among the precious things that can be destroyed."[4] On the other, as the teenaged Levi Belsey thinks to himself, "In universities people forgot how to live" (406). Yet despite its importance to *On Beauty*, Wellington College is perhaps the least representative university in Smith's universe.

In fact, elsewhere in the novels a different kind of institution can be glimpsed, one more recognizably part of a multicultural postwar Britain. In *NW*, Keisha Blake, unable to afford the train tickets for interviews at Manchester and Edinburgh, ends up in a sleepy provincial school, in "a 60s-build dormitory of indifferent architectural design," trailed by the boyfriend who has followed her from their council estate in London.[5] The unnamed narrator of *Swing Time* (2016) finds herself in her "second-choice university . . . half a mile from the gray English Channel."[6] In Smith's debut, *White Teeth* (2000), the warring brothers Millat and Magid meet after eight years in a university building in their old neighborhood, in "a room used for study. . . . Contents: one blackboard, several tables, some chairs, two lamps, an overhead projector, a filing cabinet, a computer. The university itself was only twelve years old. . . . as neutral a place as anywhere."[7] And yet Millat and Magid cannot reconcile: they "make a mockery of that idea, a neutral place; they cover the room with history . . . they take what was blank and smear it with the stinking shit of the past" (383). Leah Hanwell, in *NW*, can recall from university only "warbling posh boys" and "being more bored than you have been in your life" (36). Michelle Holland, one of Smith's sharply drawn minor characters in *NW*, will vanish in her final year, "having been asked to pass the entirety of herself through a hole that would accept only part" (251). The status of this university is ambiguous. Indifference, second choices, cheap furniture; provincial, underfunded; isolation, even rejection.

We are meant to hear irony when *NW*'s narrator declares, in the language of an admissions brochure, "University is a time of experimentation and metamorphosis" (239). Yet at times in these novels the institution *can* provide that time, in moments carved out of life in the city (Smith's other preoccupation). There are some empty rooms, some furniture, a computer, time to think. The idea of a neutral place, a place of possibility, remains. *NW*'s Keisha Blake, not without cost, gets "crazy busy with self-invention," becomes Natalie Blake, "los[es] God" and finds "politics and literature, music, cinema," and eventually a career as a high-powered lawyer (247). In *Swing Time*, as the narrator says, "the institution was almost as fresh as we were . . . it was our place to invent," and by *we* she means Black students like herself, listening to "Gang Starr or Nas," "applying high theory to shampoo ads, philosophy to NWA videos," becoming "conscious" (286). Her mother reads *The Black Jacobins* while the daughter is at dance class, watches "lectures from the Open University, pad and pencil in her hand, looking beautiful, serene" (23). She is always in search of "more time, more peace, more quiet, so she can study . . . Sociology & Politics" (23). She leaves her husband, goes to

Middlesex Polytechnic, gets a PhD, and becomes a member of Parliament. The institution of the university takes different forms at different times in Smith's novels, not containing lives behind its gates but passing through them. Neither an ivory tower nor an object of satire, it's one among many places where, if the conditions are right, people can change, intersect, and diverge, sometimes modestly, sometimes dramatically. Each of these novels incorporates upward-mobility stories of Black British women in which institutions enable rather than constrict the creation of new selves.[8]

My approach in this book has attended to the concept of the institution broadly and to the role it plays in modernist constructions of novelistic character. But the history *Institutional Character* traverses has carried with it some particular institutions: of the military, telecommunications, law, finance, colonial administration, espionage, medicine, labor, and others. Smith's novels, which demonstrate the continued relevance of modernist form, and of institutional character, to any discussion of literary form in the present, direct attention to yet another specific institution: the university. Perhaps this is inevitable given that the university is both where modernism and its practitioners ended up and where their works endure as objects of study. What I hope to have shown here is that ideas about the institution typically conceived of as external to modernist texts are in fact immanent to the works we study and teach. Seeing how these works—from those of Conrad to those of Smith and others—theorize institutions affords one way of following the aesthetic energies of modernism and institutional character across the twentieth century and perhaps into the present.

NOTES

Introduction

1. E. M. Forster, *A Passage to India* (New York: Harcourt, 1924), 50.
2. E. M. Forster, "The Challenge of Our Time," in *Two Cheers for Democracy* (New York: Harcourt, 1951), 56; Forster, *A Passage to India*, 208.
3. Scott Selisker, *Human Programming: Brainwashing, Automatons, and American Unfreedom* (Minneapolis: Univ. of Minnesota Press, 2016), 72.
4. Ian Watt, *The Rise of the Novel: Studies in Defoe, Richardson, and Fielding* (Berkeley: Univ. of California Press, 1957), 12; Georg Lukács, *The Theory of the Novel*, trans. Anna Bostock (Cambridge, MA: MIT Press, 1974), 81.
5. On "network novels," see Patrick Jagoda, *Network Aesthetics* (Chicago: Univ. of Chicago Press, 2016), 43–72; and Sam McBean, "The Queer Network Novel," *Contemporary Literature* 60.3 (Fall 2019): 427–52. Jagoda includes in the category works such as Thomas Pynchon's *Gravity's Rainbow* (1973) and Don DeLillo's *Underworld* (1997); McBean adds Hanya Yanagihara's *A Little Life* (2015).
6. Dora Zhang's *Strange Likeness: Description and the Modernist Novel* (Chicago: Univ. of Chicago Press, 2021) similarly situates modernist writing as expanding and innovating on realist concerns, though on the grounds of description rather than character.
7. Lawrence Rainey, *Institutions of Modernism* (New Haven, CT: Yale Univ. Press, 1999), 5–6.
8. See Peter Kalliney, *Commonwealth of Letters: British Literary Culture and the Emergence of Postcolonial Aesthetics* (New York: Oxford Univ. Press, 2013); and Jeremy Braddock, *Collecting as Modernist Practice* (Baltimore: Johns Hopkins Univ. Press, 2013). Other work on modernism and literary institutions includes Mark McGurl, *The Program Era* (Cambridge, MA: Harvard Univ. Press, 2009); Andrew Goldstone, *Fictions of Autonomy: Modernism from Wilde to de Man* (New York: Oxford Univ. Press, 2013); Greg Barnhisel, *Cold War Modernism: Art, Literature, and American Cultural Diplomacy* (New York: Columbia Univ. Press, 2015); Evan Kindley, *Poet-Critics and the Administration of Culture* (Cambridge, MA: Harvard Univ. Press, 2017); Laura Heffernan and Rachel Sagner Buurma, *The Teaching Archive* (Chicago: Univ. of Chicago Press, 2021); and work on particular institutions such as the BBC in Emily Bloom's *The Wireless Past*

(New York: Oxford Univ. Press, 2016) and Ian Whittington's *Writing the Radio War* (Edinburgh: Edinburgh Univ. Press, 2018).
9. Rainey, *Institutions of Modernism*, 6.
10. D. A. Miller's classic study *The Novel and the Police* (Berkeley: Univ. of California Press, 1988) is representative in this regard: as Miller writes by way of introduction, "This work centers not on the police, in the modern institutional shape they acquire in Western liberal culture during the nineteenth century, but on the ramification within the same culture of less visible, less visibly violent modes of 'social control'" (viii). Eve Sedgwick was possibly among the first to criticize this passage's evocation of the dangers of "the intensive and continuous 'pastoral care' that liberal society proposes to take" (viii), in terms that indirectly anticipate the more institutionally affirmative approach of more recent criticism: "As if! I'm a lot less worried about being pathologized by my therapist than about my vanishing mental health coverage." Sedgwick, "Paranoid Reading and Reparative Reading, or, You're So Paranoid, You Probably Think This Essay is About You," in *Touching Feeling* (Durham, NC: Duke Univ. Press, 2004), 141.
11. Amanda Claybaugh, "Government is Good," *minnesota review* 78 (2008): 165. See also Sean McCann, *Gumshoe America* (Durham, NC: Duke Univ. Press, 2000); Bruce Robbins, "The Smell of Infrastructure: Notes toward an Archive," *boundary 2* 34 (2007): 25–33; Robbins, *Upward Mobility and the Common Good: Toward a Literary History of the Welfare State* (Princeton, NJ: Princeton Univ. Press, 2007); Michael Rubenstein, *Public Works: Infrastructure, Irish Modernism, and the Postcolonial* (Notre Dame, IN: Notre Dame Univ. Press, 2010); Michael Szalay, *New Deal Modernism: American Literature and the Invention of the Welfare State* (Durham, NC: Duke Univ. Press, 2000); Matthew Hart and Jim Hansen, eds., "Contemporary Literature and the State," special issue, *Contemporary Literature* 49.4 (Winter 2008); Lauren Goodlad, *Victorian Literature and the Victorian State: Character and Governance in a Liberal Society* (Baltimore: Johns Hopkins Univ. Press, 2003); Lisi Schoenbach, *Pragmatic Modernism* (New York: Oxford Univ. Press, 2012); James Purdon, *Modernist Informatics: Literature, Information, and the State* (New York: Oxford Univ. Press, 2015); and Zarena Aslami, *The Dream Life of Citizens: Late Victorian Novels and the Fantasy of the State* (New York: Fordham Univ. Press, 2012).
12. John Marx, *Geopolitics and the Anglophone Novel, 1890–2011* (Cambridge: Cambridge Univ. Press, 2012), 1. Other critics who propose a more active role for modernist literature in the formation of state and institutional discourses include Joseph Slaughter, *Human Rights, Inc.* (New York: Fordham Univ. Press, 2007); Janice Ho, *Nation and Citizenship*

in the Twentieth-Century British Novel (Cambridge: Cambridge Univ. Press, 2015); Jessica Berman, *Modernist Commitments: Ethics, Politics, and Transnational Modernism* (New York: Columbia Univ. Press, 2011); and Matthew Hart, *Extraterritorial: A Political Geography of Contemporary Fiction* (New York: Columbia Univ. Press, 2020).

13. A foundational text of the new institutionalism is *The New Institutionalism in Organizational Analysis*, ed. Paul J. DiMaggio and Walter W. Powell (Chicago: Univ. of Chicago Press, 1991). See also Bert A. Rockman, Sarah Binder, and R. A. W. Rhodes, eds., *The Oxford Handbook of Political Institutions* (New York: Oxford Univ. Press, 2006); and Tulia G. Falleti, Adam D. Sheingate, and Karl Orfeo Fioretos, eds., *The Oxford Handbook of Historical Institutionalism* (New York: Oxford Univ. Press, 2016). See also Peter B. Evans, Dietrich Rueschemeyer, and Theda Skocpol, eds., *Bringing the State Back In* (Cambridge: Cambridge Univ. Press, 1984); Mary C. Brinton and Victor Nee, eds., *The New Institutionalism in Sociology* (New York: Russell Sage, 1998); André Lecours, ed., *New Institutionalism: Theory and Analysis* (Toronto: Univ. of Toronto Press, 2005); Hugh Heclo, *On Thinking Institutionally* (Boulder, CO: Paradigm, 2008); Karol Soltan, Eric M. Uslaner, and Virginia Haufler, eds., *Institutions and Social Order* (Ann Arbor: Univ. of Michigan Press, 1998); James G. March and Johan P. Olsen, *Rediscovering Institutions* (New York: Free Press, 1989); Douglas North, *Institutions, Institutional Change and Economic Performance* (Cambridge: Cambridge Univ. Press, 1991); and Jack Knight, *Institutions and Social Conflict* (Cambridge: Cambridge Univ. Press, 1992). Patricia H. Thornton, William Ocasio, and Michael Lounsbury's *The Institutional Logics Perspective* (New York: Oxford Univ. Press, 2012) recaps and synthesizes this work, making a case for the centrality of the "institutional logics" approach, which places particular emphasis on the overlapping and simultaneous institutional orders in which individuals and organizations take shape and act. See also Douglas Allen, *The Institutional Revolution: Measurement and the Economic Emergence of the Modern World* (Chicago: Univ. of Chicago Press, 2012); and Leo J. Blanken, *Rational Empires: Institutional Incentives and Imperial Expansion* (Chicago: Univ. of Chicago Press, 2012). The term has become the subject of debate in the art world; see, e.g., the collection *How Institutions Think: Between Contemporary Art and Curatorial Discourse*, ed. Paul O'Neill, Lucy Steeds, and Mick Wilson (Cambridge, MA: MIT Press, 2017).

14. Megan Faragher and Caroline Krzakowski, "Rainey's Institutions: Twenty Years Later," in "Modernist Institutions," ed. Faragher and Krzakowski, *Modernism/modernity Print Plus* 5, cycle 2 (9 November 2020), https://doi.org/10.26597/mod.0155.

15. Gabriel Hankins, *Interwar Modernism and the Liberal World Order: Offices, Institutions and Aesthetics after 1919* (Cambridge: Cambridge Univ. Press, 2019), 13.
16. See Caroline Levine, *Forms: Whole, Rhythm, Hierarchy, Network* (Princeton, NJ: Princeton Univ. Press, 2015), 49–81.
17. James G. March and Johan P. Olsen, "Elaborating the New Institutionalism," in Rockman, Binder, and Rhodes, *Oxford Handbook of Political Institutions*, 3.
18. See Anna Kornbluh, *The Order of Forms: Realism, Formalism, and Social Space* (Chicago: Univ. of Chicago Press, 2019).
19. Marta Figlerowicz, *Flat Protagonists* (New York: Oxford Univ. Press, 2016), 14. See Alex Woloch, *The One vs. the Many* (Princeton, NJ: Princeton Univ. Press, 2003); Aaron Kunin, "Characters Lounge," *Modern Language Quarterly* 70.3 (2009): 291–317; and Omri Moses, *Out of Character: Modernism, Vitalism, and Psychic Life* (Stanford, CA: Stanford Univ. Press, 2014). See also Matthew Burroughs Price, "Old Formalisms: Character, Structure, Action," *New Literary History* 50 (2019): 247, which argues for "the networked nature of agency" in the Victorian novel.
20. Jill Galvan, "Character," in "Keywords for Victorian Studies," special issue, *VLC: Victorian Literature & Culture* 46.3/4 (2018): 614–15.
21. Levine, *Forms*, 111.
22. Joseph Conrad, *Nostromo*, ed. Martin Seymour-Smith (New York: Penguin, 1990), 432.
23. See, e.g., Douglas Mao and Rebecca Walkowitz, "The New Modernist Studies," *PMLA* 123 (2006): 737–48; Eric Hayot, *On Literary Worlds* (New York: Oxford Univ. Press, 2012); and Susan Stanford Friedman, *Planetary Modernisms: Provocations on Modernity Across Time* (New York: Columbia Univ. Press, 2015).
24. Emily Steinlight, *Populating the Novel: Literary Form and the Politics of Surplus Life* (Ithaca, NY: Cornell Univ. Press, 2018), 15.
25. Michael Tratner's *Modernism and Mass Politics: Joyce, Woolf, Eliot, Yeats* (Stanford, CA: Stanford Univ. Press, 1995) is a key study of how modernist writing deals with collectivity. As Tratner argues, "Modernism was an effort to escape the limitations of nineteenth-century individualist conventions and write about distinctively 'collectivist' phenomena" (3). Tratner is concerned primarily with the figure of "the masses" and mass movements, though in the book's eighth chapter, "Social(ist) Institutions in *Ulysses*," he argues that Joyce saw permanent social change as inhering in institutions, not in potentially transitory political movements. Tratner suggests that "[*Ulysses*] has a decidedly artificial structure that emphasizes the dominance of institutional forces over individual concerns" (187).

26. See Jed Esty, "Realism Wars," *Novel: A Forum on Fiction* 49.3 (2016): 316–42; and the essays in "Peripheral Realisms," ed. Joe Cleary, Esty, and Colleen Lye, special issue, *Modern Language Quarterly* 73.3 (2012).
27. Allen, *Institutional Revolution*, 77.
28. Thomas Carlyle, "Signs of the Times," in *The Collected Works of Thomas Carlyle*, 16 vols. (London: Chapman & Hall, 1858), 3:100, 106.
29. Carlyle, "Signs of the Times," 3:107–8.
30. Matthew Arnold, "The Literary Influence of Academies," in Arnold, *Essays Literary & Critical*, ed. Ernest Rhys (London: J. M. Dent, 1906), 31–32, 50.
31. Arnold, "The Literary Influence of Academies," 30–31; Matthew Arnold, *Culture and Anarchy* (London: Smith, Elder, 1869), xi.
32. Charlotte Brontë, *Jane Eyre*, ed. Stevie Davies (New York: Penguin, 2006), 59. This passage has elicited notice from other institutionally minded critics. See Levine, *Forms*, 1–2; and Mary Mullen, *Novel Institutions: Anachronism, Irish Novels, and Nineteenth-Century Realism* (Edinburgh: Edinburgh Univ. Press, 2019), 17. Mullen's book is a major contribution to thinking about the role of institutions in the novel, and her position parallels my own in many respects, drawing on the new institutionalism in the social sciences and suggesting that "realist novels engage with both institutions and institutionalism as they explore the power that inheres in enclosed material structures as well as the social and temporal forms that underwrite that power" (18). Where I am interested in questions of character, however, Mullen's primary concern is with questions of temporality and anachronism as exemplified in nineteenth-century Irish writing.
33. Nancy Armstrong, *How Novels Think: The Limits of British Individualism from 1719–1900* (New York: Columbia Univ. Press, 2005), 8.
34. Elizabeth Gaskell, *North and South* (London: Chapman & Hall, 1855), 353.
35. Charles Dickens, *Great Expectations*, ed. Edgar Rosenberg (New York: Norton, 1999), 155.
36. Joe Cleary, "Realism after Modernism and the Literary World-System," in Cleary, Jed Esty, and Colleen Lye, "Peripheral Realisms," 261, 268.
37. Daniel Stout, *Corporate Romanticism: Liberalism, Justice, and the Novel* (New York: Fordham Univ. Press, 2017).
38. Carlyle, "Signs of the Times," 3:117; Arnold, *Culture and Anarchy*, 50.
39. Paul Johnson, *Making the Market: Victorian Origins of Corporate Capitalism* (Cambridge: Cambridge Univ. Press, 2010), 24.
40. See Aslami, *Dream Life of Citizens*, 2–3, for an overview of the disciplinary terms in which historicist literary scholars have figured the rise of late Victorian institutions.
41. See Max Weber, *The Protestant Ethic and the Spirit of Capitalism*, trans. Peter Baehr (New York: Penguin, 2002); and Emile Durkheim, *The Rules*

of Sociological Method, trans. W. D. Halls (New York: Simon & Schuster, 1982), 45.
42. Perry Anderson, "Components of the National Culture," *New Left Review* 50 (July/August 1968), 7.
43. See Jed Esty, *A Shrinking Island: Modernism and National Culture in English* (Princeton, NJ: Princeton Univ. Press, 2004), 182–98.
44. Arnold White, *Efficiency and Empire* (London: Methuen, 1901), 309.
45. George Bernard Shaw, *Fabianism and Empire* (London: Grant Richards, 1900), 3–4. I am grateful to Matthew Eatough for directing me to Shaw.
46. John Darwin, *The Empire Project: The Rise and Fall of the British World-System, 1830–1970* (Cambridge: Cambridge Univ. Press, 2009), 272.
47. Virginia Woolf, "A Sketch of the Past," in *Moments of Being,* ed. Jeanne Schulkind (New York: Harcourt, 1976), 152. The image of society as a machine is a recurring one in Woolf's writing. In *The Voyage Out,* Richard Dalloway could be echoing Arnold White and G. B. Shaw when he says, "Look at it this way, Miss Vinrace; conceive of the state as a complicated machine; we citizens are parts of that machine; some fulfill more important duties; others (perhaps I am one of them) serve only to connect some obscure parts of the mechanism, concealed from the public eye. Yet if the meanest screw fails in its task, the proper working of the whole is imperiled." Woolf, *The Voyage Out* (New York: Harcourt, 1920), 66. See also Mary Jean Corbett's reading of this imagery in "A Sketch of the Past" in her *Family Likeness: Sex, Marriage, and Incest from Jane Austen to Virginia Woolf* (Ithaca, NY: Cornell Univ. Press, 2008), 182–84, which parallels my own.
48. On social forces as "invisible presences" in Woolf, see esp. Alex Zwerdling, *Virginia Woolf and the Real World* (Berkeley: Univ. of California Press, 1986), 3. Zwerdling's classic study takes as one of its central themes the relationship in Woolf's writing between the "inside" of consciousness and the "outside" of society, history, and politics, but he generally sees this relationship as one of influence or reflection on a thematic level, rather than mutual imbrication and reproduction at the level of form, as I do; Zwerdling refers to *The Years* only in passing.
49. Joseph Conrad, "Author's Note," in *Under Western Eyes* (New York: Doubleday, Page, 1923), viii.
50. Virginia Woolf, *The Letters of Virginia Woolf,* ed. Nigel Nicolson and Joanne Trautman, vol. 6 (New York: Harcourt, 1980), 116.
51. See Heclo, *On Thinking Institutionally.*

1. Joseph Conrad and the Institutions of Empire

1. Joseph Conrad to Edward Garnett, 6 July 1904, in *The Collected Letters of Joseph Conrad*, ed. Frederick R. Karl and Laurence Davies, 5 vols. (Cambridge: Cambridge Univ. Press, 1988), 3:150.
2. Joseph Conrad, "Anatole France," in Conrad, *Notes on Life and Letters*, ed. J. H. Stape and Andrew Busza (Cambridge: Cambridge Univ. Press, 2004), 30.
3. Ford Madox Ford, *Joseph Conrad: A Personal Remembrance* (London: Duckworth, 1924), 58.
4. Other critics who have dealt with the issue of politics and the nation in Conrad include Pericles Lewis, "His Sympathies Were in the Right Place: *Heart of Darkness* and the Discourse of National Character," *Nineteenth-Century Literature* 53.2 (1988): 211–44; and Paul Armstrong, "Conrad's Contradictory Politics: The Ontology of Society in *Nostromo*," *Twentieth-Century Literature* 31.1 (1985): 1–21.
5. Jed Esty, "Global Lukács," *Novel: A Forum on Fiction* 42 (2009): 370.
6. See Avrom Fleishman, *Conrad's Politics: Community and Anarchy in the Fiction of Joseph Conrad* (Baltimore: Johns Hopkins Press, 1967). Fleishman also includes most of the major English novelists of the Victorian period in this genealogy. Incidentally, according to Ford, "It pleased Conrad to write at a Chippendale bureau . . . which had once belonged to Thomas Carlyle." Ford, *Joseph Conrad*, 35.
7. Fleishman, *Conrad's Politics*, 10.
8. Fleishman, *Conrad's Politics*, 110.
9. Fleishman, *Conrad's Politics*, 68.
10. Joseph Conrad, *The Mirror of the Sea*, in Conrad, *"A Personal Record" and "The Mirror of the Sea,"* ed. Mara Kalnins (New York: Penguin, 1998), 299.
11. Geoffrey Galt Harpham, *One of Us: The Mastery of Joseph Conrad* (Chicago: Univ. of Chicago Press, 1996), 3.
12. See, e.g., Zdislaw Najder, "Conrad in his Historical Perspective," in *Conrad in Perspective: Essays on Art and Fidelity* (Cambridge: Cambridge Univ. Press, 1997), 188–98. Conrad was both vilified as a deserter and hailed for his literary successes by the Polish intelligentsia of his time; see Fleishman, *Conrad's Politics*, 13–15.
13. Najder, "Conrad in his Historical Perspective," 192. See by Najder: *Joseph Conrad: A Life* (New Brunswick, NJ: Rutgers Univ. Press, 1983); *Conrad's Polish Background*, trans. Halina Carroll (Oxford: Oxford Univ. Press, 1964); and *Conrad Under Familial Eyes*, trans. Carroll (Cambridge: Cambridge Univ. Press, 1983).

14. See F. R. Leavis, *The Great Tradition* (New York: New York Univ. Press, 1964), 1–27, 173–226; and Francis Mulhern, "English Reading," in *Nation and Narration*, ed. Homi Bhabha (London: Routledge, 1989), 250–63.
15. Harpham, *One of Us*, 13.
16. Christopher GoGwilt, *The Invention of the West: Joseph Conrad and the Double-Mapping of Europe and Empire* (Stanford, CA: Stanford Univ. Press, 1995), 7.
17. Stephen Ross, *Conrad and Empire* (Columbia: Univ. of Missouri Press, 2004), 5–6.
18. Regina Martin, "Absentee Capitalism and the Politics of Conrad's Imperial Novels," *PMLA* 130 (2015): 584–85. Rebecca Walkowitz, in her *Cosmopolitan Style: Modernism Beyond the Nation* (New York: Columbia Univ. Press, 2006), takes a different approach to overcoming the national paradigm for Conrad, arguing that the author "brought to his work diverse, sometimes conflicting strategies of national and international affiliation" as a means of authorial self-fashioning (36).
19. Versions of my point here—in brief, that Conrad's writing consistently partakes aesthetically of phenomena it derides politically—recur throughout the criticism, reinforcing the sense that his major works really do represent a kind of hinge point in the history of the novel as currently constituted. See, e.g., Cannon Schmitt, who argues that "*Nostromo* prosecutes a critique of the culture of investment as mandating a society at the mercy of misprision even as it exemplifies a development in novelistic form—call it modernism—that may itself be seen to derive its distinctive qualities from the function of language in such a society." Schmitt, "Rumor, Shares, and Novelistic Form: Joseph Conrad's *Nostromo*," in *Victorian Investments: New Perspectives on Finance and Culture*, ed. Nancy Henry and Schmitt (Bloomington: Indiana Univ. Press, 2009), 184.
20. Michael Levenson, *Modernism and the Fate of Individuality* (Cambridge: Cambridge Univ. Press, 1991), 43.
21. Ronald Hyam, "The British Empire in the Edwardian Era," in *The Oxford History of the British Empire, Volume IV: The Twentieth Century*, ed. Robin W. Winks (Oxford: Oxford Univ. Press, 2005), 59.
22. Daron Acemoglu, Simon Johnson, and James A. Robinson, "The Colonial Origins of Comparative Development: An Empirical Investigation," *American Economic Review* 91 (2001): 1369–1401.
23. Leo J. Blanken, *Rational Empires: Institutional Incentives and Imperial Expansion* (Chicago: Univ. of Chicago Press, 2012).
24. Joseph Conrad, "Confidence," in Conrad, *Notes on Life and Letters*, 159.
25. The novelty of this state of affairs was asserted by the historian and Liberal MP Ramsay Muir, who writes in 1917 of the British Empire that "this

amazing political structure, which refuses to fall within any of the categories of political science, which is an empire and not yet an empire, a state and yet not a state, a supernation incorporating in itself an incredible variety of peoples and races, is not a structure which has been designed by the ingenuity of man." Muir, *The Expansion of Europe: The Culmination of Modern History* (New York: Houghton Mifflin, 1917), 287.

26. I owe this distinction to Daniel Stout; see his "Nothing Personal: The Decapitation of Character in *A Tale of Two Cities*," *Novel: A Forum on Fiction* 41 (2007): 32.
27. Georg Lukács, *The Theory of the Novel*, trans. Anna Bostock (Cambridge, MA: MIT Press, 1974), 81.
28. James G. March and Johan P. Olsen, "Elaborating the New Institutionalism," in *The Oxford Handbook of Political Institutions*, ed. Bert A. Rockman, Sarah Binder, and R. A. W. Rhodes (New York: Oxford Univ. Press, 2006), 3.
29. See Joseph Conrad and Ford Madox Ford, *The Inheritors* (New York: Carroll & Graf, 1985), 57–58.
30. On character development in Conrad, see Tobias Boes, "Beyond the Bildungsroman: Character Development and Communal Legitimation in the Early Fiction of Joseph Conrad," *Conradiana* 39.2 (2007): 113–34.
31. Michel Foucault, "Of Other Spaces," quoted in *Our Conrad*, by Peter Mallios (Stanford, CA: Stanford Univ. Press, 2010), 24. See also Robert Hampson, "Conrad's Heterotopic Fiction: Composite Maps, Superimposed Sites, and Impossible Spaces," in *Conrad in the Twenty-First Century: Contemporary Approaches and Perspectives*, ed. Carola M. Kaplan, Peter Mallios, and Andrea White (New York: Routledge, 2005), 121–35; Cesare Casarino, *Modernity at Sea: Melville, Marx, Conrad in Crisis* (Minneapolis: Univ. of Minnesota Press, 2002), 12; and Natalie Melas, *All the Difference in the World: Postcoloniality and the Ends of Comparison* (Stanford, CA: Stanford Univ. Press, 2007).
32. Ford, *Joseph Conrad*, 147.
33. McGurl, *The Program Era* (Cambridge, MA: Harvard Univ. Press, 2009), 151.
34. Joseph Conrad, "The Crime of Partition" (1919), in *Notes on Life and Letters* (London: J. M. Dent, 1921), xx.
35. The phrase seems not to actually be Gramsci's, though it is "ubiquitously attributed to him." Joseph Buttigieg, "The Contemporary Discourse on Civil Society: A Gramscian Critique," *boundary 2* 32 (2005): 50n21.
36. McGurl, *Program Era*, 151.
37. Joseph Conrad, *Nostromo*, ed. Martin Seymour-Smith (New York: Penguin, 1990), 120.

38. Eloise Knapp Hay, *The Political Novels of Joseph Conrad: A Critical Study* (Chicago: Univ. of Chicago Press, 1963), 177.
39. Franco Moretti, *The Way of the World*, 2nd ed. (New York: Verso, 2000), 232.
40. Jed Esty, *Unseasonable Youth: Modernism, Colonialism, and the Fiction of Development* (New York: Oxford Univ. Press, 2012), 67. A sample of other work on the twentieth-century bildungsroman would include Tobias Boes, *Formative Fictions: Nationalism, Cosmopolitanism, and the Bildungsroman* (Ithaca, NY: Cornell Univ. Press, 2012); Urmila Seshagiri, "Modernist Ashes, Postcolonial Phoenix: Jean Rhys and the Evolution of the English Novel in the Twentieth Century," *Modernism/modernity* 13 (2006): 487–505; Joseph Slaughter, *Human Rights, Inc.* (New York: Fordham Univ. Press, 2007); and Benjamin Kohlmann, "Toward a History and Theory of the Socialist Bildungsroman," *Novel: A Forum on Fiction* 48.2 (2015): 167–89.
41. J. A. Hobson, *Imperialism* (New York: James Pott, 1902); V. I. Lenin, *Imperialism: The Highest Stage of Capitalism* (New York: International Publishers, 1988); Hannah Arendt, *The Origins of Totalitarianism* (New York: Schocken, 1951); Eric Hobsbawm, *The Age of Empire, 1875–1914* (London: Weidenfeld & Nicolson, 1987).
42. Esty, *Unseasonable Youth*, 20. See also Gregory Castle, *Reading the Modernist Bildungsroman* (Gainesville: Univ. Press of Florida, 2006); Seshagiri, "Modernist Ashes, Postcolonial Phoenix"; and Slaughter, *Human Rights, Inc.* Sarah L. Townsend's "The Drama of Peripheralized Bildung: An Irish Genre Study," *New Literary History* 48 (2017): 337–62, questions the centrality of the *novel* to accounts of social development on the periphery of the imperial system, examining drama, but retains a focus on the bildung plot.
43. John Gallagher and Ronald Robinson, "The Imperialism of Free Trade," *Economic History Review*, 2nd ser., 6 (1953): 1–15.
44. P. J. Cain and A. G. Hopkins, *British Imperialism, 1688–2015*, 3rd ed. (London: Routledge, 2016); Darwin, *Empire Project*.
45. Stephanie Insley Hershinow, *Born Yesterday* (Baltimore: Johns Hopkins Univ. Press, 2019), 16.
46. Likewise, Lisa Siraganian points out that naturalist and modernist writers "illuminated capitalism's potent structures and scaffolds, without relying on the usual bildungsroman timeframe and its narrative conventions of an individual's rise and fall." See Siraganian, "Dreiser's Anti-Corporate Tools: Veil-Piercing and the Novel of Corporate Agency," *American Literary History* 30.2 (2018): 272.
47. Fredric Jameson, *The Political Unconscious: Narrative as a Socially Symbolic Act* (Ithaca, NY: Cornell Univ. Press, 1981), 269, 264.

48. Joseph Conrad, *Lord Jim* (New York: McClure, Phillips, 1903) 263, quoted in Michael Valdez Moses, *The Novel and the Globalization of Culture* (New York: Oxford Univ. Press, 1995), 76.
49. Moses, *Novel and the Globalization of Culture*, 85.
50. On infrastructure, see Robbins, "Smell of Infrastructure"; and Rubenstein, *Public Works*. While *Nostromo* could indeed be read as a major novel of infrastructure, Conrad himself has no interest in what Robbins and Rubenstein argue is infrastructure's buried utopian potential. In *Nostromo*, the development of infrastructure relies on and produces a commitment to institutions that leaches away individual agency and eliminates the potential for heroic action.
51. The broad spectrum of critical opinion about how Conrad wants us to evaluate Gould testifies to the complexity of character in *Nostromo*. Seymour-Smith calls Gould "the most repulsive character in the book" with "the sadistic and murderous impulse of dictators in his breast" (Conrad, *Nostromo*, 15), while C. Brook Miller argues that Gould "embodies the ideals of British culture" that Conrad sees as basically insufficient to late imperialism but admirable nonetheless. Miller, "Holroyd's Man: Tradition, Fetishization, and the United States in *Nostromo*," in *Nostromo: Centennial Essays*, ed. Allan H. Simmons and J. H. Stape (Amsterdam: Rodopi, 2004), 14. The difficulty stems, at least in part, from a standard take on the novel that sees its baffling chronology and apparent absence of psychological insight as concealing a deeper interest in individual character and motivation. I am arguing that one of Conrad's major innovations in *Nostromo* involves doing away with character as a property of the individual, the better to depict a social world structured almost entirely by institutional possibilities and limits.
52. Joseph Conrad, "Autocracy and War," in Conrad, *Notes on Life and Letters*, 107, 111.
53. Elizabeth Langland, in her essay "Society as Formal Protagonist: The Examples of *Nostromo* and *Barchester Towers*," *Critical Inquiry* 9 (1982): 359–78, refers to these phrases as "social tags." The term *type-phrase* more effectively conveys their characterological significance for my argument, but my reading parallels her point that "these tags stimulate our identification with social aspirations and principles as opposed to individual fates" (368). Langland's larger argument, that in these works "society— a set of principles or social ideas—function in the narrative in the same way as would a human hero" (361), likewise informs my own.
54. See, e.g., Joshua Gooch, who argues that the theft initiates an "opportunist turn" in Nostromo, who steals the shipment of silver because of the subjectively isolating effects of finance capital. Gooch, "'The Shape of Credit':

Imagination, Speculation, and Language in *Nostromo*," *Texas Studies in Literature and Language* 52 (2010): 273. This seems correct as far as it goes, but it does not account for the more fundamental continuities in the novel's plot of material interests.

55. For a critique of *Nostromo*'s conclusion, see Albert Guerard, *Conrad the Novelist* (Cambridge, MA: Harvard Univ. Press, 1958), 202–10.
56. Joseph Conrad, *The Secret Agent* (New York: Penguin, 1963), 126–27.
57. See Amanda Anderson, *The Powers of Distance: Cosmopolitanism and the Cultivation of Detachment* (Princeton, NJ: Princeton Univ. Press, 2001).
58. Joseph Conrad, *Under Western Eyes* (New York: Penguin, 2007), 5.
59. Unsigned review of *Under Western Eyes* by Edward Garnett, *Nation*, 21 October 1911, quoted in Keith Carabine, *The Life and the Art: A Study of Conrad's "Under Western Eyes"* (Amsterdam: Rodopi, 1996), 209.
60. Eloise Knapp Hay refers to the language teacher as a "nonentity" able to "explain without understanding." Hay, *Political Novels of Joseph Conrad*, 296. Frank Kermode calls him "the father of lies, a diabolical narrator" in his "Secrets and Narrative Sequence," *Critical Inquiry* 7 (1980): 100.
61. See Gail Fincham, "'To make you see': Narration and Focalization in *Under Western Eyes*," in *Joseph Conrad: Voice, Sequence, History, Genre,* ed. Jakob Lothe, Jeremy Hawthorn, and James Phelan (Columbus: Ohio State Univ. Press, 2008), 60–80; and Daniel Darvay, "The Politics of Gothic in Conrad's *Under Western Eyes*," *Modern Fiction Studies* 55 (2009): 693–715.
62. Darvay, "Politics of Gothic," 707.
63. Conrad, *Under Western Eyes*, 315–16.
64. Edward Said, "Conrad: The Presentation of Narrative," in *The World, the Text, and the Critic* (Cambridge, MA: Harvard Univ. Press, 1983), 92.
65. Conrad, *Collected Letters of Joseph Conrad*, 3:30.
66. Conrad, *Secret Agent*, 110.
67. Nicole Rizzuto, *Insurgent Testimonies: Witnessing Colonial Trauma in Modern and Anglophone Literature* (New York: Fordham Univ. Press, 2015), 72.
68. See Eloise Knapp Hay, "*Under Western Eyes* and the Missing Center," in *Joseph Conrad's "Under Western Eyes": Beginnings, Revisions, Final Forms,* ed. David R. Smith (Hamden, CT: Archon, 1991), 121–51.
69. Levenson, *Modernism and the Fate of Individuality*, 57.

2. Virginia Woolf and Political Possibility in the Gendered Institution

1. See Ben Harker, "'On different levels ourselves went forward': Pageantry, Class Politics and Narrative Form in Virginia Woolf's Late Writing,"

ELH 78 (2011): 433–56; and Sam See, "The Comedy of Nature: Darwinian Feminism in Virginia Woolf's *Between the Acts*," *Modernism/modernity* 17 (2010): 639–67.
2. Virginia Woolf, 20 January 1931, in *The Diary of Virginia Woolf*, ed. Anne Olivier Bell, 5 vols. (New York: Harcourt, 1977–84), 4:6.
3. Virginia Woolf, 2 November 1932, in *Diary*, 4:129.
4. Virginia Woolf, *The Pargiters: The Novel-Essay Portion of "The Years,"* ed. Mitchell Leaska (New York: Harcourt, 1977), 9. The scene that follows is headed "Chapter Fifty-Six," chapters 1–55 presumably having brought us from 1800 to 1880.
5. Virginia Woolf, *The Years*, ed. Eleanor McNees (New York: Harcourt, 2008), 336. This edition is cited throughout, but see also the edition of *The Years* edited by Anna Snaith for *the Cambridge Edition of the Works of Virginia Woolf* (Cambridge: Cambridge Univ. Press, 2012). Snaith's annotations are exhaustive, and the edition's introduction is perhaps the best comprehensive account of the novel's composition history and background.
6. Virginia Woolf, *Three Guineas*, ed. Jane Marcus (New York: Harcourt, 2006), 126–27, 136. Mark David Kaufman notes that institutional critique is the basic posture of Woolf's political writings as well as many of her short stories: "Woolf's primary targets are the military, the university, the church, and the professions, organizations with the ostensible goal of producing 'good people' and making the world a safer and more productive place." Kaufman tracks a structure of "espionage" across Woolf's work and life that he terms a "spy-function," arguing that she repeatedly stages scenes in which "a group of women infiltrate various strongholds of male power." See Kaufman, "True Lies: Virginia Woolf, Espionage, and Feminist Agency," *Twentieth-Century Literature* 64 (2018): 326, 335, 320. This argument reinforces the dialectical nature of the Society of Outsiders: the agency of the female spy is to some extent founded on the existence of the institution she infiltrates.
7. Baruch Hochmann, *The Test of Character: From the Victorian Novel to the Modern* (Teaneck, NJ: Fairleigh Dickinson Univ. Press, 1983), 157.
8. Edward Bishop, "The Subject in *Jacob's Room*," *Modern Fiction Studies* 38 (1992): 148.
9. Jesse Matz, *Literary Impressionism and Modernist Aesthetics* (Cambridge: Cambridge Univ. Press, 2001), 1. Thirty-plus years of scholarship on Woolf, inaugurated by feminist critics such as Jane Marcus and Rachel Blau DuPlessis and catalyzed in the 1980s by Alex Zwerdling's monumental *Virginia Woolf and the Real World* (Berkeley: Univ. of California Press, 1986), itself a critique of earlier feminist scholarship, have demolished the

image of Woolf as a fragile and isolated "woman writer." We have become accustomed to a view of Woolf that emphasizes her feminism, her activism, and her place in what Christine Froula terms "the Bloomsbury avant-garde," a politically and culturally engaged milieu that situated Woolf at the epicenter of political and artistic innovation in England. Froula, *Virginia Woolf and the Bloomsbury Avant-Garde: War, Civilization, Modernity* (New York: Columbia Univ. Press, 2005).

10. Emily Steinlight, *Populating the Novel: Literary Form and the Politics of Surplus Life* (Ithaca, NY: Cornell Univ. Press, 2018), 210.
11. Virginia Woolf, "Modern Fiction," in *The Common Reader* (New York: Harcourt, 1925), 149–50.
12. Virginia Woolf, "Mr. Bennett and Mrs. Brown," in *The Essays of Virginia Woolf*, ed. Andrew McNeillie and Stuart Clarke, 6 vols. (London: Hogarth, 1986–2011), 3:384–85.
13. The exploration of the relationship of consciousness to reality, and in particular that relationship's imbrication with turn-of-the-century Cambridge philosophy, is an important facet of Woolf's career, as established authoritatively by Ann Banfield in her *The Phantom Table* (Cambridge: Cambridge Univ. Press, 2000). Woolf's innovation in this area, I want to suggest, does not overshadow her work's continuities with realist practice.
14. Woolf, "Modern Fiction," 151.
15. As Rachel Bowlby observes, even when Woolf is most focused on psychology, the "complex internal world [of the mind] is, nonetheless, externally derived." Bowlby, foreword to *A Concise Companion to Realism*, ed. Matthew Beaumont (Oxford: Wiley-Blackwell, 2010), xx.
16. Jessica Berman, *Modernist Fiction, Cosmopolitanism and the Politics of Community* (Cambridge: Cambridge Univ. Press, 2000), 133.
17. Virginia Woolf, "Character in Fiction," in *Essays of Virginia Woolf*, 3:426.
18. For a different reading of Woolf's emphasis on character in these essays, see Amanda Anderson, "Thinking with Character," in *Character: Three Inquiries in Literary Studies*, by Anderson, Rita Felski, and Toril Moi (Chicago: Univ. of Chicago Press, 2019), 127–70. Anderson emphasizes that Woolf "works . . . in a way that does not imagine any problematic gap between character in life and character as it is realized on the page," but I share her sense that "understanding character within the larger context of a life and over time is of supreme importance for Woolf" (128, 129).
19. Andrew Goldstone, *Fictions of Autonomy: Modernism from Wilde to de Man* (New York: Oxford Univ. Press, 2013), 5.
20. Virginia Woolf, *The Letters of Virginia Woolf*, ed. Nigel Nicolson and Joanne Trautman, vol. 6 (New York: Harcourt, 1980), 116.
21. Woolf, 30 November 1936, in *Diary*, 5:38.

22. Woolf, 31 May 1933, in *Diary*, 4:161; Virginia Woolf, "Women and Fiction," in *Selected Essays*, ed. David Bradshaw (New York: Oxford Univ. Press, 2008), 138.
23. Virginia Woolf, "The Leaning Tower," in *Collected Essays*, 2:175–76.
24. Virginia Woolf, "Why Art Today Follows Politics," in *Selected Essays*, 213.
25. Virginia Woolf, *A Room of One's Own* (New York: Harcourt, 1929), 41.
26. John Maynard Keynes, "Art and the State," in *Social, Political and Literary Writings*, vol. 28 of *The Collected Writings of John Maynard Keynes* (London: Macmillan, 1982), 344. See also D. E. Moggridge, "Keynes, the Arts, and the State," *History of Political Economy* 37 (2005): 535–55.
27. Woolf, *Pargiters*, 43, ellipses in original.
28. See Woolf, *Pargiters*, xiv. Much of the critical history of *The Pargiters* has circled around the question of the work's failure or success, and implicitly around whether it has been under- or overappreciated in Woolf's oeuvre. Molly Hite offers a comprehensive account of this debate in the epilogue to her *Woolf's Ambiguities: Tonal Modernism, Narrative Strategy, Feminist Precursors* (Ithaca, NY: Cornell Univ. Press, 2017), 165–86, arguing that rather than being "impracticably hybrid" (168) and thus doomed to failure, *The Pargiters* was in fact "succeeding too well" in Woolf's stated mission to write about "the sexual lives of women," and that Woolf decided not to go forward with it because, as she stated in a speech that became her essay "Professions for Women," "I am not a hero." Woolf, "Speech before the London/National Society for Women's Service, January 21 1931," in *Pargiters*, xxxix, quoted in Hite, 185. While I do not share Hite's estimation of the work's aesthetic promise, I agree that it is absolutely indispensable to understanding how Woolf's thinking evolved in the 1930s and her goals for *The Years*. Notably, the contributors to the 1977 issue of the *Bulletin of the New York Public Library* that accompanied Leaska's publication of *The Pargiters* drew criticism in the opposite terms: Gloria Fromm, in "Re-inscribing *The Years*: Virginia Woolf, Rose Macaulay, and the Critics," *Journal of Modern Literature* 13.1 (1986): 288–306, takes those critics to task for their excessive enthusiasm for *The Pargiters*, arguing that their enthusiasm for the imagined radical feminist work they found there had led to the devaluation of the work Woolf actually produced, *The Years*. Fromm stresses Woolf's authorial agency, while somewhat idiosyncratically positing Rose Macaulay as a crucial influence on *The Years*.
29. Woolf, *Diary*, 4:151.
30. Virginia Woolf to Julian Bell, 21 May 1936, in *Letters*, 6:38.
31. James G. March and Johan P. Olsen, "Elaborating the New Institutionalism," in *The Oxford Handbook of Political Institutions*, ed. Bert A.

Rockman, Sarah Binder, and R. A. W. Rhodes (New York: Oxford Univ. Press, 2006), 11.
32. Woolf, *Pargiters*, 9.
33. Elizabeth F. Evans argues that these interludes serve both to dramatize and to undercut an "authoritative version of the world seen from 'on high,'" an aerial perspective associated, in Evans's argument, with fascist aesthetics. Evans, "Air War, Propaganda, and Woolf's Anti-Tyranny Aesthetic," *Modern Fiction Studies* 59 (2013): 71.
34. Rachel Blau DuPlessis, *Writing beyond the Ending: Narrative Strategies of Twentieth-Century Women Writers* (Indianapolis: Indiana Univ. Press, 1985), 162–63. Similarly, Alison Booth argues that Woolf's "work increasingly enacts the breakdown of ego boundaries . . . to turn to the first-person pronoun 'we'" (*Greatness Engendered* [Ithaca, NY: Cornell Univ. Press, 1992], 5), and Maria DiBattista points out Woolf's "creative conjunctions of the first-person plural that invoked neither a royal nor an editorial but a choric we" (*Imagining Virginia Woolf* [Princeton, NJ: Princeton Univ. Press, 2009], 25).
35. Margaret Comstock, "The Loudspeaker and the Human Voice: Politics and the Form of *The Years*," *Bulletin of the New York Public Library* 80.2 (1976/77): 254.
36. B. B. Misra, *The Bureaucracy in India: An Historical Analysis of Development up to 1947* (Delhi: Oxford Univ. Press, 1977), 91.
37. Gabriel Hankins finds in *Jacob's Room* a similar means of constructing character to the one I examine here in *The Years*, arguing that that novel demonstrates a "fascination with the institutional scaffolding of individuation that structures Jacob's life and fate." See Hankins, *Interwar Modernism and the Liberal World Order: Offices, Institutions and Aesthetics after 1919* (Cambridge: Cambridge Univ. Press, 2019), 53.
38. As Jane Marcus writes, "The patriarchal family is violently assaulted as the source of fascism in *The Years*." Marcus, *Virginia Woolf and the Languages of Patriarchy* (Bloomington: Indiana Univ. Press, 1987), 77. Marcus and numerous other feminist critics have drawn out the implications of this aspect of Woolf's politics; it is also the aspect for which she has historically been criticized the most, perhaps most famously by her nephew Quentin Bell in his *Virginia Woolf: A Biography* (New York: Harcourt, Brace, Jovanovich, 1972).
39. Carl Sandburg, "Virginia Woolf's Personal Decision," in *Home Front Memo* (New York: Harcourt, 1943), 54.
40. DuPlessis, *Writing beyond the Ending*, 162.
41. This quote is taken from a draft manuscript of *The Pargiters* and cited in Grace Radin, *Virginia Woolf's "The Years"* (Knoxville: Univ. of Tennessee

Press, 1981), 69. Radin's book, a scrupulous recounting of Woolf's process of composition, is the only full-length work on *The Years*. It played a central role in the revival of the novel in the 1970s and 1980s and remains a critical touchstone. Radin discusses how Woolf altered initial drafts into the finished novel, focusing in particular on the excision of much material related to women's sexuality.

42. As Lisa Weihman points out, although Woolf does not specify Robin Burke's profession in the novel's earlier drafts, she makes clear in the published version that he is also a military man. Likewise, whereas in early drafts of *The Pargiters* the loss of the Colonel's fingers is attributed to a fictional incident "off . . . the Coromandel Coast" (13), in *The Years* it is tied specifically to a real historical event, the Mutiny. Weihman is correct to argue that thematically "such small editing choices expand the ideological implications of these details" and "reinforce the connections between sexual aggression and English militarism in the colonies," but they also reinforce the novel's formal logic, where character is tied to institutional history. See Weihman, "Virginia Woolf's Harum-Scarum Irish Wife," *Comparative Critical Studies* 4.1 (2007): 38–39.

43. Standard works on professionalization include Harold Perkin, *The Rise of Professional Society: England Since 1880* (London: Routledge, 1989); and Magali Sarfatti Larson, *The Rise of Professionalism* (Berkeley: Univ. of California Press, 1977).

44. Steve Ellis, *Virginia Woolf and the Victorians* (Cambridge: Cambridge Univ. Press, 2006), 121.

45. Kathy Phillips, *Virginia Woolf against Empire* (Knoxville: Univ. of Tennessee Press, 1994), 37, 32, 28.

46. Lisa Weihman argues that Delia is ultimately a "*faux* Irish nationalist"; her "romantic attachment to Parnell is sexual, not political, and her adolescent rebellion is grounded in her frustrated, unhealthy attachment to her father . . . Woolf critiques nationalist politics in general as short-sighted, divisive, and particularly unhealthy for women." But to read Delia's predicament as sexual rather than political overlooks the broader context of institutional exclusion, in which Delia's relationship to both the sexual *and* the political takes on an air of dream-like unreality. Woolf's critique in these passages is less of Parnell's nationalism than of the ways in which women are denied access to *any* form of political agency. See Weihman, "Virginia Woolf's Harum-Scarum Irish Wife," 39–40, 40, 45.

47. Thomas S. Davis, *The Extinct Scene: Late Modernism and Everyday Life* (New York: Columbia Univ. Press, 2016), 86.

48. Virginia Woolf, "A Sketch of the Past," in *Moments of Being*, ed. Jeanne Schulkind (New York: Harcourt, 1976), 152.

49. DuPlessis calls her "a character whose visionary chants pose challenges to dominant ways of seeing"; Allison Booth sees her as "a kind of Antigone ... a true radical"; Jane Marcus argues that she is a clear forerunner of *Three Guineas*'s Outsiders. DuPlessis, *Writing beyond the Ending*, 172; Booth, *Greatness Engendered*, 221; Marcus, *Languages of Patriarchy*, 64. See also Phillips, *Virginia Woolf against Empire*, 26–51; Comstock, "Loudspeaker and the Human Voice," 273–74; and Patricia Cramer, "Loving in the War Years: The War of Images in *The Years*," in *Virginia Woolf and War*, ed. Mark Hussey (Syracuse, NY: Syracuse Univ. Press, 1994), 203–24. Robert Caserio, in a more qualified assessment, sees Sara as incorporating a particularly modernist element of chance into the otherwise totalizing political and historical scheme of the novel; despite her difficulty, "the character suggests what Woolf thinks history and politics would best look like, what they might become. . . . the idea of an art that looks and sounds like Sara—parodic, wacky, annoyingly silly, and irrelevant—is shadowed forth as the hope of the political and historical world, even as it looks like its unworldly, unaccountable opponent." Caserio, *The Novel in England, 1900–1950: History and Theory* (New York: Twayne, 1999), 79.
50. Froula, *Virginia Woolf and the Bloomsbury Avant-Garde*, 244.
51. Stephen M. Barber also notes the critical tendency to base readings of *The Years* on a theory of authorial repression, arguing instead that the novel intentionally "stages a formal or textual practice that aspires both to diagnose fascism and to fight against a totalizing or unifying political, aesthetic, and moral system." Barber, "States of Emergency, States of Freedom: Woolf, History, and the Novel," *Novel: A Forum on Fiction* 42.2 (2009): 204.
52. DuPlessis, *Writing beyond the Ending*, 167.
53. Maren Linett, "The Jew in the Bath: Imperiled Imagination in Woolf's *The Years*," *Modern Fiction Studies* 48 (2002): 341–61; Linett, *Modernism, Feminism, and Jewishness* (Cambridge: Cambridge Univ. Press, 2007).
54. Paul K. Saint-Amour, *Tense Future: Modernism, Total War, Encyclopedic Form* (New York: Oxford Univ. Press, 2015), 124–25.
55. Davis, *Extinct Scene*, 83.
56. Hermione Lee, *Virginia Woolf* (New York: Knopf, 1997), 623.
57. Woolf, *Room of One's Own*, 80, 83.
58. See Froula, *Virginia Woolf and the Bloomsbury Avant-Garde*, 189–98; and Berman, *Modernist Fiction, Cosmopolitanism*, 114–56.
59. See Froula, *Virginia Woolf and the Bloomsbury Avant-Garde*, 251–56.
60. The issue of deviation from institutional norms was a going concern in sociology at this time. See, e.g., Robert K. Merton's "Social Structure and Anomie," *American Sociological Review* 3.5 (1938): 672–82, in which

Merton suggests "that certain phases of social structure generate the circumstances in which infringement of social codes constitutes a 'normal' response" (672).
61. James Naremore, "Nature and History in *The Years*," in *Virginia Woolf: Revaluation and Continuity*, ed. Ralph Freedman (Berkeley: Univ. of California Press, 1980), 75. See also Woolf, *Three Guineas*, 9.
62. Barber similarly suggests that *The Years* and *Three Guineas* propose "a relation of combination between the internal and the external ... the public and private ... making of oneself one of those heterogeneous elements whose relation to the whole renders that whole—in *Three Guineas*, the state—*variable*." Barber, "States of Emergency, States of Freedom," 205. Barber's interesting argument begins with a focus on Woolf's interest in ethical and spiritual work on the self, moving to show how Woolf related that ethical work to "the state"—a term that, my argument should suggest, is not sufficient to capture the varied set of institutions with which Woolf engages in these texts.
63. Erich Auerbach, *Mimesis*, trans. Willard Trask (Princeton, NJ: Princeton Univ. Press, 1968), 463.
64. See Fredric Jameson, "Modernism and Imperialism," in *The Modernist Papers* (New York: Verso, 2007), 152–69.
65. John Whittier-Ferguson suggests that North and Peggy, as members of the novel's youngest generation, do not "feel at home in language" and "lament their alienation from words." Whittier-Ferguson, "Repetition, Remembering, Repetition: Virginia Woolf's Late Fiction and the Return of War," *Modern Fiction Studies* 57 (2011): 244. In this they exemplify the condition of Woolf's late work, which, in the face of another world war, turns away from the modernist imperative to create language anew and toward an attention to the everyday, commonplace and repetitive use of language. Language, though debased by war, remains the only stay against violence. Whittier-Ferguson's argument is important and follows my own in noting that North and Peggy turn the novel toward the future, but it overlooks the ways that the novel's clichés, repetitions, and habits of speech are often institutionally conditioned and disseminated, especially in Peggy's case, and thus refer back to the language of specific institutions rather than to language as such. Randi Saloman links *The Years*'s reliance on repetition and linguistic confusion to Woolf's attempt to combine the essay and novel in her late-career writing. Failed communication in *The Years*, for Saloman, is an expression of Woolf's awareness as an essayist of the need to abnegate the authority and control over language that are the novelist's stock-in-trade. See Saloman, *Virginia Woolf's Essayism* (Edinburgh: Edinburgh Univ. Press, 2012), 138–68.
66. Woolf, *Diary*, 5:38.

3. Institutional Picaresque

1. Merve Emre, *Paraliterary: The Making of Bad Readers in Postwar America* (Chicago: Univ. of Chicago Press, 2017), 10. Lawrence Rainey, in *Institutions of Modernism* (New Haven, CT: Yale Univ. Press, 1999), also attends to the importance of "authorial self-construction" (4).
2. Jessica Berman's work on Anand, included in *Modernist Commitments: Ethics, Politics, and Transnational Modernism* (New York: Columbia Univ. Press, 2011), has been particularly significant in this regard.
3. On Anand's work at the BBC, see Daniel Ryan Morse, "An 'Impatient Modernist': Mulk Raj Anand at the BBC," *Modernist Cultures* 10.1 (2015): 83–98. On his time in Bloomsbury, see Anna Snaith, "The Hogarth Press and the Networks of Anti-Colonialism," in *Leonard and Virginia Woolf, the Hogarth Press and the Networks of Modernism*, ed. Helen Southworth (Edinburgh: Edinburgh Univ. Press, 2010), 103–27; and Kristen Bluemel's *George Orwell and the Radical Eccentrics: Intermodernism in Literary London* (New York: Palgrave, 2004). Peter Kalliney's *Commonwealth of Letters: British Literary Culture and the Emergence of Postcolonial Aesthetics* (New York: Oxford Univ. Press, 2013) does not address Anand at length, but demonstrates how the modernism incubated in places like Harlem and Bloomsbury connected across midcentury to postcolonial aesthetics through a shared aspiration to aesthetic autonomy.
4. Mulk Raj Anand, *Apology for Heroism*, 3rd ed. (New Delhi: Arnold, 1975), 144.
5. Simon Gikandi, "Modernism in the World," *Modernism/modernity* 13 (2006): 420.
6. John Lehmann to Anand, 26 June 1936, John Lehmann Papers, Series: Letters, Harry Ransom Center, University of Texas at Austin.
7. Pascale Casanova, *The World Republic of Letters*, trans. M. B. Debevoise (Cambridge, MA: Harvard Univ. Press, 2004), 200.
8. Mulk Raj Anand, "The Barber's Trade Union," in *The Barber's Trade Union, and Other Stories* (London: Jonathan Cape, 1944), 7–16, 10. When the story was collected in this volume, Anand dedicated it to Lehmann.
9. The protagonist of *Untouchable*, Bakha, similarly adopts English dress. Rosemary Marangoly George notes Anand's knowledge of Dalit (untouchable) writing and activist movements, and the importance of clothing to these movements, in her indispensable *Indian English and the Fiction of National Literature* (Cambridge: Cambridge Univ. Press, 2013), 233n70.
10. Rob Nixon, *Slow Violence and the Environmentalism of the Poor* (Cambridge, MA: Harvard Univ. Press, 2011), 55. Annie McClanahan argues that the picaresque genre has become increasingly relevant in the era of

"tipworkification." See McClanahan, "TV and Tipworkification," *Post45*, 10 January 2019.
11. Mulk Raj Anand, *Author to Critic: The Letters of Mulk Raj Anand to Saros Cowasjee*, ed. Cowasjee (Calcutta: Writers Workshop, 1973), 98.
12. Chad Harbach, "MFA vs. NYC," in *MFA vs. NYC*, ed. Harbach (New York: N+1 Books, 2013), 9–30, 10.
13. Anand, *Author to Critic*, 104.
14. Mulk Raj Anand, *Conversations in Bloomsbury* (London: Wildwood House, 1981).
15. For example, Anand states in *Conversations* that he did editorial work for Eliot's *Criterion* and the Hogarth Press (103, 118, 124, 129, 144). There seems to be no other documentation of these activities. Similarly, Anand claims in a number of places that Gandhi himself revised *Untouchable* for publication, a story frequently cited by critics with varying degrees of skepticism. See George, *Indian English*, 126–32, for an extensive review of the evidence; George ultimately suggests that this encounter is unlikely to have actually taken place.
16. Matthew Garrett, "Subterranean Gratification: Reading after the Picaro," *Critical Inquiry* 42.1 (Autumn 2015): 100.
17. Mulk Raj Anand, "Self-Obituary," in *Mulk Raj Anand: A Reader; Selections from his Fictional and Non-Fictional Writings*, ed. Atma Ram (New Delhi: Sahitya Akademi, 2005), xvi–xxxi. I borrow the phrase *institutionalized anti-institutionalism* from Paul O'Neill, Lucy Steeds, and Mick Wilson's introduction to *How Institutions Think: Between Contemporary Art and Curatorial Discourse* (Cambridge, MA: MIT Press, 2017).
18. Geeta Kapur, "Partisan Modernity," in *Mulk Raj Anand: Shaping the Indian Modern*, ed. Annapurna Garimella (Mumbai: Marg Publications, 2005), 28–41, 30.
19. See Emre, *Paraliterary*, 94–134.
20. Timothy Mitchell, *Rule of Experts* (Berkeley: Univ. of California Press, 2002), 54.
21. John Marx, *Geopolitics and the Anglophone Novel, 1890–2011* (Cambridge: Cambridge Univ. Press, 2012), 1. Drawing on the work of Timothy Mitchell, Marx argues that this formal definition of institutions "enabled colonial officers and policy wonks to generate 'principles true in every country,' and thereby to justify their involvement in the nitty-gritty of social life everywhere from Egypt to Bengal" (27–28). It enables something similar if more politically salutary for the novelists that Marx reads, from Conrad and Rabindranath Tagore to Amitav Ghosh to Chimamanda Ngozie Adichie, constructing a genealogy of fiction that has imagined more just modes of governance while criticizing imperialism (at the opening of the

twentieth century) and neoliberalism (at its close). Yet Marx's juxtaposition of works across the century occludes, to some extent, the moment of decolonization itself, when the question of what newly independent nations would inherit from the empire was asked most pointedly and negotiated most intensely, in both literature and politics. See also Mitchell, *Rule of Experts.*

22. Mulk Raj Anand, *Coolie* (Delhi: Penguin, 1993), 63.
23. Leela Gandhi, "Novelists of the 1930s and 1940s," in *A History of Indian Literature in English,* ed. Arvind Krishna Mehrotra (New York: Columbia Univ. Press, 2003), 178.
24. Anand's experiments with Anglicized dialogue influenced writers whose work has received substantially more attention than his own. As Salman Rushdie points out: "English is an Indian literary language, and by now, thanks to writers like [Rabindranath] Tagore, [G. V.] Desani, [Nirad] Chaudhuri, Mulk Raj Anand, Raja Rao, Anita Desai and others, it has quite a pedigree." Rushdie, "Commonwealth Literature Does Not Exist," in *Imaginary Homelands* (New York: Penguin, 1983), 65.
25. Berman, *Modernist Commitments,* 119. Berman's work has been key in bringing Anand to the attention of scholars of modernism. See also Ben Conisbee Baer on Anand's experiments with language in *Untouchable:* "Shit Writing: Mulk Raj Anand's *Untouchable,* the Image of Gandhi, and the Progressive Writers' Association," *Modernism/modernity* 16 (2009): 582–86.
26. On *Untouchable*'s modernism and place in Dalit literary history, by contrast, see Toral Jatin Garajawala, "The Casteized Consciousness: Literary Realism and the Politics of Particularism," *Modern Language Quarterly* 73.3 (2012): 329–49.
27. Sonali Perera, *No Country: Working-Class Writing in the Age of Globalization* (New York: Columbia Univ. Press, 2014), 35.
28. Munoo repeatedly and insistently reminds himself of his caste status in the course of the novel, suggesting a self-consciousness on Anand's part about which aspects of Indian society are being excluded—in particular, untouchability.
29. Certainly *Coolie* registers in various ways the problems of language and representation; it is worth noting that the speech rendered most strange in *Coolie* is that of a Cockney woman rather than that of any of the Indian characters—perhaps a suggestion on Anand's part that "regionalism" has its metropolitan components as well.
30. Jessica Berman, "Toward a Regional Cosmopolitanism: The Case of Mulk Raj Anand," *Modern Fiction Studies* 55 (2009): 157. Perera's reading of the strike is similar to my own; see Perera, *No Country,* 37.

31. Mulk Raj Anand, *Untouchable* (1935; New York: Penguin, 1989), 39; Anand, *Coolie*, 40.
32. See Gregory Castle, *Reading the Modernist Bildungsroman* (Gainesville: Univ. Press of Florida, 2006); and Jed Esty, *Unseasonable Youth: Modernism, Colonialism, and the Fiction of Development* (New York: Oxford Univ. Press, 2012).
33. Jerome Hamilton Buckley, *Season of Youth: The Bildungsroman from Dickens to Golding* (Cambridge, MA: Harvard Univ. Press, 1974), 17.
34. Douglas Mao, *Fateful Beauty: Aesthetic Environments, Juvenile Development, and Literature, 1860–1960* (Princeton, NJ: Princeton Univ. Press, 2008), 119.
35. J. A. Garrido Ardila, "Origins and Definition of the Picaresque Genre," in *The Picaresque Novel in Western Literature*, ed. Garrido Ardila (Cambridge: Cambridge Univ. Press, 2015), 15–16.
36. Claudio Guillén, *Literature as a System* (Princeton, NJ: Princeton Univ. Press, 1971), 77. For a particularly insightful theorization of the picaro that presents this figure as the basis of how we think about the experience of reading in modernity, see Garrett, "Subterranean Gratification," 97–123.
37. Gail Day, "Realism, Totality and the Militant *Citoyen*: Or, What Does Lukács Have to Do with Contemporary Art?," in *Georg Lukács: The Fundamental Dissonance of Existence: Aesthetics, Politics, Literature*, ed. Timothy Bewes and Timothy Hall (London: Continuum, 2011), 209.
38. Perera's *No Country* opens with a reading of this same passages, to argue that the kind of "interruption" the narrator enacts here—along with "breaks in the storyline, key moments of textual irony, speech interferences"—lends international working-class writing a constitutive unfinishedness that solicits readerly action. Her reading is persuasive, though I am less sure about the perhaps tongue-in-cheek suggestion that in this moment Munoo "becomes caught up in a rumination on the opaqueness of world-systems theory" (all quotations from p. 2). This kind of theoretical exercise is precisely what the narrator's intrusion makes clear Munoo isn't quite capable of enacting.
39. See Paul Johnson, *Making the Market: Victorian Origins of Corporate Capitalism* (Cambridge: Cambridge Univ. Press, 2010).
40. Aaron Kunin, "Characters Lounge," *Modern Language Quarterly* 70.3 (2009): 299.
41. Note the parallel with *Nostromo*'s proliferations of type-phrases.
42. For a related discussion of corporate personhood and liability, see Lisa Siraganian, "Dreiser's Anti-Corporate Tools: Veil-Piercing and the Novel of Corporate Agency," *American Literary History* 30.2 (2018): 249–77.

43. *Chaprasi* is a term for a minor functionary, particularly with messenger or gofer duties (as the novel makes clear). Calling Daya Ram "*the* Chaprasi," as though he were the only one, thus satirically indicates his interchangeability with any number of other individuals occupying the same role.
44. Alex Woloch, *The One vs. the Many* (Princeton, NJ: Princeton Univ. Press, 2003), 249.
45. See Partha Chatterjee, "Whose Imagined Community?," in *The Nation and Its Fragments: Colonial and Postcolonial Histories* (Princeton, NJ: Princeton Univ. Press, 1993), 3–13.
46. Anand, *Apology for Heroism*, 86.
47. Thus, as Kristin Bluemel puts it, women in the novel are divided into "two camps of perversely sexual virgins and frigid whores." *George Orwell and the Radical Eccentrics*, 86. Given that Bluemel shows how Anand addresses women and patriarchal mores in far more nuanced ways in his later writing, the portrayal of female characters in *Coolie* is a more significant, and more ideological, failure of craft than his "love of detail." But Bluemel further suggests that the portrayal of women in Anand's early novels was partially responsible for those novels' relative commercial success: "Anand's fictional women provided the majority of his readers . . . with an essential and essentialized referent that could smooth away threats of cross-cultural difference posed by his male protagonists. . . . [H]is novels threatened many members of London's intellectual circles with their tendency to lead readers from a criticism of India's caste and class systems to a criticism of British imperialism. The fact that Anand's novels do not require his readers in Britain or India to extend that same criticism to the patriarchal structures of British institutions implies that Anand was on some level asking his readers to accept sexism in order to uproot imperialism" (80–81). The upshot is that "the reader can finish *Coolie* with the impression that it is women who condemn Munoo to death" (86). When it comes to the reception of Anand's novels, Bluemel's claim is certainly plausible, although the evidence she provides is ultimately circumstantial. However, the suggestion that the text itself turns imperial oppression into oppression at the hands of women is not quite the whole story, not because it is clear that Munoo's death is due to other identifiable causes but because of the novel's consistent emphasis on the contingency of his demise.
48. The extent to which tradition and the domestic are debunked in *Coolie* suggests the insufficiency of characterizations of Anand as "India's Dickens." See, e.g., Premila Paul, "Major Themes in the Novels of Mulk Raj Anand," in *The Novels of Mulk Raj Anand*, ed. R. K. Dhawan (New Delhi: Prestige Books, 1992), 19.

49. Bluemel cites an exchange between Anand and Saros Cowasjee in the late sixties and early seventies that suggests an even closer connection between the novel's representation of women and its criticisms of Indian categories of identity. Cowasjee suggests that Anand revise *Coolie*'s ending because of its extended and offensive treatment of May Mainwaring. Anand responds that "there was no racial attack intended." "It is interesting," Bluemel notes, "that in the 1970s Anand thought readers might accuse him of offensive racial, rather than sexual, stereotypes." *George Orwell and the Radical Eccentrics*, 195n24. Certainly it suggests that Anand continued to overlook issues around gender in his writing. But in its insistence that he not be understood as drawing on racial types, the exchange also highlights Anand's consistent refusal, for better or worse, to understand conflict as ultimately driven by racial or cultural difference.
50. See Ashis Nandy, *The Intimate Enemy: Loss and Recovery of Self under Colonialism* (Delhi: Oxford Univ. Press, 1983).
51. B. B. Misra, *The Bureaucracy in India: An Historical Analysis of Development up to 1947* (Delhi: Oxford Univ. Press, 1977), ix.
52. On this type of generic comparison, see Simon During, *Exit Capitalism* (New York: Routledge, 2010), 97.
53. Walter Benn Michaels, *The Beauty of a Social Problem* (Chicago: Univ. of Chicago Press, 2015), 38–39.
54. Leo J. Blanken, *Rational Empires: Institutional Incentives and Imperial Expansion* (Chicago: Univ. of Chicago Press, 2012), 111–38.
55. Rebecca Walkowitz, *Cosmopolitan Style: Modernism Beyond the Nation* (New York: Columbia Univ. Press, 2006), 26; see also Michael de Certeau, *The Practice of Everyday Life*, trans. Steven Rendell (Berkeley: Univ. of California Press, 1984).
56. Anna Kornbluh, *The Order of Forms: Realism, Formalism, and Social Space* (Chicago: Univ. of Chicago Press, 2019), 31.
57. Frances Ferguson, *Pornography, the Theory: What Utilitarianism Did to Action* (Chicago: Univ. of Chicago Press, 2004), 23.
58. Of course, as Edward Said writes, citing Eric Stokes, "the influence of Bentham and the Mills on British rule in the Orient (and India particularly) was considerable." *Orientalism* (New York: Random House, 1978), 214. See also Stokes, *The English Utilitarians and India* (Oxford: Clarendon, 1959). Ranajit Guha demonstrates that utilitarian theory and practice played a key role in the development of British rule in India as a form of "dominance without hegemony," that is, to use Guha's terms, a situation in which coercion outweighs persuasion in establishing dominance. In this situation, the colonizing power and the Indian bourgeoisie competed to acquire hegemony by attempting to assimilate the bulk of Indian civil

society to their projects of rule (such attempts, Guha argues, always failed). Although this is not the place to make the argument at length, I would suggest that Anand's rendering of modern institutions as analogous to utilitarian social structures registers the political hope that the autonomy of such institutions, and their potential to articulate individuals regardless of identity, would make them arenas in which a genuinely Indian national hegemony could be established. *Coolie*'s exclusion of specifically subaltern experience, in this reading, would dovetail with Guha's argument, and that of the Subaltern Studies Group, of which he was a member, that bourgeois nationalism was ultimately not able to represent the South Asian masses. See Ranajit Guha, *Dominance without Hegemony: History and Power in Colonial India* (Cambridge, MA: Harvard Univ. Press, 1997); see also, though, Vivek Chibber's critique of the Subaltern Studies paradigm in *Postcolonial Theory and the Specter of Capital* (New York: Verso, 2013), especially his discussion of institutions, 192–200.

59. Mulk Raj Anand, *Letters on India* (London: Routledge, 1942), 115–16.
60. Mulk Raj Anand, preface to *Apology for Heroism*, unpaginated.
61. Anand, *Apology for Heroism*, 154.
62. Jed Esty and Colleen Lye, "Peripheral Realisms Now," introduction to "Peripheral Realisms," ed. Joe Cleary, Esty, and Lye, special issue, *Modern Language Quarterly* 73.3 (2012): 280.
63. George, *Indian English*, 124.
64. Ulka Anjaria, *Realism in the Twentieth-Century Indian Novel* (Cambridge: Cambridge Univ. Press, 2012), 29.
65. See Gloria Fisk, *Orhan Pamuk and the Good of World Literature* (New York: Columbia Univ. Press, 2017).
66. It is striking to consider that Anand's writing career overlapped with that of Salman Rushdie for more than twenty-five years, for example. Susheila Nasta points out that Rushdie's lecture "The Indian Writer in England" was first delivered at a conference in India, with Anand, Raja Rao, and Nirad Chauhuri all in attendance. Nasta, *Home Truths: Fictions of the South Asian Diaspora in Britain* (London: Palgrave, 2002), 139.
67. In this sketch of *Marg*'s history I draw on Rachel Lee and Kathleen James-Chakravorty, "*Marg* Magazine: A Tryst with Architectural Modernity," *Architecture Beyond Europe* 1 (2012), http://journals.openedition.org/abe/623; doi: 10.4000/abe.623.
68. Mulk Raj Anand, "Planning and Dreaming," *Marg* 1.1 (October 1946): 4.
69. Jawaharlal Nehru, "The Temples of New India," in *Selected Works of Jawaharlal Nehru*, 2nd ser., vol. 26 (New Delhi: Jawaharlal Nehru Memorial Fund, 2000), 131.
70. Mulk Raj Anand, "Letter to an Englishman," *Marg* 2.2 (1948).

71. Mulk Raj Anand, "Acknowledgements," in *Story of the Indian Post Office*, ed. Anand (New Delhi: Indian Posts and Telegraphs Dept., 1954).
72. Chinmay Tumbe, "Toward Financial Inclusion: The Post Office of India as a Financial Institution, 1880–2010," *Indian Economic and Social History Review* 52.4 (2015): 210.
73. Mulk Raj Anand, introduction to *Story of the Indian Post Office*, xiv–xv.
74. Gulammohammed Sheikh, "Mulk and *Marg*," in Garimella, *Mulk Raj Anand: Shaping the Indian Modern*, 50.

4. Elizabeth Bowen

1. Elizabeth Bowen, "A Conversation between Elizabeth Bowen and Jocelyn Brooke," interview by Jocelyn Brooke, in Bowen, *Listening In: Broadcasts, Speeches, and Interviews by Elizabeth Bowen*, ed. Allan Hepburn (Edinburgh: Edinburgh Univ. Press, 2010), 274.
2. Elizabeth Bowen, "Frankly Speaking: Interview, 1959," in *Listening In*, 343.
3. Victoria Glendinning's *Elizabeth Bowen: A Biography* (New York: Knopf, 1978) refers to Bowen's wartime work as "reporting" (193), but the truth is considerably more complicated. Claire Wills, in *That Neutral Island: A Cultural History of Ireland during the Second World War* (Cambridge, MA: Harvard Univ. Press, 2007), contextualizes Bowen's wartime activities among those of many other Irish writers and members of Ireland's cultural elite "whose wartime writing has to be understood as a challenge to neutrality" (12)—a neutrality that the vast majority of Irish supported throughout the war. See also Elizabeth Bowen, *Notes on Éire: Espionage Reports to Winston Churchill, 1940–2*, ed. Jack Lane and Brendan Clifford (Aubane, County Cork: Aubane Historical Society, 2009), which reproduces Bowen's reports with supplemental material and an introduction criticizing her as a traitor. Patricia Laurence, in *Elizabeth Bowen: A Literary Life* (New York: Palgrave, 2019), 191–221, presents a careful investigation Bowen's espionage work and the controversies it has occasioned. On the issue of neutrality in Bowen's literary work, see Anna Teekell, *Emergency Writing: Irish Literature, Neutrality, and the Second World War* (Evanston, IL: Northwestern Univ. Press, 2018), 127–58.
4. Elizabeth Bowen, *Bowen's Court*, 2nd ed. (New York: Ecco, 1978), 259.
5. See Paul Fussell, *The Great War and Modern Memory* (Oxford: Oxford Univ. Press, 1976).
6. Hugh Heclo, "Thinking Institutionally," in *The Oxford Handbook of Political Institutions*, ed. Bert A. Rockman, Sarah Binder, and R. A. W. Rhodes (New York: Oxford Univ. Press, 2006), 736.

7. Virginia Woolf, *The Years*, ed. Eleanor McNees (New York: Harcourt, 2008), 389.
8. See also Paul K. Saint-Amour, *Tense Future: Modernism, Total War, Encyclopedia Form* (New York: Oxford Univ. Press, 2015).
9. Elizabeth Bowen, *The Heat of the Day* (New York: Knopf, 1949), 109.
10. Elizabeth Bowen, "The Bend Back," in *The Mulberry Tree: Writings of Elizabeth Bowen*, ed. Hermione Lee (New York: Harcourt, Brace, Jovanovich, 1986), 54.
11. Heather Bryant Jordan's *How Will the Heart Endure: Elizabeth Bowen and the Landscape of War* (Ann Arbor: Univ. of Michigan Press, 1992) surveys Bowen's entire career in the context of the European and world wars that she lived through. Jordan's is a feminist reading, and she argues convincingly that Bowen, who rejected the term *feminist* herself, nonetheless avidly pursued in her life and writing the expanded social possibilities for women that war helped to produce: "The perspectives imposed by war caused Bowen to take many more risks than she might otherwise have done, both in choice of subject and style. . . . The shifting and uncertain civilization she had inherited impelled her to paint her reactions on a far larger canvas than had she lived in a time of peace" (190–91). Other key early feminist studies of Bowen include Phyllis Lassner, *Elizabeth Bowen* (Savage, MD: Barnes & Noble, 1989); and Hermione Lee, *Elizabeth Bowen: An Estimation* (London: Vision, 1981).
12. Barbara Brothers, "Pattern and Void: Bowen's Irish Landscapes and *The Heat of the Day*," *Mosaic* 12.3 (1979): 130–31.
13. Elizabeth Bowen, "The Big House," in *Mulberry Tree*, 28–29.
14. Elizabeth Bowen, "Women's Place in the Affairs of Man," in Bowen, *People, Places, Things*, ed. Allan Hepburn (Edinburgh: Edinburgh Univ. Press, 2008), 378.
15. See Jordan, *How Will the Heart Endure*, 114, citing a letter from John Hayward to Frank Morley. Hayward was a London literary figure; Morley was at the time editor in chief of Harcourt Brace in the United States.
16. On the "English garrison," see J. C. Beckett, *The Anglo-Irish Tradition* (Ithaca, NY: Cornell Univ. Press, 1976), 87–89. Beckett's book is itself a historical defense of the Anglo-Irish, and the complexities of the Anglo-Irish position in Ireland and in the broader structure of the British Empire are captured in his discussion of the term *English garrison*: "If the Irish Protestants [after 1800] were in truth a garrison, they were a garrison in peculiar and difficult circumstances. . . . They had neither means nor authority to organize their own defence. . . . They had no power to come to terms on their own behalf; but they lived in constant fear that terms would be arranged behind their backs; that a vital outwork might suddenly be

surrendered; and even that, sooner or later, the whole fortress would be abandoned and they themselves left to their fate" (88).

17. Standish O'Grady, *Selected Essays and Passages* (Dublin: Talbot, 1918), 180. The legacy of the Anglo-Irish remains a topic of debate, particularly in Ireland itself.

18. In *Bowen's Court*, Bowen recounts the family legend of how their land was acquired. Colonel Bowen "loved his hawks and hawking, doubted God and cared almost nothing for man" (36). Called before Cromwell to discuss some military matter, he was distracted by the bird he carried on his arm, at which point Cromwell, in a fit of rage at being ignored, wrung its neck. Colonel Bowen, having sometime later either reformed or become notable enough to be reckoned with, received an apology and was granted as much land as one of his other hawks would fly over. See *Bowen's Court*, 67–69.

19. W. B. Yeats, "Under Ben Bulben," in *The Variorum Edition of the Poems of W. B. Yeats*, ed. Peter Alt and R. K. Alspach (London: Macmillan, 1973), 638; Bowen, *Bowen's Court*, 87. An oft-quoted and less flattering though quite nuanced definition of the Anglo-Irish is offered by the Irish working-class playwright Brendan Behan in *The Hostage* (New York: Grove, 1958):

> Pat: He was an Anglo-Irishman.
> Meg: In the name of God, what's that?
> Pat: A Protestant with a horse.
> Ropeen: Leadbetter.
> Pat: No, no, an ordinary Protestant like Leadbetter, the plumber in the back parlour next door, won't do, nor a Belfast orangeman, not if he was as black as your boot.
> Meg: Why not?
> Pat: Because they work. An Anglo-Irishman only works at riding horses, drinking whiskey, and reading double-meaning books in Irish at Trinity College. (11)

20. It is difficult to say whether Bowen is entirely serious in the passage's conclusion, which produces a kind of reverse bathos as it offers an opinion that seems nonetheless to be Bowen's own. Lee refers to Bowen's "complexity of tone, in which regret and parody rub shoulders," which captures something of the strangeness of these lines, though they seem odder still when one considers that "1939" refers to the calamity of the world war whose effects Bowen was directly experiencing in London at the time she wrote. Lee, *Elizabeth Bowen*, 18.

21. Bernard McKenna, "Yeats, *On the Boiler,* the Aesthetics of Cultural Disintegration and the Program for Renewal 'of our own rich experience,'" *Journal of Modern Literature* 35.4 (2012): 73.
22. W. B. Yeats, "Bishop Berkeley," in *Essays and Introductions* (New York: Macmillan, 1961), 402.
23. See Raymond Williams, *Culture and Society, 1780–1950* (London: Chatto & Windus, 1958), xiv.
24. Seamus Deane, "The Literary Myths of the Revival," in *Celtic Revivals* (London: Faber & Faber, 1985), 29, 32. Deane briefly links Bowen to Yeats, suggesting that Yeats's "transposition of the political theory of aristocracy into the realm of literature" (31) informs a swath of twentieth-century Irish writing, including Bowen's *The Last September,* that Deane summarizes as concerned with "the Big House surrounded by the unruly tenantry, Culture besieged by barbarity, a refined aristocracy beset by a vulgar middle class" (31). This reductive characterization of the novel overlooks the self-conscious irony that pervades *The Last September*'s depiction of the Anglo-Irish, whom the novel portrays as a class almost helplessly out of sync with the times and at the mercy of political circumstance. On this irony, see Maria DiBattista, "Elizabeth Bowen's Troubled Modernism," in *Modernism and Colonialism,* ed. Richard Begam and Michael Valdez Moses (Durham, NC: Duke Univ. Press, 2007), 226–45. Indeed, the novel is significantly less optimistic than *Bowen's Court* about what might be salvaged from Anglo-Ireland. Deane's palpable distaste for Anglo-Irish mythmaking is highly instructive in the case of Yeats, but his essay does not allow for the possibility that writers like Bowen may have found alternative, even if still suspect, forms of value in looking back on Anglo-Ireland.
25. Neil Corcoran, *Elizabeth Bowen: The Enforced Return* (New York: Oxford Univ. Press, 2004), 25.
26. Henry III is a character reminiscent of Conrad's Singleton, the elemental sailor of *The Nigger of the Narcissus.* As Conrad writes, "Singleton with an education is impossible . . . he would become conscious—and much smaller—and very unhappy." Conrad to Cunninghame Graham, 14 December 1897, in *The Collected Letters of Joseph Conrad,* ed. Frederick R. Karl and Laurence Davies, 5 vols. (Cambridge: Cambridge Univ. Press, 1988), 1:424.
27. Sharon Cameron, *Impersonality* (Chicago: Univ. of Chicago Press, 2007), ix.
28. In a late fragment of autobiography, Bowen does offer an account of Anglo-Irish cultural achievement that is explicitly indebted to that of Yeats. "Bravado," she writes, "characterizes much Irish, all Anglo-Irish

writing: gloriously it is sublimated by Yeats. . . . As beings we are at once brilliant and limited; our unbeatables, up to now, accordingly, have been those who best profited by that: Goldsmith, Sheridan, Wilde, Shaw, Beckett." Elizabeth Bowen, "Pictures and Conversations," in *Mulberry Tree*, 276. Bowen, however, maintains an emphasis on Anglo-Irish constraints ("we are . . . limited"), and unlike Yeats, she draws only two of her exemplars from the eighteenth century. What is most significant for Bowen about the height of Anglo-Irish power in her post–*Bowen's Court* writing is still not the culture it produced.

29. Lee traces the many novelistic parallels to aspects of *Bowen's Court*; see Lee, *Elizabeth Bowen*, 34–42.
30. Maud Ellmann, *Elizabeth Bowen: The Shadow Across the Page* (Edinburgh: Edinburgh Univ. Press, 2004), 67.
31. Corcoran adds an interesting footnote to the history of Bowen's Court: "When I made a program about Elizabeth Bowen for BBC Radio 3 in 1998, I interviewed people in Farahy and Kildorerry and was told that, while Elizabeth was in London, the local branch of the IRA—some of whose members worked, or had worked, in the house—took a vote *in the house itself* about whether to burn it. The vote was, of course, not to do so." Corcoran, *Elizabeth Bowen*, 25n9. Exactly when this might have occurred is an object for speculation, as Bowen herself notes that she was in Italy when the neighboring houses were burned (see *Bowen's Court*, 440), and her absence would not have implied that the house was vacant; Henry Bowen ("Henry VI"), her father, would presumably have been either at the house or in Dublin throughout the 1920s.
32. Vera Kreilkamp, *The Anglo-Irish Novel and the Big House* (Syracuse, NY: Syracuse Univ. Press, 1998), 142.
33. A May 1934 letter from Virginia Woolf to Vanessa Bell somewhat humorously reinforces the idea that architecture has less to do with the set of institutional values presented in *Bowen's Court*. Of a visit to the house, Woolf writes, "The remarkable thing about Ireland is that . . . There is no architecture of any kind . . . so Elizabeths home was merely a great stone box . . . however they insisted upon keeping up a ramshackle kind of state, dressing for dinner and so on." Virginia Woolf, *The Letters of Virginia Woolf*, ed. Nigel Nicolson and Joanne Trautman, vol. 5 (New York: Harcourt, 1979), 299–300.
34. See, e.g., Ellmann, *Elizabeth Bowen*; Kreilkamp, *Anglo-Irish Novel*; and Lee, *Elizabeth Bowen*.
35. Allan Hepburn discusses what he terms "this remote relation between narrator and character" in Bowen's writing in his "French Translations: Elizabeth Bowen and the Idea of Character," *University of Toronto Quarterly*

79 (2010): 1058. Hepburn argues that Bowen looked for examples of unsympathetic relationships between narrators and characters to French novelists, and especially to Gustave Flaubert, Henri de Montherlant, Guy de Maupassant, and Marcel Proust. In his *Intrigue: Espionage and Culture* (New Haven, CT: Yale Univ. Press, 2005), Hepburn suggests that Stella is "a translator in the Ministry of Information," but crucially the novel never actually says this (134). Hepburn argues that "Bowen places love at the core of narrative" (139), against which I would suggest that the novel's crypto-institutionalism in fact occludes what exactly *is* at "the core of narrative." Because of this, my reading stands at an oblique angle to Hepburn's argument that "*The Heat of the Day* conceives character as an entity detachable from action" (158) and that character is "an ontology apart from action" (163); it is difficult to say what character could be in a world where the truth of individual lives, insofar as it can be discerned, is mediated entirely through institutions.

36. Jacqueline Rose, "Bizarre Objects: Mary Butts and Elizabeth Bowen," *Critical Quarterly* 42.1 (2003): 81.
37. As Anna Teekell puts it, "*Bowen's Court* provides a secret subtext to Bowen's novel of secrecy, in both the novel's structural echoes of Bowen's own wartime travel to and from Ireland and London and, less transparently, its syntactical negativity and contortion. In *The Heat of the Day*'s syntactical features, Bowen directly borrows—even copies—many of the structures of *Bowen's Court*. However, she applies these structures not to the fiction estate Mount Morris but to her depiction of London under the Blitz." Teekell, *Emergency Writing*, 144. Teekell's broader discussion specifically concerns the genre of plantation gothic, which she suggests both works evoke, and the ways in which Bowen's uniquely difficult literary language is tied to questions of Irish neutrality. I am interested in Bowen's and her characters' relationships to the British state and its institutions, less so Ireland.
38. Rochelle Rives, in her *Modernist Impersonalities* (New York: Palgrave, 2011), situates Bowen "within a larger modernist genealogy . . . concerned with the asymmetries that develop between subject and object, human and external world. For Bowen, such imbalances occur particularly through a promotion of personality that subjugates the object of the world to its subject" (151). My argument here accords with that of Rives insofar as I see Bowen as privileging impersonality over the personal in order to show the generative effects of institutions on character. Where Rives suggests that Bowen "looks toward an impersonal organization of space in hopes of creating a more empathic, less cruel, material setting" (151), though, I would suggest that in her wartime and late-career work ethical concerns such as these are made secondary to an interest in impersonal style.

39. Jordan, *How Will the Heart Endure*, 153.
40. As Bowen writes in *Seven Winters*, a short memoir of her Dublin childhood, "The first male Bowen in each generation had been christened either Robert or Henry. My grandfather had been Robert, my father Henry—there was no doubt which name was waiting for me." Elizabeth Bowen, *Seven Winters* (Dublin: Cuala, 1942), 21.
41. Andrew Bennett and Nicholas Royle, *Elizabeth Bowen and the Dissolution of the Novel* (New York: St. Martin's, 1995), 93. Robert Caserio makes the related (and more compelling) argument that *The Heat of the Day* is a riposte to widespread notions of narrative, indebted to Paul de Man, as "by its very nature a structure of lurid opposites"—most notably for Caserio that of "tychism and totality," chance and necessity, choice and no choice. Bowen's novel, by contrast, shows us a world in which "the careers of love are agonizing because they belong to history and to fiction and therefore to narrative as Bowen practices it. They belong to a narrative network of distinctions and disjunctions that is simultaneously a network of likenesses and continuities; they belong to a sequence of choices and decisions that undoes choice and decision." Caserio, *The Novel in England, 1900–1950: History and Theory* (New York: Twayne, 1999), 268, 269.
42. See Ashley Maher, "'Swastika Arms of Passage Leading to Nothing': Late Modernism and the 'New' Britain," *ELH* 80 (2013): 251–85. Maher argues convincingly that late modernists like Bowen, George Orwell, and Christopher Isherwood "examined interior and architectural design as a means of expressing their apprehension about their own style and its political implications in years when form had become newly politicized" (251).
43. See Teekell, *Emergency Writing*, 143–51, for a reading that parallels mine with regard to the significance of the Big House in *The Heat of the Day*. For a significantly different reading of the role of state institutions in *The Heat of the Day*, see Janice Ho, *Nation and Citizenship in the Twentieth-Century British Novel* (Cambridge: Cambridge Univ. Press, 2015), 85–115. Ho argues that Bowen "counters the state's attempts at locating good citizenship in the domain of character . . . by opposing the instabilities of novelistic character . . . to the stasis of the state's citizen-subject" (101) and suggests that "Ireland . . . stands for a site of freedom from the civic demands of war" (113). While I agree that Bowen rejects the forms of institutional drudgery that might fall into the category "good citizenship," my argument here imagines a more positive role for character's instability in the novel: it is that instability that enables Bowen's ethos of stylish impersonality.
44. Elizabeth Bowen, "Careless Talk," in *The Collected Stories of Elizabeth Bowen*, intro. Angus Wilson (London: Jonathan Cape, 1981), 670.

45. Elizabeth Bowen, "Green Holly," in *Collected Stories*, 719.
46. Elizabeth Bowen to William Plomer, quoted in Glendinning, *Elizabeth Bowen*, 160. I am grateful to Vaclav Paris for pointing out the quoted phrase's echo of the apocryphal last words of another Anglo-Irish wit, Oscar Wilde: "Either the wallpaper goes, or I do."
47. On Bowen's relationship with Isaiah Berlin, see Laurence, *Elizabeth Bowen: A Literary Life*, 87–95 and *passim*. The first scholarly biography of Bowen, Laurence's study is particularly insightful regarding Bowen's friendships, intellectual and otherwise.
48. Elizabeth Bowen, "Without Coffee, Cigarettes, or Feeling," in *People, Places, Things*, 99.
49. Glendinning, *Elizabeth Bowen*, 263–67, provides a useful overview of Bowen's endeavors at American universities. In a curious parallel, some Big Houses themselves also found homes in the United States, as Terence Dooley notes in "The Destruction of the Country House in Ireland, 1879–1973," in *Lost Mansions: Essays on the Destruction of the Country House*, ed. James Raven (London: Palgrave, 2015), 44–62. "Throughout the late nineteenth century and long after Irish independence in 1922," writes Dooley, "sold-off contents made their way across the Atlantic to adorn the homes of rich and aspirant American families" (48–49), with William Randolph Hearst in particular acquiring entire rooms and staircases. For a reading that complements my own, see Ian d'Alton, "Bowen's Court as 'an Aesthetic of Living': A Lost Mansion's Significance in the Imagining of the Irish Gentry," 63–79 in the same volume. D'Alton discusses what he terms "the anthropomorphic house" (70) and its role in maintaining "the fiction of Anglo-Irish nostalgia" (74).
50. See Elizabeth Bowen to Blanche Knopf, 11 July 1963, Alfred A. Knopf Inc. Records, box 686, folder 1, Harry Ransom Center, University of Texas at Austin.
51. See Glendinning, *Elizabeth Bowen*, 288–92.
52. Elizabeth Bowen and Charles Ritchie, *Love's Civil War: Letters and Diaries, 1941–1973*, ed. Victoria Glendinning with Judith Robertson (Toronto: McLelland & Stewart, 2008), 301–2, final ellipsis in Glendinning's volume.
53. Clark Kerr, *The Uses of the University*, 5th ed. (Cambridge, MA: Harvard Univ. Press, 2001).

Conclusion

1. Georg Lukács, *The Theory of the Novel*, trans. Anna Bostock (Cambridge, MA: MIT Press, 1974), 77.
2. Joseph Cleary, "Realism after Modernism and the Literary World-System," *Modern Language Quarterly* 73 (2012): 261, 268.

3. David James and Urmila Seshagiri, "Metamodernism," *PMLA* 129.1 (2014): 87–100.
4. The epigraph is borrowed from Elaine Scarry, *On Beauty and Being Just* (Princeton, NJ: Princeton Univ. Press, 1999), 8, quoted in Zadie Smith, *On Beauty* (New York: Penguin, 2006), 127.
5. Zadie Smith, *NW* (New York: Penguin, 2012), 236.
6. Zadie Smith, *Swing Time* (New York: Penguin, 2016), 285.
7. Zadie Smith, *White Teeth* (New York: Random House, 2000), 378.
8. On the relationship between state institutions and upward-mobility narratives, see Bruce Robbins, *Upward Mobility and the Common Good: Toward a Literary History of the Welfare State* (Princeton, NJ: Princeton Univ. Press, 2007). See also Helen Small, "Fully Accountable," *New Literary History* 44 (2013): 539–60, on the complicated politics of the university in *NW* in relation to UK higher education policy.

INDEX

Acemoglu, Daron, 30
Africa, 30, 31
Allen, Douglas, 9–10
All-India Progressive Writers' Union, 134
Althusser, Louis, 5
Anand, Mulk Raj: *Across the Black Waters*, 117; *Apology for Heroism*, 112, 119–20, 132, 133; autobiography of, 108–9, 133; "The Barber's Trade Union," 22, 103–5, 107, 108, 110, 111, 117; Bloomsbury and, 101, 106–8, 134, 198n3; caste and traditional Indian life in, 103–4, 114, 136, 200n28; collective agency and, 105, 118, 130–32, 138; collective authorship like an institution and, 22, 134–38; *Conversations in Bloomsbury*, 22, 106–8, 110, 199n15; globalization and, 133; imprisoned in independence movement, 102, 107; in institutional picaresque genre, 21–22, 101–2, 104–5, 108–11, 117–18, 128–29, 134–38, 164; institutions' ameliorative capacity and, 2, 101, 112, 129–30, 137, 164; international status of, 105, 106, 134; *Lament on the Death of a Master of Arts*, 102; later career of, 106, 134–38; *Letters on India*, 132–33, 136, 138; "Letter to an Englishman," 136; love of detail in, 113, 120; as modernist, 106, 133, 134, 200n25; *Morning Face*, 106; nationalism and, 101, 104, 108, 125, 132, 134–35, 137; Nehru/Gandhi connections of, 104, 106, 107, 135–37, 199n15; as outsider's insider, 22, 106, 108–9, 134; political commentary of, 101–2, 104, 109–10, 164; in prewar British literary world, 102, 105, 107, 134; Progressive Writers' Association and, 102; realism and, 102–3, 108, 118; return to India (1945), 105–6, 134; Sahitya Academy Award received by, 106; "Self-Obituary," 22, 108–10, 138; self-presentation of, 22, 102–3, 106, 108–12; *Story of the Indian Post Office* (ed.), 22, 105, 134, 137–38; *The Sword and the Sickle*, 106, 117; *Two Leaves and a Bud*, 117; *Untouchable*, 101, 102, 106, 111, 114, 115, 134, 198n9, 199n15, 200nn25–26; *The Village*, 117. See also *Coolie*; *Marg*
Anderson, Amanda, 55, 192n18
Anderson, Perry, 13–14, 16
Anglo-Irish: Bowen's family history and, 23, 139–42, 144; Deane on mythmaking of, 208n24; definition of, 207n19; dominance in 1750s, 146; Gaelic League's role, 148; history of, 146, 206n16; idea of living vs. culture of, 145, 147–48, 149, 153, 209n28; impersonal institutionalism of, 141–42, 143–54, 164, 166; insufficiency of ethos of, 169; as landowner class, 139–42, 144; legacy of, 207n17; sold-off contents from Big Houses transferred to America, 212n49; thread of future potential in, 167; in Victorian era, 148, 168; women's suffering in, 167; Yeats's construction of culture of, 147–48, 208n24, 208–9n28. See also *Bowen's Court*
Anjaria, Ulka, *Realism in the Twentieth-Century Indian Novel*, 133
anti-institutional ethos of Cold War era, 2
anti-Semitism, 14, 90–91
Ardila, J. A. Garrido, 117

Arendt, Hannah, 114; *Origins of Totalitarianism,* 40
Armstrong, Nancy, 11
Arnold, Matthew, 12, 26, 27; *Culture and Anarchy,* 10; "The Literary Influence of the Academies," 10–11
Arnold, Thomas, 26
Association Internationale Africaine, 31
Auerbach, Erich, *Mimesis,* 96
Austen, Jane, 40
authenticity, 27, 95, 166, 171
autonomy: female, 65, 90–91; of institutions, 7, 118, 132, 164; literary, 69

Baer, Ben Conisbee, 114, 200n25
Balzac, Honoré de, 4
Banfield, Ann, 192n13
Barber, Stephen M., 196n51, 197n62
Baxter, Richard, *Worlds of Spirits,* 145
BBC, Anand working at, 101, 105, 110, 134, 138, 198n3
Beckett, J. C., 206n16
Beckett, Samuel, 209n28
Behan, Brendan, 207n19
Bell, Julian, 74
Bell, Quentin, 107, 194n38
Bennett, Andrew, *Elizabeth Bowen and the Dissolution of the Novel* (with Royle), 163–64
Bennett, Arnold, 66
Bentham, Jeremy, 130
Berkeley, George, 87, 147
Berlin, Isaiah, 139, 171
Berman, Jessica, 68, 95, 113–15, 198n2, 200n25
Bharatiya Janata Party (BJP), 110
bildungsroman: Anand's *Coolie* viewed in terms of, 111, 114–16, 127, 129; Conrad and, 20, 40–44; effect of institutional character on, 27, 175, 188n42; scholarship on, 3, 39–40, 188n40
Binschtok, Viktoria, 129
Bishop, Edward, 66
Bland, Bill, 107

Blanken, Leo J., 129; *Rational Empires,* 30
Bloomsbury: Anand and, 101, 106–8, 134, 198n3; Bowen and, 139, 167; nostalgia of 1970s and 1980s, 107
Bluemel, Kristin, 132–33
Boer War, 14, 16
Boes, Tobias, 44, 188n40
Booth, Alison, 194n34, 196n49
Bowen, Elizabeth: aestheticization of institutions by, 143, 173; affair with Charles Ritchie, 140; American universities and, 23, 140, 143, 168, 172–73, 212n49; Anglo-Ireland and, 139–42, 144; "The Bend Back," 142, 152; Big House's role in fiction of, 142, 151–52, 164–69, 171, 208n24, 211n43; Bloomsbury and, 139, 167; Bowen Court property of, 139–40; Brooke's interview of, 139; "Careless Talk," 168; collective change and commitment in, 141–42, 144, 151, 153, 172–73; consciousness vs. unconsciousness in, 150–51; disdain for welfare state, 170–71, 173; *Encounters,* 139; family background of, 139; feminism and, 206n11; "Green Holly," 168; "The Happy Autumn Fields," 168–69; impersonality of institutional life and, 141–54, 156–59, 163–67, 172, 175, 210n38, 211n43; as journalist in post-WWII Germany, 171–72; Kent and, 139–40; *The Last September,* 154, 166, 208n24; later career of, 23, 140, 143, 167–68, 172–73; in London during wartime 1940s, 140–42, 168, 205n3; marriage of, 139–40; modernism and, 142, 210n38, 211n42; narrator and character relationship in, 155, 209–10n35; plantation gothic and, 210n37; politics shunned by, 143, 157, 164, 173; Rives's reading of, 210n38; *Seven Winters,* 211n40; "Without Coffee, Cigarettes, or Feeling,"

171–72; Woolf and, 139, 209n33; Yeats and, 208n24, 208–9n28. See also *Bowen's Court; Heat of the Day, The*
Bowen, Robert (father), 139
Bowen's Court (Bowen), 22–23, 143–54; afterword in second edition, 150–51, 153–54; Anglo-Irish idea of living and form of life, 145, 147–48, 149, 153; Anglo-Irish impersonal institutionalism and, 23, 141–54, 164; Anglo-Irish legacy, attempt to reconceive, 149–50; Bowen Court (the Big House) representing concept of institution in, 23, 142, 151–52; Colonel Bowen as progenitor of family arriving in Ireland, 145, 207n18; compared to Conrad's *The Nigger of the Narcissus*, 208n26; era of "Personal Life" in, 149; Henry III as builder of Bowen's Court and creating impersonal pattern for all succeeding Bowens, 145–47, 150, 167, 208n26; Henry V's Dublin experience, 149; human agency of lesser interest in, 149–51; Irish Civil War of 1920s and destruction of nearby houses, 140, 153, 209n31; life of family and life of house in, 23, 143–45, 207n18; narrator and character relationship in, 155, 209–10n35; prose style of historical formality used in, 152–53, 159; pseudo-monarchical names used for forebears in, 149, 211n40; similarities to Bowen's *The Heat of the Day*, 156, 162–65, 210n37; wartime conditions in, 141–42
Bowlby, Rachel, 192n15
Bowra, Maurice, 139
Braddock, Jeremy, *Collecting as Modernist Practice*, 5
Bradley, F. H., 26
Brecht, Bertolt, 129
British culture: compared to French culture and the Academy, 10; cultural studies as distinctly English, 13–14; lack of historical materialism and classical sociology, 13; Shaw and White, comparison of views on, 16
British Empire: causes of decline of, 14; effect of formation on intellectual climate, 12–13; institutions of, 1, 13–14, 16, 31, 127, 132; Muir on, 186–87n25; political-economic model of, 41; protest movement against, 132; Woolf on Englishmen in, 16–17, 77–78. See also *Coolie*
Brontë, Charlotte, 12, 40; *Jane Eyre*, 11
Brontë, Emily, 40
Brooke, Jocelyn, 139
Brothers, Barbara, 142
Buckley, Jerome Hamilton, 115–16
Burke, Edmund, 26, 147

Cain, P. J., *British Imperialism 1688–2015* (with Hopkins), 41
Cambridge school of historiography, 41
Cameron, Alan, 139, 140
Cameron, Sharon, 148
Cape, Jonathan, 143
capitalism: Conrad and, 28, 42; imperial, 119; nation-based, 40; naturalist and modernist writers on, 188n46
Carlyle, Thomas, 11, 12, 26, 27, 185n6; "Signs of the Times," 10
Casanova, Pascale, 103, 108
Caserio, Robert, 196n49, 211n41
Catholics and Catholicism, 144–46
Center for Contemporary Cultural Studies (University of Birmingham), 13
Charles I (king of England), 144
Chatterjee, Partha, 125
Churchill, Winston, 170–71
civil service, 3, 10, 65
Claybaugh, Amanda, "Government Is Good," 6
Cleary, Joseph, 12, 175
Cold War, 140

Coleridge, Samuel Taylor, 26
collectivities: Anand and, 105, 118, 130–32, 138; Bowen and, 141–42, 144, 151, 153, 172–73; colonialism's effect on, 26, 30; Conrad and, 20, 25, 26, 29, 42, 50, 53, 57; impersonality of, 9, 77, 151; manifest in modernist writing, 9, 92, 175, 181n13, 182n25; minor characters in relation to, 4; nineteenth-century novel grappling with, 9; Woolf and, 21, 65, 75–76, 81, 83, 92, 98
colonialism: anticolonial nationalist thought in, 125; economic development and, 30; forms of rule in, 30; left-wing British intellectuals' views of, 105, 110; unsettling effects on national culture, 39. *See also* imperialism
coming-of-age novel. *See* bildungsroman
Commonwealth and Afro-Asian Writers' Conferences, 106
Comstock, Margaret, 76
Connelly, Cyril, 140
Conrad, Joseph: "Autocracy and War," 25, 47, 100; belief in perfectibility of human institutions, 25; bildungsroman and, 39–44; career of, 27–28; *Chance*, 58; collective action and, 20, 25, 26, 29, 42, 50, 53, 57; Congo experience of, 31; "The Crime of Partition," 35; criticism of, 57, 189n51; distrust of institutions and, 2, 25, 31, 38, 54; Fleishman on, 26–27; on Anatole France, 25, 26; *Heart of Darkness*, 29, 31, 61; "heterotopic" sensibility of, 33–34; on human reproduction of the institution, 8; imperialism and, 20–21, 28, 30–32, 36–38, 41, 189n51; individual action and, 20–21, 25–27, 29, 38, 42, 44, 47, 51, 55; influence of, 100; *Lord Jim*, 20, 27, 28, 39, 42–44; *The Mirror of the Sea*, 27; national identity and, 22, 26–28, 33, 50–52, 58, 186n18; *The Nigger of the Narcissus*, 208n26; organicism and, 27, 35, 38; pessimism of, 20, 38, 44, 57, 61–62; Polish background of, 27–28, 185n12; political institutions and politics in, 20–21, 25–26, 29, 38, 55, 62, 100, 185n4; problems of character development for, 44; *The Secret Agent*, 25, 31, 53, 54–55, 60; *A Set of Six*, 25; *The Shadow Line*, 42; social uses of literary form by, 101; *Victory*, 28; Woolf influenced by, 97. *See also Inheritors, The; Nostromo; Under Western Eyes*
consciousness: Bowen and, 150–51; modernism's shift to, 3, 9, 77; Woolf and, 20, 66–69, 73, 77, 90–91, 184n48, 192n13
Coolie (Anand), 22, 111–33; anticipating institutions' ameliorative capacity, 22, 112, 129–30, 137, 164; bank's institutional hierarchy in, 125, 128, 131; bildungsroman genre and, 111, 114, 115–16, 127, 129; biographical form of, 106, 112; caste status in, 128, 200n28; compared to Conrad's *Nostromo*, 53; compared to Joyce's *A Portrait of the Artist as a Young Man*, 114, 116–17; continuity with Anand's other work in picaresque genre, 117; cruelty and hypocrisy of feudal life in, 125–26; cultural misunderstanding between English and Indian men in, 128; Dalit experience ignored in, 114, 200n28; Daya Ram's imperious behavior, 124–25, 129; death of Munoo, 112, 127; domestic sphere and search for surrogate mothers in, 126–27; everyday Indian life in late colonial period depicted in, 113, 115, 117, 123, 131; foreman (Jimmie Thomas) as institutional character in, 116, 120–23, 129; on India's imperial inheritance,

111–13; institutional character in, 21–22, 111–31, 175; institutional picaresque realm of, 21–22, 111, 117–18, 128–29; mill's production and extractive functions, 122–23; Munoo's experiences of exploitation, 22, 111–12, 114, 122–23, 129; narrator's independence and knowledge in, 116, 118–20; peripheral realism of, 133; political economy in, 118–19, 122, 129; political formalism of, 130; popularity of, 101; publication of, 102, 111, 134; Ratan (Munoo's friend), 123, 135; regional languages rendered into English in, 113–15, 200n24; union rally ended by religious discord, 112, 126, 131
Corbett, Mary Jean, 184n47, 209n31
Corcoran, Neil, 148, 163
Cowasjee, Saros, 106
Cromwell, Oliver, 34, 144, 145, 207n18
crypto-institutionalism, 143, 157, 159, 161–64, 166, 168, 170, 210n35
Cunard, Nancy, 107

d'Alton, Ian, 212n49
Darvay, Daniel, 58
Darwin, John, *The Empire Project: The Rise and Fall of the British World-System 1830–1970*, 41
Davis, Thomas S., 85, 91–92
Day, Gail, 118
Deane, Seamus, 147–48, 208n24
de Certeau, Michel, 130
decolonalization, 200n21
de Man, Paul, 211n41
De Silva, Anil and Minette, 135
detachment, 19, 54–62, 95–96
DiBattista, Maria, 194n34
Dickens, Charles, 4, 40; *Bleak House*, 4; Bowen taking characterization from, 12, 170; *Great Expectations*, 12
Dobree, Bonamy, 106
Dooley, Terence, 212n49
Duckworth, George, 17–19

DuPlessis, Rachel Blau, 76, 79, 88, 191n9, 196n49
Durkheim, Émile, *The Rules of Sociological Method*, 13
dynamism: Carlyle and, 10; Conrad and, 27

Eatough, Matthew, 184n45
Edgeworth, Maria, *The Absentee*, 149
Edwardian novelists, 66–67, 69, 73
Eliot, George, 26, 55
Eliot, T. S., 101, 106, 107, 136, 147, 199n15
Ellis, Steve, 83–84
Ellmann, Maud, 150, 154, 162, 169
Emre, Merve, 101, 110
essay-novel form, Woolf's experimenting with in *The Pargiters*, 63–64, 70, 87, 197n65
Esty, Jed, 13–14, 26, 40, 42, 133; *Unseasonable Youth*, 39
Evans, Elizabeth F., 194n33

Fabian Society, 15
Faragher, Megan, "Modernist Institutions" (with Krzakowski), 7
fascism, 63, 76, 79, 194n33, 194n38, 196n51
feminism: Bowen and, 206n11; Woolf and, 21, 64–65, 76, 87, 91, 94–95, 191–92n9, 193n28, 194n38
Ferguson, Frances, 130
Figlerowicz, Marta, 8
Fisher, Herbert, 16–17, 19
Fisk, Gloria, 134
Flaubert, Gustave, 159, 210n35
Fleishman, Avrom, 38, 185n6; *Conrad's Politics*, 26–27
Ford, Ford Madox, 185n6; on Conrad's belief in perfectibility of human institutions, 25. See also *Inheritors, The*
Forster, E. M.: Anand and, 101, 107; distrust of institutions and, 2; *Howards End*, 176; influence on Zadie Smith, 176; *A Passage to India*, 1–2; on round or flat characters, 48

Foucault, Michel, 5, 74
fragmentation, 3, 20, 80, 99–100, 176
France, Anatole, 25, 26
Fromm, Gloria, 193n28
Froula, Christine, *Virginia Woolf and the Bloomsbury Avant-Garde*, 87, 95, 192n9
Fussell, Paul, *The Great War and Modern Memory*, 141

Gaelic League, 148
Gallagher, John, "The Imperialism of Free Trade" (with Robinson), 41
Galsworthy, John, 66
Galvan, Jill, 8
Gandhi, Leela, 113
Gandhi, Mahatma, 104, 106, 125, 136, 199n15
Garajawala, Toral Jatin, 200n26
Garnett, Edward, 57
Garrett, Matthew, 108
Gaskell, Elizabeth, 12; *North and South*, 11
gender. *See* women
George, Rosemary Marangoly, 133; *Indian English and the Fiction of National Literature*, 107, 198n9, 199n15
Germany after World War II, 171–72
Gikandi, Simon, 102
Gill, Eric, 107
Glendinning, Victoria, 140, 148, 171, 172, 205n3, 212n49
globalization: Anand and, 133; Conrad and, 28, 33; literary culture and, 101–2; Woolf and, 79, 97
GoGwilt, Christopher, 28
Goldsmith, Oliver, 147, 209n28
Goldstone, Andrew, 69
Gooch, Joshua, 189n54
Gramsci, Antonio, 36, 187n35
Green, Henry, 139
Green, T. H., 26
Greene, Graham, 139
Guillén, Claudio, 117

Hankins, Gabriel, *Interwar Modernism and the Liberal World Order*, 7, 194n37
Harbach, Chad, 106
Hardt, Michael, 28
Harpham, Geoffrey Galt, 27–28
Hay, Eloise Knapp, 38, 61, 190n60
Hayward, John, 206n15
Hearst, William Randolph, 212n49
Heat of the Day, The (Bowen), 23, 154–67; Anglo-Irishness of, 164; Caserio's reading of, 211n41; compared to Conrad's *Nostromo*, 162; confusing chronology depicting how time passes in wartime, 160; crypto-institutions of wartime in, 141–43, 156–57, 159, 161–71, 210n35; demolition of the moment in, 157–58; Dickens's characterization appearing in, 12, 170; doppelganger effect in, 163–64; Harrison's blackmail of Stella, 159–62; Hepburn's reading of, 209–10n35; Ho's reading of, 211n43; individuals as agents of their times in, 151, 164; institutional impersonality of, 3, 23, 156–59, 163–67, 172, 175, 210n38, 211n43; Louie and her friend Connie in final subplot of, 169–70; as present-day historical novel, 157; promise of new kinds of intimacy in, 158; reader limited to imperfect knowledge of the main characters, 161; Robert's admission to being a German spy, 161, 163; Robert's family home of Home Dene in, 161, 166; Roderick, Stella's son, inheriting Mount Morris (Big House) in, 165–67, 211n43; similarities to *Bowen's Court*, 156, 162–65, 210n37; similarities to "The Happy Autumn Fields," 169; Stella and Robert's love story in, 157–59; style shift from deliberate and descriptive to contradictory and abstruse in, 156; wartime making

INDEX 221

individuals interchangeable, 159, 163–64; welfare state in, 23, 170
Heclo, Hugh, 22, 141
Hepburn, Allan, 209–10n35
Hershinow, Stephanie Insley, 41–42
Hinduism, 112, 126
Hindu Right, 110
Hite, Molly, 193n28
Ho, Janice, 211n43
Hobsbawm, Eric, 29; *The Age of Empire, 1875–1914*, 40
Hobson, J. A., *Imperialism*, 36, 40
Hochman, Baruch, 66
Hogarth Press, 22, 102, 110, 199n15
Hone, Joseph, *Bishop Berkeley* (with Rossi), 147
Hopkins, A. G., *British Imperialism 1688–2015* (with Cain), 41
Huxley, Aldous, 107
Hyam, Ronald, 29–30

imperialism: age of empire, 39, 40, 111; Anand and, 112; bildungsroman and, 40–41; Cambridge school of historiography and, 41; characterized by formal institutions, 29, 199–200n21; Conrad and, 20–21, 28, 30–32, 36–38, 41, 189n51; continuity in British expansion, 41; disruption of self-sufficiency of nationhood and narratives of development, 39; formal vs. informal periods of, 40–41; global effects on institutions, 14–15, 30, 119–20; historiography of, 42, 175; Marxist account of, 40; Woolf and, 16–17, 79, 84, 97. *See also* British Empire
impersonal institutions. *See* Bowen, Elizabeth
India: caste and other hierarchical distinctions in, 103–4, 114, 126, 128, 131, 136, 200n38; cruelty and hypocrisy of feudal life in, 125–26; cultural Left in, 134, 137; Dalits in, 114, 198n9, 200n28; imperial governance of, 30; independence movement in, 132; independence of, 128, 135, 137; *Marg*'s depiction of independent India and its heritage, 135–36; politics in, 109–10, 134. *See also* Anand, Mulk Raj; British Empire
individualism, 1–4; institutions' relationship with, 7–9, 16–22; methodological individualism of the Victorians, 3, 11, 39; in Victorian prehistories, 9–13
Industrial Revolution, 9–10
Inheritors, The (Conrad and Ford), 20, 32–37; compared to Conrad's *Under Western Eyes*, 59; critique of imperialism in, 28, 31, 32, 36–37; efficiency and, 32–37; individual action in, 54; institutionality's effect on social cohesion and, 25–26, 35; institutions as technology in, 35–37, 100; key passage attributed solely to Conrad, 34; popular press as social force in, 29, 32–33
institutional character, 1–9; central role in novelistic narrative, 4, 175; complementary aspect of natural characteristics, 11; cross-period resonances between Victorian and modernist studies and, 8; identity generated by institutional attachment, 12; legacy of, 175–76; meaning of, 3, 38; Victorian prehistories of, 9–13, 182n19
institutionalism: ameliorative capacity of, 2, 22, 101, 112, 129–30, 137, 164; biography of an institution, 31; inevitability of institutions, 13–20; institutionalized anti-institutionalism, 108, 199n16; institutional reform, need for, 16; institutional revolution of measurement and merit, 9–10; meaning of institution, 5, 7, 35, 37–38, 74–75, 111, 199n21; modernism and new institutionalism, 7–8; visibility of state power and, 5–6

"institutional logics" approach, 181n13
institutional picaresque, 21–22, 101–2, 104–5, 108–11, 117–18, 128–29, 134–38, 164
interiority. *See* consciousness
international literary world, 15, 101, 108, 111, 134, 172
Ireland: Act of Union (1800), 144, 149; Constitution (1782), 144; history of "English" in, 143–44; Irish Free State, 139, 144; Irish home rule, campaign for, 85; neutrality during wartime, 205n3, 210n37; Protestant Ascendancy in, 144, 206n16; Ulster Rebellion (1641), 144. *See also* Anglo-Irish
irony: Anand and, 114; Bowen and, 148, 160, 208n24; Conrad and, 50–51, 55, 57; Smith and, 177; Woolf and, 79, 85
Isherwood, Christopher, 211n42

Jagoda, Patrick, 179n5
James, David, 176
James, Henry, 37
Jameson, Fredric, 42, 44, 97; *The Political Unconscious*, 42
Jews, 14, 89–90, 98
Johnson, Paul, *Making the Market: Victorian Origins of Corporate Capitalism*, 13, 119
Johnson, Simon, 30
joint-stock companies, 13
Jordan, Heather Bryant, 159, 206n11
Joyce, James, 37, 39, 66, 68, 176; *A Portrait of the Artist as a Young Man*, 114, 116–17; *Ulysses*, 68, 182n25
justice, individual vs. institution in pursuit of, 12

Kalliney, Peter, *Commonwealth of Letters*, 5, 198n3
Kapur, Geeta, 109
Kaufman, Mark David, 191n6
Kermode, Frank, 190n60
Keynes, John Maynard, "Art and the State," 71
Knopf, Blanche, 172
Koenigsberger, Otto, 135
Kornbluh, Anna, 8, 130
Kreilkamp, Vera, 154, 166
Krzakowski, Caroline, "Modernist Institutions" (with Faragher), 7
Kunin, Aaron, 8, 121

Langland, Elizabeth, 189n53
language: Anand and Joyce both using character's language abilities, 114; Anand's making Cockney strangest language in *Coolie*, 200n29; Anand's regional Indian vocabularies rendered into English, 113–15, 200n24; Bowen's use of contradictory and abstruse language, 156, 210n37; Conrad's choice of English as his literary language, 28; English as Indian literary language, 113, 200n24; type-phrases used to reinforce characterization in Conrad's *Nostromo*, 47–50, 189n53; Woolf's use of repetition, 78, 86, 94, 95, 197n65
Larson, Magali Sarfatti, 195n43
Laurence, Patricia, 212n47
Lawrence, D. H., 66, 107
Leaska, Mitchell, 63, 73, 193n28
Leavis, F. R., 28
Le Corbusier, 105, 135, 137
Lee, Hermione, 93, 169, 206n11, 207n20, 209n29
left-wing British intellectuals, 105, 110, 136–37
left-wing poets, Woolf's criticism of, 71
Lehmann, John, 102–4, 105, 110, 198n8
Lehmann, Rosamond, 139
Lenin, V. I., 29; *Imperialism: The Highest Stage of Capitalism*, 40
Leopold II (king of Belgium), 31
Levenson, Michael, 29, 61

INDEX 223

Levine, Caroline, 37; *Forms: Whole, Rhythm, Hierarchy, Network*, 7, 8
Lewis, Pericles, 185n4
liberal humanism, 8, 74
liberalism, 2, 16; parody of conservative liberalism, 60–61; pastoral care and, 180n10
Linett, Maren, 90–91
literary branding, 101, 108, 110
Lukács, Georg, 3, 26, 31, 92, 112, 118
Lye, Colleen, 133

Maher, Ashley, 211n42
Mallios, Peter, *Our Conrad*, 50
Mao, Douglas, 115
March, James, *Rediscovering Institutions* (with Olsen), 6–8, 31, 74–75
Marcus, Jane, 191n9, 194n38, 196n49
Marg (journal founded by Anand), 22, 105, 109, 110, 134–38
marriage as female ambition, 85
Martin, Regina, 28–29
Marvell, Andrew, "The Garden," 89
Marx, John, *Geopolitics and the Anglophone Novel*, 6, 111, 199n21
Marxism, 40, 42
masculinity and imperialism, 14
material interests, 20, 29, 31, 38, 43, 46–47, 50–53, 141, 190n54
Matz, Jesse, 66
McBean, Sam, 179n5
McClanahan, Annie, 198–99n10
McGurl, Mark, 35–37
McKenna, Bernard, 147
mechanism and mechanics: Anand and, 120, 123, 129, 131, 135; Conrad and, 27; modern institutions and, 10, 12; Woolf and, 65, 95, 184n47
Merton, Robert K., 196–97n60
Michaels, Walter Benn, 129
military bureaucracy, 17, 75–79, 195n42. *See also* imperialism
Miller, C. Brook, 189n51

Miller, D. A., 180n10
Misra, B. B., 77; *The Bureaucracy in India*, 128
Mitchell, Timothy, 111, 199n21
modernism: Anand and, 106, 133, 134, 200n25; anti-bildungsroman in, 40; approaches to character and narrative form, 2–9, 23, 41, 175–76; Bowen and, 23, 142, 210n38, 211n42; collectivity and, 9, 92, 175, 181n13, 182n25; consciousness or character in, 3, 9, 66–69, 77; cross-pollination with other genres, 108; de-emphasis on exceptionality in, 8; function of language in society and, 186n19; global, 101–2; high modernist works, 110–11, 136, 139; inception of, 5; late modernist works, 12, 92, 211n42; legacy of, 176; metropolitan perception as precondition for, 97; new institutionalism and, 3, 6–8, 180n12; realism's relationship with, 4, 9, 12, 26, 31, 53, 69, 96–97, 175, 179n6, 192n13, 192n15; transition to post-war era's international literary world, 101, 111, 134. *See also specific authors and titles*
"Modernist Institutions" (online forum), 7
Moretti, Franco, 38; *The Way of the World*, 39
Morley, Frank, 206n15
Moses, Michael Valdez, 42–43
Moses, Omri, 8
Muir, Ramsay, 186n25
Mullen, Mary, 183n32
multiculturalism, 15
Murry, John Middleton, 107
Muslim vs. Hindu conflict, 126

Najder, Zdislaw, 28
Nandy, Ashis, 128
Napoleon, 35
Naremore, James, 96

nationalism and national identity: Anand and, 101, 104, 108, 125, 132, 134–35, 137; Arnold and, 10, 12; colonial encounter with, 39; Conrad and, 22, 26–28, 33, 50–52, 58, 186n18; Woolf and, 63, 195n46; Yeats and, 147–48, 166
Negri, Antonio, 28
Nehru, Jawaharlal, 106, 107, 135–37
"network novels," 4, 179n5
Neutra, Richard, 135
new institutionalisms in social sciences, 5–9, 181n13, 183n32
New Left Review, 13
New Writing (magazine), 102–3, 105, 110
Nixon, Rob, 104
Nostromo (Conrad), 20, 37–54; as always-already-begun story, 42; bildungsroman and, 41; blankness and fictional quality of Nostromo's character, 50–51; character depth in, 29, 45–46, 189n51; chronological order among Conrad's works, 25; compared to Bowen's *The Heat of the Day*, 162; compared to Conrad's *Lord Jim*, 42–44; compared to Conrad's other bildung narratives, 42; compared to Conrad's *Under Western Eyes*, 59; compared to Woolf's *The Years*, 21, 53; as critique of culture of investment, 186n19; engineer-in-chief of railway's institutional role in, 43, 49, 53–54, 100; fixations of significant figures in, 44–45; Fleishman on, 38; imperialist system and, 28, 41; individualism and, 38, 42, 44, 47, 51, 55, 175; on infrastructure, 43, 189n50; institutional agency in, 25–26, 37–54, 100, 189n51; institutions as technology in, 44; Lukács on, 31; material interests in, 29, 38, 43, 46–47, 190n54; as modern political novel, 38; nationhood as failed concept in, 51–52; as pivot point in Conrad's career, 31, 38; realist tradition brought into conclusion of, 53, 190n55; romance plot in, 52–53; Ross on, 28–29; type-phrases used to reinforce characterization in, 47–50, 189n53; war in, 141
novel: essay-novel, Woolf's experimenting to create new form of, 63–64, 70, 87, 197n65; historiography of, 40–42, 175; "network novels," 4, 179n5. *See also* bildungsroman; institutional character; institutional picaresque; modernism; realism; *specific authors and works*

O'Grady, Standish, 144
Olsen, Johan, *Rediscovering Institutions* (with March), 6–8, 31, 74–75
optimism: of Anand, 22, 112, 129–30, 137, 164; of Bowen, 208n24; of Woolf, 64, 66, 70, 84, 92, 96
organicism in Conrad, 27, 35, 38
Orwell, George, 211n42; Anand and, 101; "Killing an Elephant," 104

Pargiters, The (Woolf), 63–65, 70–73; attempt to create a new literary form of essay-novel in, 63–64, 70, 74, 87, 197n65; binaries of inside/outside, private/public in, 73; definition of "pargeter," 73; exclusion of women from professions in, 80–81; feminism and, 64, 193n28; Leaska's publication of drafts of, 63, 73, 193n28; relationship to *The Years*, 63, 65, 87, 193n28, 195n42; relationship to *Three Guineas*, 63; social critique in, 71–72
Paris, Vaclav, 212n46
Parnell, Charles Stewart, 85, 195n46
patriarchy, 16–17, 65, 79, 84, 87, 91, 194n38
Pereira, Sonali, 114, 200n30
Perkin, Harold, 195n43
pessimism: of Conrad, 20, 38, 44, 57, 61–62; of Woolf, 19, 63

Phillips, Kathy, 84
picaro and picaresque genre, 21–22, 101, 104–5, 108, 117, 198–99n10. *See also* institutional picaresque
plantation gothic, 210n37
Plomer, William, 169
Poland: Conrad's roots from, 27–28, 185n12; "The Crime of Partition" (Conrad) and, 35
political economy, 118–19, 122, 129
political institutions and politics: Anand and, 101–2, 104, 109–10, 164; Bowen's evasion of, 143, 157, 164, 173; Conrad and, 20–21, 25–26, 29, 38, 55, 62, 100, 185n4; Woolf and, 21, 71, 74, 86–87, 100, 191n6, 194n38, 195n46
popular press, 29, 32–33, 92
post-colonial state: Anand's role in, 105, 110, 134; within framework of Western hegemony, 30; literary forecasting of, 6, 111
Price, Matthew Burroughs, 8
Progressive Writers' Association, 102

Radin, Grace, 194–95n41
Rainey, Lawrence, *Institutions of Modernism*, 5, 198n1
Ram, Jagiwan, 137
Read, Herbert, 107
realism: Anand and, 102–3, 108, 118, 133; Conrad's *Nostromo* and, 53, 190n55; Conrad's *Under Western Eyes* and, 61; engagement with institutions and institutionalism, 96, 183n32; individualism of nineteenth century and, 3; modernism's relationship with, 4, 9, 12, 26, 31, 53, 69, 96–97, 175, 179n6, 192n13, 192n15; Woolf's encoding of, 69, 96–97, 192n13, 192n15
Rickword, C. H., 68
Ritchie, Charles, 140, 172–73
Rives, Rochelle, 210n38
Rizzuto, Nicole, 61

Robinson, James, 30
Robinson, Ronald, "The Imperialism of Free Trade" (with Gallagher), 41
Romanticism, 148
Rose, Jacqueline, 156
Ross, Stephen, *Conrad and Empire*, 28–29
Rossi, Mario, *Bishop Berkeley* (with Hone), 147
Rousseau, Jean-Jacques, 26
Royle, Nicholas, *Elizabeth Bowen and the Dissolution of the Novel* (with Bennett), 163–64
Rushdie, Salman, 200n24
Russo-Japanese War (1905), 25

Sahitya Academy Award, 106
Said, Edward, 58
Saint-Amour, Paul, 91–92
Saloman, Randi, 197n65
Sandburg, Carl, 79
Schmitt, Cannon, 186n19
Schoenbach, Lisi, 37
Sedgwick, Eve, 180n10
Selisker, Scott, 2
Sen, Nikhil, 108
Seshagiri, Urmila, 176
Sex Disqualification (Removal) Act (1916), 96
sexism. *See* feminism; patriarchy
Seymour-Smith, Martin, 189n51
Shakespeare, William: *The Merchant of Venice*, 121; *The Tempest*, 89
Shaw, George Bernard, 209n28; *Fabianism and Empire*, 15–16, 20
Sheikh, Gulammohammed, 138
Sheridan, Richard Brinsley, 209n28
Siraganian, Lisa, 188n46
Smith, Zadie, 23, 176–78; *NW*, 176–78; *On Beauty*, 176; *Swing Time*, 177; "Two Paths for the Novel," 176; *White Teeth*, 177
Snaith, Anna, 191n5
socialism, 15–16

social sciences: development of sociology, 13; deviation as theme in sociology, 196n60; new institutionalisms in, 5–9, 181n13, 183n32
society as machine (Woolf), 16–20, 80–81, 86, 184n47
Spender, Stephen, 70
state power, 5–6. *See also* political institutions and politics
Steinlight, Emily, 66; *Populating the Novel*, 9
Stout, Daniel, 187n26; *Corporate Romanticism: Liberalism, Justice, and the Novel*, 12
Swift, Jonathan, 147

Tata, J. R. D., 135
technology as institutions: in Conrad and Ford's *The Inheritors*, 35–37, 100; in Conrad's *Nostromo*, 38, 44; digital technology, effect of, 176; in India, 135–36
Teekell, Anna, 210n37, 211n43
Thackeray, William Makepeace, 40; *Pendennis*, 68
Tomkins, Harry, 107
totalization, 14
Townsend, Sarah L., 188n42
Tratner, Michael, 182n25
Tumbe, Chinmay, 137

Under Western Eyes (Conrad), 20–21, 54–62; alternatives to institutionality in, 29; author's note on impartiality as goal, 58; collective agency and, 57; compared to Conrad's *The Inheritors* and *Nostromo*, 59; compared to Woolf's *The Years*, 84; as Conrad's last political novel, 25, 55; criticism of, 57; Darvay on, 58; detachment's diminishing returns in, 54–62; futility of political action in, 55, 62; individual agency and, 20–21, 53, 57; institutionality's effect and, 25–26, 31, 55, 57, 59–62, 100; irony in, 57; pessimism in, 61–62; post-Enlightenment navigation between rationality and sympathy in, 57; revolutionists vs. representatives of autocracy in, 59–60; unnamed Teacher of Languages as narrator in, 21, 55–59, 61, 84
university, institutional role of: Bowen and, 23, 140, 143, 172–73, 212n49; Smith and, 176–77; Woolf and, 17

Victoria (queen of England), 14
Victorian era and values: Anglo-Ireland in, 148, 168; Conrad's work influenced by, 20–21, 27; critical detachment in, 55; end of, 14, 183n40; interiority replacing outward social expression in, 66; methodological individualism of, 3, 11, 39; political economy of, 119; prehistories of institutional character, 9–13, 182n19; Woolf's work influenced by, 69, 80, 83–84. *See also* realism

Waley, Arthur, 107
Walkowitz, Rebecca, 186n18; *Cosmopolitan Style*, 130
Watt, Ian, 3
Waugh, Evelyn, 139
Weber, Max, *The Protestant Ethic and the Spirit of Capitalism*, 13
Weihman, Lisa, 195n42, 195n46
welfare state, 6, 23, 173
Wells, H. G., 66
White, Arnold, *Efficiency and Empire*, 14–16, 20
white racial supremacy, 14
Whittier-Ferguson, John, 197n65
Wilde, Oscar, 55, 209n28, 212n46
Williams, Jeffrey, 37
Williams, Raymond, 97, 147
Woloch, Alex, 8, 12, 79, 124–25
women: in Anglo-Irish decline, 167; Black British women in Smith's

novels, 178; exclusion from institutions and professions, 3, 21, 65, 80–91; imperial machinery and, 17, 80–81, 86; inclusion in institutions, 21, 95–96, 100; lack of political agency, 195n46; marriage as female ambition, 85; Sex Disqualification (Removal) Act (1916), 96; sexual lives of, 63, 72, 87, 193n28, 195n41, 202n47; in wartime, 206n11; Woolf's perspective of women as institutional outsiders, 3, 19–20, 65, 80–91, 191n6. *See also* feminism

Woolf, Leonard, 90, 101, 107, 132

Woolf, Virginia: Anand and, 101, 107; anti-Semitism and, 90–91; *Between the Acts*, 63, 74, 91, 99; biography by Quentin Bell, 107, 194n38; Bowen and, 139, 209n33; character as focus of later works, 67–68, 74, 91, 192n18; "Character in Fiction," 66, 68–69, 91; collective agency and, 21, 65, 75–76, 81, 83, 92, 98, compared to White and Shaw, 20, 184n47; consciousness ("inside") vs. society and politics ("outside"), 20, 66–69, 73–74, 77, 90–91, 184n48, 192n13; on dominance of institutionalized life, 17–20; ego boundaries and, 88, 194n34; feminism of, 21, 64–65, 76, 91, 191–92n9, 193n28, 194n38; fiction of autonomy, 69; imperialism and, 16–17, 79, 84, 97; influence of, 100, 176; institutional character in, 3–4, 21, 69, 75–99, 100, 194n37, 195n42, 197n62; *Jacob's Room*, 194n37; "The Leaning Tower," 71, 73; "Modern Fiction," 66–67; modernism and, 66, 69, 77, 92, 97, 197n65; "Mr. Bennett and Mrs. Brown," 66–67, 68; *Mrs. Dalloway*, 71, 92, 141; nationalism and, 63, 195n46; optimism of, 64, 66, 70, 84, 92, 96; *Orlando*, 63; Outsiders Society of, 20, 191n6; pessimism of, 63; politics and, 21, 71, 74, 86–87, 191n6, 194n38, 195n46; "Professions for Women," 193n28; realism and, 69, 96–97, 192n13, 192n15; repetitive use of language by, 78, 86, 94, 95, 197n65; *A Room of One's Own*, 63, 71, 94; sexual abuse suffered by, 17; on sexual lives of women, 63, 72, 87, 193n28, 195n41; "A Sketch of the Past," 16–20, 63, 86, 91, 96, 99; social critique by, 71–72, 79; social uses of literary form by, 101; society as machine in, 16–20, 80–81, 86, 184n47; stylistic innovations of, 63–64, 70–72; supranational institutions and, 79, 97; *Three Guineas*, 20, 63, 65, 71, 74, 79, 91, 95, 96, 100, 196n49, 197n62; *To the Lighthouse*, 141; *The Voyage Out*, 39, 184n47; *The Waves*, 63, 99; "Why Art Today Follows Politics," 71, 73; "Women and Fiction," 70. See also *Pargiters, The*; *Years, The*

"world republic of letters," 108, 198n3

World War I literature, 141, 142

World War II, as setting for Bowen's *The Heat of the Day*, 23, 140–43, 210n37

Wright, Frank Lloyd, 135

Years, The (Woolf), 21, 75–99, 184n48; anonymous collectivity in, 75–76, 81, 83; anti-Semitism in, 90–91; character's relationship to institutions in, 65, 74, 77–78, 86, 91, 96–97, 175; compared to Conrad's *Nostromo*, 21, 53; compared to Conrad's *Under Western Eyes*, 84; composition history of, 63–64, 70, 191n5, 195n41; Conradian elements of, 97; criticism of, 79, 196n51; domestic context of, 78–79, 194n38; egalitarian character-system of, 79–81; Eleanor's protagonist-like role in, 81, 92;

Years, The (Woolf) (*continued*)
exclusion of women from professions in, 3, 80–91; feminist view in institutional terms in, 65, 76, 80, 87, 94–95; futurity's possibilities and, 21, 80, 92–99, 100, 196n49, 197n65; historical novel genre reconfigured by, 92; as imperial fiction, 79; inclusion of women into professions in, 21, 95–96, 100; institutional character in, 3–4, 21, 69, 75–99, 100, 194n37, 195n42, 197n62; liberal humanism and, 74; military bureaucracy and, 75–79, 92; North implicating institutional and individual in his character, 97–99; optimism of, 70, 92; Peggy illustrating tensions between individual and institutional practice, 64–65, 93–96; Peggy's critical detachment, 95–96; plotless narrative of, 65, 77, 79; politics and, 86–87, 100; relationship to "A Sketch of the Past," 86; relationship to *The Pargiters*, 63, 65, 87, 193n28, 195n42; relationship to *Three Guineas*, 65, 91, 95, 100, 197n62; repetitious language in, 78, 86, 94, 95, 197n65; Sara as negative example of institutional characterization, 21, 86–91, 196n49; social critique in, 79; Victorian characteristics of, 80, 83–84; World War I's effect in, 141

Yeats, W. B., 145, 147–49, 166, 208n24, 208–9n28

Young, Arthur, 149

Zahir, Sajjad, 102
Zhang, Dora, 179n6
Zwerdling, Alex, 184n48, 191n9

RECENT BOOKS IN THE SERIES
Cultural Frames, Framing Culture

Walk the Barrio: The Streets of Twenty-First-Century Transnational Latinx Literature
Cristina Rodriguez

Fashioning Character: Style, Performance, and Identity in Contemporary American Literature
Lauren S. Cardon

Neoliberal Nonfictions: The Documentary Aesthetic from Joan Didion to Jay-Z
Daniel Worden

Dandyism: Forming Fiction from Modernism to the Present
Len Gutkin

Terrible Beauty: The Violent Aesthetic and Twentieth-Century Literature
Marian Eide

Women Writers of the Beat Era: Autobiography and Intertextuality
Mary Paniccia Carden

Stranger America: A Narrative Ethics of Exclusion
Josh Toth

Fashion and Fiction: Self-Transformation in Twentieth-Century American Literature
Lauren S. Cardon

American Road Narratives: Reimagining Mobility in Literature and Film
Ann Brigham

The Arresting Eye: Race and the Anxiety of Detection
Jinny Huh

Failed Frontiersmen: White Men and Myth in the Post-Sixties American Historical Romance
James J. Donahue

Composing Cultures: Modernism, American Literary Studies, and the Problem of Culture
Eric Aronoff

Quirks of the Quantum: Postmodernism and Contemporary American Fiction
Samuel Chase Coale

Chick Lit and Postfeminism
Stephanie Harzewski

American Iconographic: "National Geographic," Global Culture, and the Visual Imagination
Stephanie L. Hawkins

Wanted: The Outlaw in American Visual Culture
Rachel Hall

Male Armor: The Soldier-Hero in Contemporary American Culture
Jon Robert Adams

African Americans and the Culture of Pain
Debra Walker King

Against the Unspeakable: Complicity, the Holocaust, and Slavery in America
Naomi Mandel

I'm No Angel: The Blonde in Fiction and Film
Ellen Tremper

Visions of the Maid: Joan of Arc in American Film and Culture
Robin Blaetz

Writing War in the Twentieth Century
Margot Norris

The Golden Avant-Garde: Idolatry, Commercialism, and Art
Raphael Sassower and Louis Cicotello

Kodak and the Lens of Nostalgia
Nancy Martha West

www.ingramcontent.com/pod-product-compliance
Lightning Source LLC
Chambersburg PA
CBHW030620230426
43661CB00053B/2077